Echoes *of* Injustice

The True Story Behind the Epic Song
'The Lion Sleeps Tonight'
and of the Battle of
Reparation

Owen H. Dean

Echoes of Injustice

First published 2025

Juta and Company (Pty) Ltd
First Floor, Sunclare Building, 21 Dreyer Street, Claremont 7708
PO Box 14373, Lansdowne 7779, Cape Town, South Africa
www.juta.co.za

© 2025 Juta and Company (Pty) Ltd

ISBN: 978 1 48515 454 9 (Print)
eISBN: 978 1 48515 468 6 (WebPDF)

Production specialist: Valencia Wyngaard-Arenz
Editor: Chris Le Roux
Proofreader: Deidre Du Preez
Cover designer: Drag and Drop (Jacques Nel)
Typesetter: Wayne Osmond

Typeset in 12 pt on 16 pt Times New Roman MT Std

Printed in South Africa by

This work is dedicated to my wife Dana
who has at all times during the past 58 years stood by me
and supported me loyally in pursuing my career and in my life
in general. In particular, she was a great comfort to me during
the stressful period of the Disney court case which assisted me
immeasurably in dealing with the pressures that I had to endure.
My achievements would not have been possible without
her devotion. I am truly deeply indebted to her.

Contents

PREFACE x

ABOUT THE AUTHOR xix

PART 1 – Ante Leo

Chapter I 3

Introducing The Lion 3

The approach 3
Enter the lion 4
Outing the jungle... 5

Chapter II 7

MBUBE 7

Ownership of Mbube 7
Mbube comes to life 9
The final nail in the ownership coffin 11

Chapter III 12

Mobilising for Action.. 12

A moment of inspiration... 12
The Dickens of a problem.. 15
Beating about the bush.. 17

Chapter IV.. 20

Preparing for the Lion 20

Setting the scene... 20
A power of good 20
Early life.. 21
Coming home to roost 24

Chapter V 29
A New Direction 29
Roosting as a legal eagle 29
Arriving in copyright 30

Chapter VI 33
Gaining Expertise 33
Legislating 33
The Copyright Act, 1978 34
Further developments in copyright 36
Creative lawyering – test cases 37
Creative lawyering – anti-piracy 43
Innovation in diverse fields 47
Academia 49
Quo vadis? 50

PART 2 – In Tempore Leo

Chapter VII 53
The Master Plan 53
The plot 53
Legal framework 55
The target 57
Developing a case 58

Chapter VIII 62
Mastering The Plan 62
Setting the ball rolling 62
The bombshell 64
Implementing Plan B 66
Assembling the team 72

Chapter IX 76
The Lion and the Mouse 76
Taking Mickey hostage 76
Disney empire strikes back 77

Fighting on two fronts 79
Finding a funder 80
Counterattack 82

Chapter X 83
The Empire Strikes Back 83
Operation hostage release 83
Going head-to-head 85
Out on a limb 87
The call in the wild 87

Chapter XI 89
Downing the Giant 89
Breaking the news 89
Clinching the victory 91
Influential factors 92
Entitlement to damages 95
The sum of the parts 97
The settlement 98
Bounteous payments 99
Consequences of the settlement 100
Glad tidings 103
The Estate and the Trust 103
Spreading the good news 107
Putting the case to bed 108

PART 3 – Post Leo

Chapter XII 113
Ambush 113
Back to the future 113
Ambush marketing 114
Ambushing World Cups 116
2010 Soccer World Cup 120

Chapter XIII.. 127

   Twilight Time 127

      Change of identity 127

      Taking a front seat 127

      Reemergence of the Linda family............................ 130

      Introspection... 135

      Taking stock... 142

Chapter XIV 146

   Copyright on the Rack 146

      Disciple of intellectual property............................ 146

      Misguided legislation – IPLAB 149

      Misguided legislation – CAB............................... 153

      Copyright warfare.. 161

      Copyright in the blood 165

Chapter XV 168

   Enter Netflix 168

      The proposition.. 168

      Getting the show on the road 169

      Opening gambit 170

      Telling it as it is 171

Chapter XVI 186

   Second Take.. 186

      The garden path 186

      The bout 188

Chapter XVII 193

   The Lion's Share 193

      Remastered stories 193

      The world according to Malan............................... 195

      Thickening plot... 197

      A dose of truth.. 199

      Raindrops of royalties.. 199

      Commission by omission 200

Constructing the truth.. 203
Monetary misinformation 204
The critical 1952 copyright assignment 207
A shot in the foot?.. 213
Summing up.. 218

Chapter XVIII.. 220
Postmortem.. 220

Effect of the settlement 220
Pricking the bubble 221
The bull and its horns 224
Paying the piper 224
Carrying on the crusade 227
Truth will out 228

Appendices 230
I – 1952 Linda Assignment Agreement 230
II – Section 5 of the Imperial Copyright Act.......................... 231
III – Particulars of Claim... 232
IV – Judgment in Disney Enterprises Inc v Griesel N.O. 251

Preface

This is the story of what started out as a trial in the High Court of South Africa but became a trial by media in a 2019 documentary film produced and flighted by Netflix under the title *Remastered – The Lion's Share*. It is all about the world famous court case in 2006 concerning the origins and commercial exploitation of the international hit song *The Lion Sleeps Tonight*. The actual court case dealt in facts, but the media version embodies a generous dollop of fiction. The wheat must be sorted from the chaff. This process unfolds in the telling of this story. So does why I am appropriately positioned to tell the true story.

The Zulu word *'mbube'* means 'lion' and was chosen by Solomon Linda as the title of a song that he composed in the 1930s. It is traditional/tribal in character and had a melody so catchy that it became the genesis of the world-famous blockbuster song The Lion Sleeps Tonight.

Solomon hailed from Zululand and came to seek his fortune in the City of Gold, Johannesburg. He found employment in the record storage warehouse at Gallo Records. By night, however, he performed with a group of entertainers called The Evening Birds in Sophiatown, an area on the fringe of Johannesburg, which was a black social and cultural hub. The group performed *Mbube* as one of their standard items.

The song's popularity prompted Gallo Records to make and release a record of it. The record was reasonably successful in the market for indigenous music. At the time of its making Gallo caused Solomon to assign the copyright in the work to them. Gallo in turn assigned the copyright in the song to American interests and it migrated to the United States of America.

The song as such made no headway in the USA but it begat a song named *Wimoweh*, an adaptation of the original, which in turn begat a further adaptation named *The Lion Sleeps Tonight*. Both these songs carried the unmistakable core of *Mbube*. They were indeed copies, direct in the case of *Wimoweh*, and indirect in the case of *The Lion Sleeps Tonight*. *Wimoweh* became successful and famous, but its renown and popularity were dwarfed by the super-hit status achieved by *The Lion Sleeps Tonight*. This song became one of the most successful items of popular music ever conceived. Its crowning glory came when it was taken up into Walt Disney's mega stage show, and subsequent animated movie, *The Lion King*.

Solomon Linda passed away in 1962 and never experienced the fame achieved by the derivative versions of his song. Nor did he participate in the millions of dollars that *The Lion Sleeps Tonight* generated in revenue, and he went unrecognised as the original composer of the song. His widow, Regina, and his children also did not derive any financial benefit from the hit song.

The exclusion of the Linda family from the fruits of the exploitation of the song was due to the fact that Solomon had divested himself of all proprietary rights to *Mbube* when he assigned his copyright to Gallo – he, as it were, had signed away his birthright. Far from basking in the glory of Solomon's achievement and wallowing in the fruits of the commercial success of *The Lion Sleeps Tonight*, the Linda family were condemned to living in abject poverty in Soweto.

The path that led to my involvement with the song began when the author and journalist, Rian Malan, became aware of their plight and the inequity of Lindas' estrangement from the success of *The Lion Sleeps Tonight* and he wrote about it in a magazine article. This article drew attention to their plight. A public outcry ensued, causing Gallo Records to feel compelled to endeavour to try and achieve some share for them in the financial success of *The Lion Sleeps Tonight*.

I, being a specialist copyright lawyer, was consulted and mandated by Gallo to find some way to achieve this outcome. This gave rise to the court case that I instituted, which forms the subject matter of this book, namely *Griesel NO v Walt Disney Enterprises and Others* (Stephanus Griesel was the Executor who was appointed in the Estate of the late Solomon Linda, and therefore the figurehead who acted as the Plaintiff). This case gave rise to a counterclaim brought by *Disney*, viz. *Disney Enterprises Inc v Griesel NO* 2006 **BIP** 29 (T);895 **JOC** (T). I will lump these two cases together and refer to them collectively as *The Lion Sleeps Tonight Case*, or the *Disney Case*, as they are commonly called.

Gallo's participation in the project of the court case was short lived. They walked away from the project when we were on the cusp of launching the litigation. Their untimely exit from the project was ignominious and abrupt. It left the protagonists of it high and dry. We were all dressed up for the litigation but suddenly had nowhere to go. What was I to do, I asked myself? I had been fully remunerated for my services to date by Gallo. Should I simply pack up my bags, move on and turn to the next case on my waiting list, as I had done on occasions in the past when cases petered out for some or other reason? That would be the comfortable and sensible thing to do. But, no! This was a special case. I felt compelled to perform a civic duty. So, instead I took a fateful decision. I embarked on a speculative Quixotic venture which put my professional reputation and career at risk and amounted to taking a leap of faith into the abyss.

Legal colleagues and I went ahead and instituted a copyright infringement action against Walt Disney in the High Court of South Africa off our own bat and, initially, relying entirely on our own resources. We had no outside funding for the venture. Were we being foolish, reckless, outrageous, or audacious, selfless, altruistic? It was difficult to say. Time would tell. This marked the real beginning of the drama that is the subject of this story. Little did we know that six years of mixed stress, anguish, disappointment, anger and joy lay ahead. We were to taste sublime success but in the end were to be crucified, figuratively speaking.

After a convoluted and arduous legal journey through the South African court, a spectacular success was achieved, which conferred unexpected and bounteous rewards upon the Linda family. The case was a real David-versus-Goliath epic with a fairy-tale ending leaving the Linda family with the potential to live happily ever after. This was the popular and accurate perception. But a different gloss was put on it from another quarter.

The case generated considerable local and foreign interest and attention. It was acclaimed as a great success, which indeed it was, particularly since it was achieved against all odds. But, alas, we were to experience that in the media happy endings do not always make for compulsive telling and viewing and they do not keep the cash register ticking over.

A few years after the conclusion of the case I was approached by Tafelberg Publishers to write a 'short book' as a part of a series of such items that they proposed to publish electronically through Amazon. I accepted the invitation and contributed a work entitled *Awakening the Lion*, giving the inside story of the Disney case. This work was duly published by Amazon as an e-book in 2013.

In around 2017, a decade after the completion of the case, I received a telephone call out of the blue from Netflix, who informed me that the company wished to make a documentary film about the Disney case. I was asked whether I would be willing to collaborate in the making of the film. I agreed to do so and suggested that they should use *Awakening the Lion* as the blueprint for the film. The caller welcomed this suggestion and thanked me for my willingness to collaborate with them. He advised me that a film maker/director would be appointed to undertake the project and that he would be contacting me in due course to get the project under way.

A short while later I was contacted by Sam Cullman who had been appointed to make the film. I did some research on him and learned that he had a long history of producing substantial documentaries, so I looked forward to working with him. Little did I know that this collaboration would ultimately turn sour.

Sam Cullman and an entourage from the United States arrived in South Africa to make the film. I learned that the film was to be one of a series of films which were collectively labelled as '*Remastered*'. It transpired that each of the films in the series dealt with prominent figures in the music industry, such as Bob Marley and Johnny Cash, and related controversial episodes about their careers and lives. The thrust of the individual films was to sensationalise the subject matter in each instance. It was not apparent to me at the outset that Cullman's film was to be in the same vein. I was, however, destined to have a rude awakening.

I participated in filmed interviews with Sam Cullman and his team on two lengthy occasions, all in all providing around eight hours of filmed question and answer sessions. I played completely open cards with

Sam Cullman and did my best to assist him in his cause. Cullman also conducted interviews with others such Rian Malan, Hanro Friederich and the Linda daughters. On the occasion of the second interview, when filming took place in my own home, Rian Malan unexpectedly also participated. The tenor of the discussions that took place made me feel uneasy. An untoward plot was beginning to unfold.

Cullman, aided by Rian Malan, was suggesting that the lawyers who acted for the Linda Estate had been guilty of some impropriety in dealing with the money involved in the matter and that the Linda family had not received all the monies that were due to them. There was no evidence to support this, and it was simply untrue.

I felt insulted and aggrieved at this innuendo as all the lawyers and the Executor, being prominent and highly respected members of their professions, had acted with the utmost propriety, resourcefulness and diligence in the matter. We had achieved a result that had surpassed everyone's wildest dreams and had done the daughters proud. Moreover, this had been accomplished at absolutely no cost or trouble to the daughters themselves. A vast amount of money, manna from heaven, had been gift wrapped and presented to them. This extremely salient point was completely glossed over in the film.

This outcome to the litigation was evident to anyone who was prepared to have regard to all the facts of the matter and not adopt only those that fitted and supported a preconceived prejudice.

When the film appeared, it was called *The Lion's Share*. The name presaged the contents of the film, making the clear inference that the lawyers had been the principal beneficiaries of the spoils of the case. This is both untrue and borders on being libelous.

Netflix describes the film as follows: 'After discovering the family of Solomon Linda, the writer of The Lion Sleeps Tonight, a reporter tries to help them fight for fair compensation.'

While the film gives a fairly competent account of the case and makes for interesting and entertaining viewing, it has an unwelcome and skewed slant to it designed to support a preconceived conclusion of convenience.

It politicises a case that was essentially apolitical. It portrays the matter as being a case of White guilt and avarice and lawyers' greed, whereas those of us at the coal face were motivated by achieving social justice and righting an economic wrong. We felt genuine empathy for the Linda family and strove to do the best for them that we could.

The case spanned around six years. For a significant part of the time that we were involved with it, we considered that we were likely to get scant remuneration, if any at all, for our considerable efforts and the risks that we took. Furthermore, I suffered dire consequences through retribution, which included being dismissed as the South African attorney for the American movie industry, a longstanding and very substantial client. I paid a high price for my troubles.

Rian Malan played an important role in setting up the matter right from the outset. He researched and wrote the article that ignited the case and is to be commended for doing so. In the early stages he was part of our team that was involved in bringing the matter to the stage where the decision to embark on litigation was taken. However, once we began to go it alone, he faded from the scene on his own volition for reasons best known to himself. Surprisingly he was aloof from, and played no role in connection with, the actual court case as such. Yet oddly he was cast in the leading role in Cullman's film.

The film paid considerable attention to Malan's political views and aspirations and attributed much of the favourable outcome to him. Indeed, the film is as much about him as it is about the court case. This contributed substantially to the inaccuracy and undue politicisation of the story. Instead of being a feel-good, rags-to-riches story it became a political drama concerning lawyers who allegedly had dubious scruples. It was described by the *Daily Dot* reviewers in 2021 as portraying 'the all too common exploitation of Black talent for white gain'. While that may be true of the American music industry in general, it is very wide of the mark as far as this saga and the court case are concerned.

I later realised that the documentary thus fitted into the pattern of Netflix's *Remastered* series with its focus on controversy. It was contrived to do so. I propose to set the record straight.

This book, *The True Lion Sleeps Tonight Story – Unpacking the Netflix documentary and the 'Remastered' Disney court case*, is the story behind the controversy.

Sam Cullman, as the director and film maker, does not himself put in an appearance as a member of the d*ramatis personae*. What the cast says is orchestrated by him, through posing questions and giving leads off camera. By means of selection of material and editing, he composed the narrative and content of the film.

In effect his storyline, though provided by the interviewees, accords with his own views and dictates. He is the ventriloquist who speaks through the medium of the cast. The 'star' of his show, and Cullman's principal mouthpiece, is Rian Malan, but he also speaks at some length through the mouths of Solomon Linda's daughters.

This book consists of three parts.

Part 1 and **Part 2** comprise a remastering and considerable expansion of *Awakening the Lion*, the short book written by me some years previously.

Part 1 is entitled *Ante Leo* (prior to *Lion*) and it deals with the arrival of *The Lion Sleeps Tonight* in my life and what went before this watershed development.

Part 2, entitled *In Tempore Leo* (during the time of *Lion*), relates the story of the conduct of the court case against Walt Disney.

Part 3, entitled *Post Leo* (after *Lion*), breaks new ground and gives an accurate factual account of what transpired after the successful conclusion of the litigation, and of the events and circumstances used by Sam Cullman to pursue his private agenda and imply that the lawyers involved in the matter had taken *the lion's share* of the spoils generated by the case.

A critical analysis of the content of the film and a discussion of the aftermath of it is given in Part 3. It also explains how Sam Cullman, in his eagerness to home in on the 'exploitation of Black talent for White gain' and the 'sins' of the lawyers who handled the case, has misguidedly presented material that injudiciously undermines the very foundation of the legal case and probably precludes any further claims for remuneration from being pursued. In so doing, the very purpose of bringing the court case in the first place is frustrated and defeated, and the daughters are placed in a position where the monies paid out to them ought to be refunded because they turn out to have been wrongfully received. The good achieved by the case is undone.

The outcome of the film has been very favourable to Cullman. He won a prestigious award for it, and it doubtless made him lots of money. The film, and for that matter Cullman, have, however, not materially benefited the Linda daughters at all. Far from it, they have done untold harm to them. This causes one to wonder whether in the final analysis, through his windfall, Cullman himself is perhaps the ultimate beneficiary of the lion's share of the spoils flowing from his story!

While I am critical of Sam Cullman, and to some extent of Rian Malan, I do not mean to demean them or suggest that they have acted improperly. However, they appear to have had their own agendas and have advanced their views tailored by those agendas. They have also acted in a large measure of ignorance regarding the salient issues and have abundantly demonstrated that they never really understood the case. They failed properly to get to grips with it, despite all the well-meaning advice and assistance given to them by me and others. Perhaps it suited their purposes to stay aloof from that advice! The result is that they have strayed from presenting an accurate picture of what actually transpired in the case and its aftermath. They have perverted the story.

My objective in telling this story is to point out where they have erred in not giving the true picture, and to set the record straight. In so doing I frequently dispute their versions of what they profess to be the 'truth'. I unequivocally disagree with their bigoted conclusions. I do not, however, deny their right to give expression to their points of view. Beyond the hallowed precincts of the courtroom, freedom of expression embraces the right to talk nonsense.

I, too, have the right of freedom of expression and to present my side of the story which is founded on reality. Read on!

There are four appendices to the main narrative, namely the following:

- The 1952 Linda assignment document – Appendix I
- An extract from the British Imperial Copyright Act – the so-called Dickens Clause – Appendix II
- The Particulars of Claim in the main court action – Appendix III

- The court decision in the preliminary case to set aside the attachment of trade marks – Appendix IV

These appendices are intended to provide those readers wishing to obtain more detail with an opportunity of doing so. They are referred to in context in the book. Yet further background detail, including recorded renditions of all the relevant songs, can be obtained from the article 'NEW eBOOK: *"Awakening the Lion"* by Owen Dean', written by Cobus Jooste which can be found on the IPSTELL website under the link:

https://blogs.sun.ac.za/iplaw/2013/02/01/awakening-the-lion-portraying -the-tip-of-the-iceberg/

Owen Dean

About the Author

Owen Dean is an attorney who specialises in the practise of copyright law with an emphasis on High Court Litigation. After retiring from over fifty years of active practice, he established a Chair of Intellectual Property Law at Stellenbosch University, where he became a professor. He continues to be active in the field of law as a consultant and an Emeritus Professor of Mercantile Law.

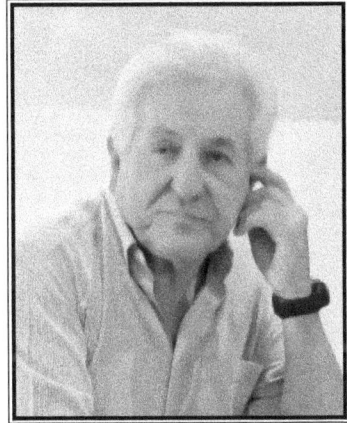

He holds a law degree and a doctorate from Stellenbosch University. He has written copiously on copyright law both in academia and the media and is the author of the standard legal textbook on the subject, *Handbook of South African Copyright Law,* as well as the principal editor and compiler of a student's guide, *Introduction to Intellectual Property Law.*

He has also published two novels, *The Summit Syndrome,* and *Reach for the Summit,* both based on one of his court cases. He considers this, his latest book, dealing with the *Lion Sleeps Tonight* case, to be a chronicle of the most interesting, challenging and worthwhile case, indeed the pinnacle, of his legal career.

He lives in Helderberg and is an active sportsman and participant in outdoor activities.

Ante Leo

I

Introducing the Lion

THE APPROACH

There was nothing about 2 September 2002 that outwardly suggested it was going to be anything but a conventional day in my life. It was a normal spring day in Pretoria, bright and sunny, without being too hot. The trees in the city were already heralding the approach of spring and there were signs of their boughs budding with greenery.

I was an attorney and partner at Spoor & Fisher, one of the leading specialist intellectual property law firms in the country. This field of law comprises mainly patents, trade marks, copyright and designs. I had been specialising in trade mark and copyright law for the past 28 years, had obtained a doctorate (LLD) in copyright law based on a thesis entitled *The Application of the Copyright Act 1978 to Works made Prior to 1979*, and had published a textbook on South African copyright law, entitled *Handbook of South African Copyright Law* which has been quoted and accepted as authority on several occasions in and by South African courts. I had somewhat to my embarrassment become known as 'Mr Copyright'.

I was sitting in my office waiting for a client named Geoff Paynter of Gallo Africa, one of the principal music companies in South Africa. It was part of a group of companies that also comprised Nu Metro Films and various other entities in the entertainment industry. Geoff Paynter was the person at Gallo who was primarily involved in copyright matters, especially the commercial exploitation of music, as distinct from recorded music. Gallo was a major client of mine, and I had acted for them in several matters, including in connection with music rights, sound recordings and the distribution of movies in the home entertainment market.

I hadn't been told what Geoff wanted to talk to me about, but I had an inkling; I had half been expecting him to see me about a certain matter for some time. This went back to a consultation I had with him some two years earlier, in June 2000, when he had raised a very interesting matter and sought a formal opinion from me on behalf of his company.

ENTER THE LION

The matter in question related to the rights in a song called *Mbube*, which had evolved over a period of several years into an international hit called *The Lion Sleeps Tonight* and become one of the most successful pop songs ever written and performed. After several visits to the international hit parade in various guises, it had been taken up into the world famous musical production *The Lion King*, which had enjoyed long and successful runs on Broadway, London's West End and in other parts of the world. The stage show, the animated movie version of its story, and its music had been produced by Walt Disney of the United States.

Two years earlier, Geoff had brought me a suitcase full of documents that represented everything Gallo had on file about the song *Mbube*. He had also handed me a copy of an article entitled *In the Jungle* by Rian Malan, an investigative journalist and writer who had made a name for himself by writing controversial articles, often of a political nature. The article, published in the US magazine *Rolling Stone* of 25 May 2000, related the sad tale of the composer of *Mbube*, Solomon Linda (also known as Ntsele), and his family.

Wikipedia describes Rian Malan as follows: '…a South African author, journalist, documentarist and songwriter of Afrikaner descent. He first rose to prominence as the author of the memoir *My Traitor's Heart* (1990), which, like the bulk of his work, deals with South African society in a historical and contemporary perspective and focuses on racial relations. As a journalist, he has written for major newspapers in South Africa, Britain and the United States.'

I subsequently got to know him as a somewhat eccentric maverick who does not shy away from controversy.

OUTING THE JUNGLE

The main thrust of Malan's article was that although Solomon Linda had composed *Mbube*, derivations of which had gone on to achieve great things and generate copious riches, none of these riches had accrued to the composer or his family, who all lived a life of poverty. The article sketched how the song had progressed to becoming a commercial property, and how it had been the subject of commercial and legal wrangles between various other parties. But all of this had passed Solomon Linda and his family by; he had simply melted away into penniless oblivion.

The article said it was grossly unfair that the original composer of the song and his family should have lived such impoverished lives, while the song was a passport to riches for others, mainly the moguls of the music industry in the United States. The plight of the composer and his family was attributed at least in part to the Apartheid system and the second-class status suffered by Black people in South Africa at the time.

Gallo, the initial usurper of the song from Solomon Linda, had given it a start along its successful road and participated in the benefits. In fact, Gallo was cast somewhat in the role of villain in what had befallen Solomon Linda and his family. And they weren't enjoying being portrayed in this light, particularly in the 'new' reformed democratic South Africa, where it had become part of a corporate group with a strong black empowerment orientation.

The purpose of that earlier visit of Geoff's had been to commission me to investigate the legal situation surrounding the rights to the song and to find out whether anything could be done to advance a claim on the part of the Linda family to the song, and to a portion of the bounteous fruits that it had produced, and thus improve their material lot.

In short, Gallo were politically embarrassed by the position Rian Malan's article had highlighted and wanted me to find some way for it to redeem them, particularly in the eyes of the public.

I had undertaken the task of ploughing through a myriad of documents, mostly contracts entered into over the years in connection with the song. I had pieced together the relevant facts and legal issues in the hope that I would miraculously find that Gallo and/or the Linda family could claim some rights in the song, which would lead them to the pot of gold. It had been a daunting task. I had spent many hours sifting through all the documents and at the end of it all I had produced a lengthy written opinion for Gallo. My efforts were not in vain. I had come to a conclusion. The position I had arrived at was an interesting one – and one that surprised everyone, including me.

II

MBUBE

OWNERSHIP OF MBUBE

Solomon Linda was an unsophisticated Zulu man with little formal education who hailed from Zululand in what was then Natal. He came to Johannesburg to seek his fortune and got work as a cleaner in Gallo's warehouse. He was also a talented musician and performing artist. Together with a group called The Evening Birds, he performed in the music halls of Black society at the height of the Sophiatown era in Johannesburg.

In or about 1938 he composed the song *Mbube* and Gallo had made a record of it. The record sold reasonably well, and Linda derived a meagre income from royalties.

At the time when Solomon Linda composed *Mbube*, South Africa's law of copyright was effectively regulated by the British Copyright Act of 1911, known as the 'Imperial Copyright Act' because Britain had it legislated and adopted in all its overseas territories, i.e. throughout the British Empire and Commonwealth. This situation came about because the South African Patents, Designs, Trade Marks and Copyright Act, 1916, rendered that Act our own domestic copyright law. This was achieved by including the Imperial Act as a schedule to it. The 1916 South African Act was subsequently repealed by the Copyright Act, 1965. It in turn was repealed by the Copyright Act, 1978, which is still the prevailing law today.

Each of these successive Copyright Acts provided that, notwithstanding the repeal of the preceding Act, the existence, ownership and duration of the copyright pertaining to works made under such a repealed Act would continue to be regulated by the Act in force at the time of the making of the work. So, if a work was made in 1930 under the 1916

Act (British Imperial Act), the 1978 Act would ensure that the existence, ownership and duration of the copyright in it continued to be regulated by the 1916 Act, even though that Act had already been consigned to the archives.

When Solomon Linda wrote *Mbube* in 1938, the song, as an original musical work, enjoyed copyright in South Africa under the 1916 Act. As the author or composer of the song, Solomon Linda was the initial copyright owner in South Africa. In addition, it also enjoyed copyright throughout the civilised world by virtue of an international treaty, the Berne Convention, of which South Africa as well as various other countries were members. In terms of the Berne Convention all works made in one member country enjoyed copyright under the laws of each and every other country that was a member of it. Each member country treated a foreign work as though it was a local work, and the local law thus governed the copyright in each foreign country.

Since the Imperial Copyright Act was in force throughout the British Empire and Commonwealth, exactly the same situation that existed in South Africa prevailed in those countries as well, and this meant that Solomon Linda was also the initial owner of the copyright in *Mbube* throughout the former British Empire and Commonwealth.

Copyright is a form of property. It can be transferred to another in a written agreement commonly known as an assignment. When the copyright in a work is assigned from one person to another, the person giving up the rights (the assignor) transfers them all to another (the assignee). Once the transfer has taken place, the assignor has no rights to the work.

Solomon Linda assigned the worldwide copyright in *Mbube* to Gallo in 1952. A copy of this agreement can be found in Appendix I on page A1. By means of this transaction he gave up all rights to that song throughout the world. For better or for worse, he surrendered all rights to claim any form of remuneration from the subsequent use and exploitation of the song. Whether this was fair or unfair, or ill-advised, is entirely irrelevant from a legal perspective. The equities of the matter may have been different, but they had no legal consequences. The equities of the matter cannot alter or affect or mitigate the legal consequences of an assignment of copyright.

Thus, on the face of it, the fact that the copyright in the song was governed by the Imperial Copyright Act, and this Act had initially awarded the copyright in it to Solomon, offered naught for comfort. As a result of the assignment the horse had bolted. Little did Solomon Linda – and no doubt Gallo – know at the time that the song would later become worth billions of US dollars.

MBUBE COMES TO LIFE

At about this time, Gallo sent Linda's record of *Mbube,* along with several other Gallo recordings, to the United States to see whether there was a market for them there. The song came to the attention of Pete Seeger, a well-known American songwriter and singer. Although there was thought to be no market for Linda's record, Pete Seeger saw potential in the song per se and he transcribed it from Linda's record and made a revised version named *Wimoweh.* ('Wimoweh' was Seeger's phonetic transcription of the Zulu word 'uyibube', meaning 'he's a lion,' as enunciated by Linda on his record.)

Wimoweh was performed and recorded by Pete Seeger and his group, The Weavers. A company Seeger was associated with, Folkways Music Publishers, claimed copyright in *Wimoweh* as a new and original work. This claim was somewhat tenuous in view of the close similarity between it and *Mbube,* but nevertheless the claim went unchallenged. In this guise, the song made it to the hit parade in the United States and became an international hit.

Folkways and Gallo entered into several agreements over the years regarding *Wimoweh,* the gist of which was to grant licence rights to Gallo for its exploitation in various African countries, while Folkways, as the copyright owner, had the exploitation rights for the rest of the world.

Around May 1961 a group called The Tokens released a record embodying an adaptation of *Wimoweh* but given the name *The Lion Sleeps Tonight.* Authorship of this version of the work was credited to Hugo Peretti, Luigi Creatore and George Weiss. Whereas *Wimoweh* was almost entirely an instrumental piece, *The Lion Sleeps Tonight* was a song with words, and it boasted some variations and innovations to the original melody. A company called Token Music Corporation claimed copyright in *The Lion Sleeps Tonight*. This claim was sustainable as the revamped song contained sufficient new elements to give it originality, despite comprising substantial material copied from *Wimoweh* and thus indirectly from *Mbube*.

Folkways and Token Music fought various legal battles in the United States as to who actually owned the copyright in *The Lion Sleeps Tonight*. Token Music, or its successor in title, Abilene Music, won the day. *The Lion Sleeps Tonight* achieved enormous fame and success and graced the hit parade for many years (in different versions and interpretations) throughout the world. It had an evergreen life and was incorporated into several movies, including Walt Disney's animated movie, *The Lion King*. The movie had a counterpart, the musical stage show by the same name. *The Lion King* became a huge money spinner.

During litigation in the United States concerning the copyright ownership of *Wimoweh/The Lion Sleeps Tonight,* it was acknowledged that *Wimoweh* had been derived from *Mbube* and that *The Lion Sleeps Tonight* was in turn derived from *Wimoweh*. Although the latter two versions of the work were arguably eligible for copyright in their own right (because they contained sufficient new material in addition to the content of each of their predecessors), they were nevertheless derivatives of *Mbube* and so the owner of the copyright in *Mbube* could potentially control the use of later versions of the work. This stemmed from the fact that both of the later versions comprised a substantial part of *Mbube* and thus fell within the orbit of the copyright in that work.

Copyright infringement occurs when reproduction or adaptation of any substantial part of a work takes place without the permission of the copyright owner. If the embodiment of *Mbube* in the latter two songs was done without the permission of the copyright owner of that song, copyright infringement would have been perpetrated. All unauthorised subsequent exploitation of the later songs would likewise have constituted copyright infringement. All uses of *Wimoweh* and *The Lion Sleep Tonight* were thus required to be authorised by the owner of the copyright in *Mbube* and that copyright owner was in a position to demand that royalties should be paid for the use of those derivative songs.

THE FINAL NAIL IN THE OWNERSHIP COFFIN

Solomon Linda died on 8 October 1962, but he had already divested himself of all rights in *Mbube*, so no rights to the song passed to his heirs. Nevertheless, adopting a belt-and-braces approach during the disputes in the United States between Folkways and Token Music over ownership of the copyright in *Wimoweh/The Lion Sleeps Tonight,* Folkways procured Regina, Solomon Linda's widow – against the possibility that she might conceivably hold some rights in the song – to transfer all her rights and interest in it to them in 1983. For good measure the daughters executed the assignment as well. But in fact Regina and the daughters held no rights in the work in 1983, so the purported assignment was inoperable. Indeed, Folkways already held the rights anyway. A copy of this agreement can be found in Appendix II on page A2.

When Regina died in February 1990 she left her entire estate to her four children, Elizabeth, Fildah, Delphi and Adelaide, in equal shares. No rights in *Mbube* were included in the assets of her estate at that time. However, no doubt in yet a further excess of caution, in March 1992 Folkways also procured Solomon Linda's children to assign 'their' right, title and interest in *Mbube* to them. By virtue of the fact that the children of course held no such rights at the time this assignment was similarly inoperable.

All this meant was that Solomon Linda, his wife Regina and his children had all done a good job of assigning away and kissing goodbye all rights in the song. They no doubt had little or no conception of what they were doing. Although Gallo and Folkways had entered into a multitude of agreements, licensing and assigning *Wimoweh* backwards and forwards, none of these agreements created any rights in favour of Solomon Linda or his family. Any claim to rights in *Mbube* on the part of the family were well and truly dead and buried at that time.

III

Mobilising for Action

A MOMENT OF INSPIRATION

On my first reading of the documentation provided by Gallo, the ability of Solomon Linda's heirs to claim any rights in *Mbube,* and therefore in *The Lion Sleeps Tonight,* didn't look at all promising. Indeed, it seemed to be a completely lost cause. By virtue of the 1952 assignment of copyright, Solomon Linda had permanently surrendered all rights and prospects of ever receiving remuneration from the use of *Mbube* and its derivatives. Rian Malan's article had made out a strong argument in equity why in an ideal world fairness and charity called for his participation in some way in the fruits of the exploitation of his song, but there was no legal leg to stand on to bring this about. In the real world it is legal rights that count. I empathised with Solomon Linda's hard luck story but feared that his family would simply have to bite the bullet. I rued the fact that the law was not always fair.

Then, while pondering the matter in the wee small hours of one morning I had a sudden inspiration – a veritable eureka moment. I remembered that while I had been researching and preparing my doctoral thesis some thirteen years earlier, I had come across a very strange provision in section 5(2) of the Imperial Copyright Act, which had made little sense to me. I had mentioned it in my thesis but had given it short shrift. Now on reflection, I realised that this provision altered the normal situation that applied in regard to ownership of copyright throughout the currency of the Act in South Africa during the period 1916 to 1965.

The standard position is that for the duration of the term of copyright – which is the lifetime of the author plus 50 years after his death – the copyright in the work belongs to the author or to the person who can claim ownership of the work through being the successor in title to the author. Where the copyright has been assigned or transferred, the most recent assignee holds ownership until the end of the term.

However, by virtue of this extraordinary provision, where the author of a work was the initial owner of the copyright in it, no assignment of copyright or any licence granted under copyright could confer on the assignee or licensee any rights in the copyright beyond the expiration of 25 years from the death of the author. The term of 50 years beyond the death of the author was effectively divided into two 25-year segments. The ownership of the most recent assignee ended at the end of the first 25 years. Ownership of the second 25-year segment (i.e. years 25 to 50 after the author's demise) of the copyright was automatically awarded or transferred back to the author's heirs. The ownership of the copyright thus reverted to them. These rights generously bestowed on the author's heirs were known as the 'reversionary interest'.

In other words, at that point the author's heirs replaced the most recent assignee as the copyright owner. The reversionary interest passed to the heirs no matter what assignments of copyright might have taken place after the initial transfer of copyright by the author.

This measure was removed from the subsequent Copyright Acts in both the United Kingdom and South Africa, but it remained applicable to works made during the currency of the Imperial Copyright Act. This was the case with Solomon Linda's song *Mbube*.

The existence of this historic reversionary interest was virtually unknown anywhere in the world in the modern era, and in particular in South Africa. I subsequently learned that it had been introduced into British law in the late 1800s to cater for the interests of the family of Charles Dickens. During his lifetime, Dickens had assigned away all his copyrights to publishers and he had not left the wherewithal to his family to enable them to cope with daily living. All the income from the sale of his books was going to his publishers. The relevant provision of the British copyright law was introduced in order to redeem the plight of the Dickens family. It became known as the Dickens Clause. It brought welcome relief to his family as they were placed in a position to receive royalties from the exploitation of his works.

I was elated by the realisation that the plight of the Linda family corresponded with that of the Dickens family all those years ago and that their financial challenges might be alleviated in the same way as had occurred with the Dickens family.

Solomon Linda both wrote and died during the time when the 1916 Copyright Act (incorporating the Imperial Copyright Act) was in force in South Africa, so it governed the ownership of the copyright in the work. The outcome was that 25 years after Linda's death in 1962 – that is, in 1987 – copyright in *Mbube* reverted to his heirs, who were his wife Regina and his four children. This was despite the fact that he had signed over the rights to Gallo in 1952. His misstep had been compensated or corrected with effect from 1987. The *Mbube* chickens had come home to roost in the Linda household! This position applied not only in South Africa but throughout all the countries of the former British Empire and Commonwealth.

The upshot of all of this was that, contrary to my initial conclusion, Solomon Linda's heirs did indeed hold copyright in South Africa and in many other countries in the world. They had effectively owned the copyright since 1987. All uses of the work in these countries since 1987 required the heirs' authorisation. Without their approval, any uses amounted to infringements of the copyright, giving rise to a claim of damages. Of course, because *Wimoweh* and *The Lion Sleeps Tonight* were derivatives of *Mbube,* the heirs also controlled the right to the use of those songs, including the use of *The Lion Sleeps Tonight* in the musical production *The Lion King.* The heirs were, as it turned out, in a very strong legal position – at least in theory. I was convinced that my academic research ought to pay dividends for the Linda family.

Providence had smiled on the Linda family and out of nowhere a right had emerged in their favour to enable them to add a legal claim to the impassioned emotional plea for compensation advanced by Rian Malan. Rian's forlorn prayer had been answered, completely against the run of play, as it were.

It is important to emphasise that this godsend did not rewrite the history between 1952 and 1987. That position remained unchanged. The family's rights in *Mbube*, having been forfeited in 1952, only recommenced in 1987 and were prospective and therefore operated solely in the post 1987 period. Rian's diatribe in his article about the sins of the American players who flaunted the 'rights' of the family when the song was earlier in its ascendency in the 60s and 70s and beyond should be viewed in this light. The American players owned, and continued to own, the copyright in *Mbube* during the period from 1952 to 1987. Sight of this situation was lost in the further development of *The Lion Sleeps Tonight* story. In particular it became conventional wisdom on the part of the uninitiated to assume (wrongly) that Solomon Linda and his family had always and inherently held the God-given right to derive the rewards that flowed from the use of the song and its derivatives (i.e. including during the period from 1952 to 1987). This factor played a significant role as the saga unfolded.

THE DICKENS OF A PROBLEM

The discovery of the applicability and effect of the reversionary interest brought about by the Dickens Clause was an earth-shattering experience. However, there appeared to be a problem. At first blush, it seemed that there was a fatal obstacle in applying the Dickens Clause to the Linda situation. This was due to the fact that, firstly both Regina and the daughters in 1983, and thereafter the daughters again in 1992, had divested themselves of their rights under the copyright by virtue of the assignments that they had entered into in favour of Folkways. Those assignments were inoperable at the time when they were executed because the 'assignors' owned no rights at the time. One cannot transfer rights that one does not hold. However, these assignments were not totally without effect. They existed as a question of fact but remained dormant. They would come to life and would take effect immediately when the 'assignors' (i.e. the Linda daughters) acquired the copyright.

It seemed as though this line of reasoning had led to a cul-de-sac. The moment the copyright in *Mbube* vested in the family by virtue of the reversionary interest, the aforementioned assignments lying in wait would be activated and the copyright would pass without any further ado to Folkways.

However, solace came from revisiting and making a detailed analysis of the Dickens Clause and reconsidering it. The section provided that the reversionary interest devolved upon the Executor as an asset of the author's estate, and not directly on the family. The Executor had the power to deal with the reversionary interest in the same way as he could deal with any asset in an estate. He could pass the reversionary interest to one or more of the heirs if he deemed it appropriate, or he could transfer it to a third party and pass to the heirs the monetary value realised by such transfer. It was necessary, no matter to whom the Executor transferred the reversionary interest, that he should enter into a written deed of assignment effecting transfer of the rights. The heirs of the author only became the owner of the reversionary interest if and when such interest was assigned to them in writing by the Executor.

This had not happened in the present instance. The ownership of the copyright in *Mbube* had not yet progressed beyond the Executor. This meant that the 1983 and 1992 assignments were still of no practical force or effect. The heirs had not yet acquired the copyright and thus held no rights to pass on in the assignments. This would remain the case for as long as the heirs never acquired the ownership of the copyright. It would be fatal to their interests if they should ever become the copyright owners. The moment that they became owners of the copyright the dormant assignments of copyright in favour of Folkways would be activated and the copyright would then, as it were, immediately fly out the window and become vested in Folkways.

On a proper construction the of the matter the copyright in *Mbube* vested in the Executor of Solomon Linda's Estate in 1987 and would remain in his hands until such time that he assigned it to another party, which in no circumstances should ever be any of the daughters. This point, not easily or always understood, was to have a significant effect on the further development of this story.

Other countries that were formerly part of the British Empire had also, perhaps unbeknown to themselves, preserved the reversionary interest created by the Dickens Clause of the 1911 Imperial Copyright Act, up to the present time. As a result, what the executor held was not only the reverted copyright in South Africa but also the reverted copyright in all countries that were former British possessions, as well as in Britain itself. Indeed, a large and valuable chicken had come home to roost with the Executor in 1987! The way forward was clear.

The Executor in the Estate of the late Solomon Linda could enforce the copyright in South Africa and in any country which was formally part of the British Empire, including the United Kingdom itself. He would be in a position to make a claim of copyright infringement against anyone performing any acts in relation to *Mbube* and its derivatives after 1987.

This revelation formed the cornerstone of my opinion that I prepared for Gallo in 2000. The punchline was that the Executor of Solomon Linda's estate could claim damages and royalties for all uses of *Mbube* and its derivatives, especially *The Lion Sleeps Tonight,* throughout the countries of the former British Empire for the post-1987 period.

I had triumphantly presented the opinion to Gallo, fully expecting that they would rejoice and now take steps forthwith to rectify the past wrongs the Linda family had suffered.

BEATING ABOUT THE BUSH

Nothing happened! There was a deafening silence.

I received no feedback from Gallo, apart from an acknowledgement of receipt. My opinion had disappeared into a void. Days, weeks and months, even years, went by without any reaction from Gallo. I was left with a feeling that it had all been a case of much ado about nothing.

In the meantime, I read in the press and learned from television that a Johannesburg attorney named Hanro Friederich, with the help of Rian Malan, had been appointed by and was representing the Linda family, and was hard at work desperately investigating any options open to the family to derive income from the exploitation of *The Lion Sleeps Tonight.* It was clear to me that they were clutching at straws to find some leg to stand on – besides appealing to notions of fair play.

They were mainly pursuing the line that undue influence had been brought to bear on Solomon Linda when he executed the 1952 assignment in favour of Gallo and that the assignment could be set aside on this account. I had considered this point while preparing my opinion, but could find no evidence to support the argument. Without cogent factual evidence to support the point, the argument was dead in the water – it was pure speculation and speculation counted for nothing before the court. Friederich was conducting a wild goose chase, and I was tempted to pick up the telephone and tell him that there was indeed a way for his clients to achieve success.

Hanro Friederich, so I learned, practised as an attorney mainly in the field of the diamond industry, and while being an industrious and competent practitioner with an altruistic bent, had little or no experience in copyright or in intellectual property in general. He was an acquaintance of Rian Malan and had been introduced into the matter by him to provide some legal assistance in his quest for justice for the Linda family. However, as much as I wished to assist, ethical considerations made it impossible for me to disclose to a third party the contents of an opinion I had written for Gallo. It was for Gallo to decide what, if anything, should be done with the opinion.

It was frustrating. I began to suspect that Gallo had expected, even wanted, me to fail to come up with a viable course of action; that they would rather I had advised them there was nothing that could be done. Had this been the case they could then have declared publicly that they had consulted a leading expert on the area of the law for some way they could help the family but, regrettably, there was nothing to be done. This would clear their public conscience.

Now, more than two years later, Geoff Paynter was coming to see me. Was he going to discuss the matter with me; explain why Gallo took no steps based on my opinion, I wondered? Or was the purpose of his visit something completely different. I simply didn't know.

My telephone rang; Paynter was waiting in reception. I picked up a note pad and my file dealing with the opinion on the off chance that the consultation might have something to do with it. As I passed through the doorway of my office into the corridor, a strange feeling came over me. I had a premonition that something momentous in my career was about to happen. It was as though all my legal experience and everything that had happened in the past had been leading up to that moment. I went to meet my client with a feeling of anticipation tinged with trepidation.

I did not know it then, but I was on the threshold of taking on the major court case of my career. The song *The Lion Sleeps Tonight* was to dominate my life for the next six years. It was as though my entire legal career, if not my life to date, was but a preparation for this undertaking. The case would call on me to utilise and rely upon all my skills, expertise, knowledge and experience to handle it and to deal with the problems, challenges, pitfalls and crises that lay ahead. The risks that I would take would be dangerous and daunting. The betrayals and disappointments that I would experience would render me disconsolate. I was in for a bumpy ride!

IV

Preparing for the Lion

SETTING THE SCENE

The *Lion* arrived in my life 25 years into my legal career. Much water had passed under the bridge by then. I was already at that time an acclaimed specialist intellectual property attorney with copyright law being my principal field of practice. It was on that basis that I was consulted by Gallo in the matter.

The consultation that was about to take place was to turn out to be the starting point of a series of events that led me to embark on a course of action that had the makings of becoming, and ultimately was, an escapade that would have done Don Quixote proud.

You may ask what there was about my background, character and personal make up that led me to take on the formidable challenge that materialised? A clue is to be found in the words of one of the songs sung by Don Quixote in the musical, 'The Man of La Mancha':

> To dream the impossible dream, To fight the unbeatable foe......To fight for the right Without question or pause, To be willing to march, march into Hell for that Heavenly cause.....To reach... the unreachable star.

Therein lies a message that is material to a proper understanding and appreciation of what was to unfold and to influence me and my conduct in due course in the *Lion* story.

A POWER OF GOOD

Without being a committed believer in the theory of predestination, throughout my life I've had a feeling that its course was being predetermined by extraneous influences, call it fate, divine guidance, or what you may. The end objective was to achieve the state as a person of being a power of good, i.e., a mission to help or benefit my fellow human beings. How and in what circumstances this goal would be attained was unknown. It was a little like being the driver of a train travelling along a predetermined track with an unknown destination. As the train driver, I could perhaps determine its speed, when it stopped and went, and to some extent the smoothness of the journey, but the tracks it was following actually determined where it was going. From time to time the tracks passed through junctions and there was a semblance of choice of direction, but the points determining the track to be followed had been set and choice was just an illusion.

As *The Lion Sleeps Tonight* matter evolved, I became more and more disposed to the view that my predetermined train track was leading me to a destination that would land me in a situation where I would be seized with, and would take on something like the litigation which followed, in which I assisted helpless people in need to take on the forces of corporate power; where I could be a benevolent force and could give expression to the power of good.

It would have been out of the question for me to embark on this undertaking if I had not been properly equipped and had the wherewithal to do so. I believed that I was, and that I had the experience, expertise and status in the relevant field of legal practice to carry me through. I was confident that I was properly qualified to take the matter on. My life leading up to this point had prepared me for it. Getting to this point was a long and winding journey. Like every journey, it began with a first step.

EARLY LIFE

I first saw the light of day in Bantry Bay, Cape Town, on the 9th of June 1944, three days after D-Day. I grew up in Camps Bay, which was at that time a small coastal hamlet with a handful of small shops and two cafés, a far cry from the present-day affluent tourist mecca. I spent a large proportion of my teenage years on Camps Bay and Clifton beaches. It was an idyllic upbringing. I matriculated at Sea Point Boys High School, where I was Head Prefect. While there I made my first tentative steps into the literary world when I published my first article, entitled 'The Art of Conversation', in the school magazine.

I then did a law degree at Stellenbosch University, graduating with a BA LLB degree in 1966. During my time as a law student I served as the Vice-Chairman of the Law Society and the co-editor of a legal journal named *Responsa Meridiana,* a joint venture between the Law Faculties of Stellenbosch and Cape Town Universities. I published an article in that journal under the title 'Solidarity' in which I argued in favour of a minority judgment in the Appellate Division of the South African court. At this early stage in the legal path that I had chosen, therefore, I showed a propensity to think independently and not follow the herd. This article, which was the forerunner of a myriad to follow in later years, was to play a not insignificant role in my journey.

Because my studies were funded by a state bursary, I was obliged to enter the civil service for six years. This necessitated my relocation to Pretoria where I spent a year together with my newly wedded wife, Dana. I served those six years in the Department of Foreign Affairs, the home of the diplomatic service. After an initial spell in Pretoria, I was deployed at the South African Embassy in The Hague, Netherlands, for most of my six-year stint. I held the post of Third Secretary initially and was then promoted to the rank of Second Secretary.

My main function at the Embassy was to do consular work. This entailed dealing with visas and passports and assisting South Africans who encountered difficulties in the Netherlands. During this tour of duty the third South West Africa case dealing with that territory's road to independence took place at the International Court of Justice in The Hague. As the most junior member of the diplomatic staff, I was detailed to assist the South African legal team in a sort of articled clerk-like capacity. The legal team conducting our case comprised some of the top legal minds in South Africa and it was a stimulating and worthwhile experience interacting with these eminent jurists and observing the proceedings before the court. This experience assisted me to form the view that my future lay in the legal profession and not in the diplomatic service, which I viewed as no more than a passing phase.

Dana and I used our time in the Netherlands to travel extensively throughout Europe during my vacation time and over weekends (one virtually couldn't travel for more than an hour or two without leaving the country) which made it a valuable and enjoyable experience. Being part of the diplomatic community and attending functions hosted by the Queen of the Netherlands and the like was an enriching experience for us as young twenty-somethings. The infamous Dr Eschel Rhoodie was the Information Counsellor at the Embassy, and I had frequent interactions with him.

On my return to South Africa, I decided that a legal career was my destiny. I wanted to pursue a career as an attorney, but for this I had to serve two years' articles of clerkship. My preference for a place to practise was my hometown, Cape Town, but my position as a returning diplomat meant taking up office once again in Pretoria. At this point we had two children, Ian and Carin, and I thus had a family to support (a third child, Bryan, followed a few years later). This was a complicating factor. My salary at the time was the princely sum of R350 per month, a meagre income, which I considered to be on the breadline. Articles of clerkship back in 1972 were notoriously badly paid; the going rate was around R100 per month. Dana was unable to work because she was nursing a two-month-old baby, so we'd be entirely reliant on my salary to sustain ourselves. My prospects for a legal career did not look promising.

I approached attorneys' firms in Cape Town, Johannesburg and Pretoria with a view to getting a position as an articled clerk. These firms would have been happy to take me on board at a salary of R100 per month, but not at R350 per month. I was told that an amount of that order could buy three articled clerks! I began to despair; a career as an attorney was probably not going to materialise.

At this time, I chanced to encounter Eschel Rhoodie in the street in Pretoria. He had returned from his posting in The Hague and had become the Secretary for Information. He invited me to come and work for him in a special unit within the Department of Information at a generous salary. The offer was tempting, but not the legal position that I wanted, so I declined it.

In the light of what later transpired with him it was just as well that I was absolutely intent on becoming an attorney! As the Secretary of Information, he had strong political connections and conducted special projects of a clandestine nature; he subsequently fell from grace, was arraigned for criminal conduct and fled the country, going into exile. I might otherwise have been led astray and suffered the same ignominious fate as his cohorts who were involved in the notorious so-called Information Scandal, a major political upheaval of the day. It was sparked by the dutiful revelation of a high court judge, Anton Mostert, who was not thanked for his efforts and subsequently resigned from his position. He later indirectly entered my life and influenced my future career.

COMING HOME TO ROOST

While still in the employment of the Department of Foreign Affairs in Pretoria, I decided to buy a house in the then Verwoerdburg area. By the nature of its location, it would give me the flexibility to work either in Pretoria or Johannesburg if I struck it lucky and secured articles of clerkship in either city. In the course of house hunting I met an estate agent named Maurice Witt, who had also gone to Sea Point Boys High School. With that as a common bond, while we travelled together looking at houses, I shared with him my aspirations and the problems I was experiencing in achieving them. He knew an attorney named Sonny Hart, the senior partner of Friedland Hart & Partners in Pretoria, and arranged an interview for me with him. He thought that Sonny Hart might have a longer range vision than other attorneys. But Hart's attitude was no different from the other attorneys I had approached; he also couldn't see his way clear to pay me more than R100 per month.

He did, however, mention his son, Laurie Hart, who was a partner of Spoor & Fisher, specialist intellectual property attorneys. He felt that perhaps an intellectual property firm might by the nature of its international practice place greater store on my diplomatic and overseas experience than an ordinary attorneys firm. He promised to tell his son about me. Some weeks later Laurie Hart invited me to an interview.

He asked me to provide him with background biographical material prior to the interview. Amongst the material that I submitted to him was my 'Solidarity' article published in *Responsa Meridiana* back in my student days. This appeared to impress him, and he said during the interview that anyone who could, as a student, write an article proclaiming that four eminent judges of the Appeal Court had got it wrong in their majority judgement must have some spirit and the courage of his convictions. The interview raised my hopes that a break might be coming my way.

I had never heard of such a thing as an intellectual property attorney, nor did I have the slightest idea of what such an attorney did, or what intellectual property law entailed. I also had no idea of whether it was an area of legal practice that would hold any appeal for me, but it had become clear to me that if an employment offer was forthcoming this might be my last opportunity to get a position as an articled clerk and, since beggars can't be choosers, I should grab it with both hands. It came good for me and Spoor & Fisher were prepared to take me on at my required salary and the rest, as they say, is history. I commenced working at Spoor & Fisher on 1 October 1972. I progressed quickly and became a partner of the firm in March 1975, immediately after completing my articles.

But at the outset I faced a daunting task. I had been out of university for six years and had lost a lot of ground in the legal profession compared to my peers at university, many of whom were already established partners in prominent attorneys firms or had several years of practice at the bar as advocates behind them. By contrast, I was a lowly articled clerk. Qualifying as an attorney and passing the attorneys' admission exams lay ahead of me.

Spoor & Fisher was a truly specialist law firm. It dealt only with intellectual property law, i.e. the law of patents, trade marks, copyright and designs (collectively known colloquially as IP), and did no general legal work at all. The practical experience that I gained while working at the firm was confined to IP and related matters such as Supreme Court litigation in that field. It accordingly was not an ideal place for an aspirant attorney to launch a general career as an attorney.

In the beginning I was by no means committed to a career in IP. I saw my role at Spoor & Fisher to be primarily a means of getting my articles behind me and qualifying as an attorney. Then I would be in a position to decide in what direction I would like to go and even where I would like to practice. Cape Town was the hot favourite.

Learning the trade, so to speak, at Spoor & Fisher, had its challenges and anxious moments. In order to get going and to make the grade I had to pass the Attorneys Admission exam, which was concerned with practical matters in the attorneys' profession to which I had little or no exposure during my clerkship. Moreover, the examination process included written papers and an oral examination by a panel of leading attorneys. I had no choice but to prepare for a practical examination on an academic basis. I learned a lot of the relevant material off by heart and muddled successfully through the examination, including the oral. It was, however, a nerve-racking process.

Buoyed by my success in winging it through the Attorneys Admission examination, I decided to tackle the Notaries Exam and qualify as a notary public as well as an attorney. My thinking was that, if after completing my articles and being admitted as an attorney, I was to seek other pastures outside Spoor & Fisher it would help if I was as widely qualified as possible.

If attorneys practise fell outside the ambit of my experience being gained at Spoor & Fisher, the problem was mild compared to notarial practise. The notaries exam involved being adept at, to me, foreign matters like winding up deceased estates, drafting mineral rights agreements and areas of law that I had barely even heard of. Like attorneys' admission, it entailed a written exam followed by an oral exam. Once again, I learned the relevant material off by heart and passed the written exam without any hitches. However, the prospect of the oral exam filled me with trepidation. There is no place to hide in an oral exam.

The oral examination was conducted by a panel of three experienced and eminent notaries. I was confronted by this imposing tribunal. Along came the first question: 'Where would you find the rules and regulations applicable to acting as a Commissioner of Oaths?' I took a deep breath.

In my time working at the Embassy in The Hague I had the status of, and acted on a daily basis as, a Commissioner of Oaths. I knew exactly where to find the rules – they were contained in a particular *Government Gazette* which I had at my elbow for four years.

I answered the panellist's question by giving the number and date of the relevant *Government Gazette*. To my astonishment he responded that I was wrong and that was not the answer he wanted. I stuck to my guns and told him that I was not wrong and that my answer was definitely correct. We entered into a debate which became fairly heated and took up some time. He finally said, 'Why are you being so obstinate? I thought I would be kind to you and begin with an easy question so that you can settle your nerves, and you have now turned it into a major issue! The simple answer I wanted is, "Hortors' Diary" (a useful voluminous custom designed diary containing pertinent information used by most attorneys). Why don't you just admit that you don't know, and we can get on with the rest of the oral examination' He was not amused, and it showed. I replied, 'That may be so, but Hortors' Diary simply refers to and quotes the *Government Gazette*'.

During this exchange the other members of the panel were bemused onlookers. The Chairman then intervened and said, 'Why don't we check and see if he is correct. Will someone please bring me a Hortors' Diary?' A copy was duly fetched and inspected by the Chairman. He looked up and said with a smile, 'He is perfectly correct, you know! Here it is,' and he quoted the *Government Gazette* reference. The atmosphere in the room changed, albeit to the embarrassment of the questioner, and the Chairman then said, 'Okay, you can go, we have no further questions'. This was heavenly music to my ears, and I departed with alacrity before they could change their minds. I was duly admitted as a Notary Public. The gods were definitely with me on the path I was following!

After my fortuitous escape in the notaries oral, I didn't want to push my luck further and decided against seeking qualification and admission as a conveyancer, the one outstanding option open to me. It was best to quit while I was ahead!

This unlikely scenario was how I came to embark on my lifelong career. It has proved to be very fulfilling, and I have no doubt there's no other branch of the law that would have suited or appealed to me more than intellectual property. Fortuity, happenstance, fate, destiny, good luck? Whatever it was, it had the result that I landed in what turned out to be exactly the right niche for me in the legal profession without my having exercised any choice in the matter. It also set in motion a course of events that played a crucial role in the unfolding of this story.

V

A New Direction

ROOSTING AS A LEGAL EAGLE

Spoor & Fisher comprised essentially two departments, viz. the Patent Department, which was exclusively engaged in registering patents, administering and enforcing them, and the Trade Marks Department, which performed a similar function in regard to trade marks. As somewhat of a side issue the Patents Department was also seized with registering, administering and enforcing designs, but this was a relatively small part of their practice, indeed of IP practice in general. Likewise, the Trade Marks Department dabbled to a minor extent in copyright, but since no registration of copyright took place its practise in this regard was limited to giving the occasional piece of advice.

The Patent Department of the firm was located in Johannesburg, while the Trade Marks Department had its home in Pretoria, the seat of the Patents and Trade Marks Registry, which was a division of the Department of Trade and Industry. Having no technical qualifications (which were essential to practise patent law), I was deployed in the Trade Marks Department. I knew absolutely nothing about trade mark law – it had never featured at our law course at Stellenbosch University. I was really starting at square one.

I was seconded to Laurie Hart and Geoff Webster, the two leading and experienced trade mark partners. They became my mentors. Laurie Hart had practised for several years as an advocate and knew all the tricks of the trade when it came to conducting litigation. Geoff Webster was indisputably the leading trade mark lawyer in the country and was the co-author of the standard text book on South African trade mark law. He was also an extremely competent and accomplished lawyer.

Here I hit the jackpot in no uncertain terms. I learnt virtually everything to know about trade mark law, and the art of IP litigation, at the feet of the masters.

Geoff Webster was also the most knowledgeable person around on copyright (although even he would have acknowledged that he was by no means an expert) of which there were not really any in South Africa. It was a case of in the land of the blind the one-eyed is king! The simple fact of the matter was that copyright was a sparsely used or encountered area of the law at that time.

ARRIVING IN COPYRIGHT

At an early stage in my career Geoff Webster became involved in a Supreme Court case which had a copyright angle. I assisted him. It involved the copying of the design on the face of a packet of breakfast cereal which was sold by one of our clients and had been copied fairly slavishly by a competitor. One of our clients' claims was that their copyright in their artistic work had been infringed by the making of unauthorised copies of it, which were featured on the packet of their competing product. Rather blatant copying had taken place, and it seemed to be an open and shut case of copyright infringement.

In defence of the claim the advocate for the other side, Fanie Cilliers (who was a junior counsel at the time but went on to become one of the leading senior advocates and IP counsel in the country; he was also an examiner in respect of my doctoral thesis in later years), advanced an argument, that by his own admission later, was a shot in the dark. The argument was that, in terms of some obscure regulation under the Designs Act, if an artistic work had been used as a design and a three-dimensional version of it had been the subject of the copying by another, that manner of copying could not constitute copyright infringement. The rationale was that such works should have been registered as designs and consequently copyright protection was forfeited.

To everyone's astonishment this unheard defence was successful and our clients' case was dismissed. This result came as a shock to Geoff Webster and to the eminent advocates who had argued our case, and they were mortified by it. The advocates offered to waive their fees on account of their failing to foresee the fatal and successful defence.

As the articled clerk and new kid on the block involved in the case, I was non-plussed by the fact that such highly respected and eminent exponents of IP law could be so completely taken by surprise by a point of law and be flummoxed by it. I decided to satisfy my curiosity and do some research into the question. There were no South African authorities that could be consulted so I was forced to have recourse to British law whence, so it appeared, the crucial point had found its way into our law had been derived.

After doing considerable homework I found that the point of law had come to the fore in a British case that had dealt with the design of a yacht. The principle that had been espoused was that where a drawing had given rise to the design of a yacht and a competitor has copied the design of the actual yacht itself by a process of reverse engineering, thus working from the derivative three-dimensional item, the resulting competing yacht's design was deemed to be an indirect reproduction of the original drawing and could constitute copyright infringement. There was a rider, however, that the copying of the drawing by reverse engineering could only constitute copyright infringement if a certain condition was satisfied. This was that the design of the yacht could not have been registered as a 'design' on account of it being ineligible for registration because it was purely functional by nature (this was a disqualification for registration of a design under the Designs Act).

In the South African breakfast cereal case, the picture on the packet would indeed have been capable of registration as a design under the Designs Act. Therefore the copyright infringement disqualification came into play and the copyright in the artistic work could not be enforced in the prevailing circumstances. Fanie Cilliers' obscure shot in the dark was good in law! Hence the failure of our client's case. I found this fascinating.

This episode came about just when I had muddled my way through the Attorney's Admission Examination, and I had been admitted as an attorney. I decided to mark my arrival in the profession by publishing an article of the British yacht case in a South African legal journal. In my article I drew attention to the possibilities that the yacht principle held for claiming copyright infringement where reverse engineering of design drawings was taking place. This was of particular relevance to the trade in alternative spare parts for machinery, motor vehicles and the like. In those areas the designs of the articles were invariably purely functional. Consequently they could not be registered as designs, which meant that copyright infringement could be validly claimed.

My article was a revelation and created considerable interest in the spare parts after market where 'pirate' parts were proliferating. I soon found myself being called upon to speak at seminars, workshops and the like on how copyright could be used as a weapon in the prevention of three-dimensional copying in the industrial field. I had arrived in the field of copyright law! I had also cut my teeth as an attorney and become a partner of Spoor & Fisher.

My preparations for equipping myself to eventually exert the power of good by dealing with *The Lion Sleeps Tonight* case had begun. My train track was heading off in that direction, but a long journey, spanning a quarter of a century, still lay ahead.

Those preparations followed two contemporaneous and parallel courses which were interrelated and fed off one another. They can be described as 'legislating' and 'creative lawyering,' respectively. They played an important role in the years that followed.

VI

Gaining Expertise

LEGISLATING

Shortly after I became a partner of Spoor & Fisher in 1975, the Registrar of Patents and Trade Marks, the state official responsible for administering IP in the Government, embarked on the process of updating our copyright law. It was decided that the 1965 Copyright Act, which had repealed the Imperial Copyright Act as embodied in the Patents, Trade Marks, Designs and Copyright Act, 1916, should be amended or replaced to keep pace with modern developments. The Imperial Copyright Act had been replaced in Britain by the Copyright Act 1956, which in turn had been the genesis of our 1965 Act.

The Registrar formed a broadly based consultative committee to assist him with his task and to provide input on what changes to the law were necessary. Various bodies and interest groups were invited to join the committee. These included, inter alia, the Bar Council, the Association of Law Societies, the publishing industry, the music and record industries, the SABC, performers societies, and the South African Institute of Intellectual Property Law, the professional body representing IP practitioners. I was designated by the IP Institute to be one of its representatives on the committee in my newfound role of being someone versed in copyright. Despite my junior status in the profession, I had become the 'one-eyed' person in the Institute.

The Registrar's committee met fairly regularly over a period of around a year, and I attended and actively participated in all its meetings. A wide range of viewpoints, providing valuable input, were aired and taken into account to by the Registrar who ultimately came forward with draft legislation which eventuated into the Copyright Act, 1978.

The Act provided for a statutory advisory committee to advise the Minister of Trade and Industry on matters relating to copyright. I was invited to become a member of that committee, which comprised a judge as chairman and five other members. I served on that committee for some 20 years. When, some years later, the mandate of the committee was expanded to include all the branches of IP law, and not only copyright, I was appointed as the chairman of the Copyright Sub-committee. The judges who successively served as Chairman of the Advisory Committee were steeped in IP law and included experts in that field, such as Louis Harms and Chris Plewman, both of whom were highly respected judges of the Appellate Division of the Supreme Court. This gave the Committee considerable stature and standing, and I benefitted immeasurably from working with such eminent jurists.

THE COPYRIGHT ACT, 1978

I will digress momentarily to discuss the 1978 Act because in recent times it has been much misrepresented and maligned by being described as 'Apartheid legislation,' with this term used in a pejorative sense. I can testify by giving direct evidence that there is absolutely no merit in the suggestion that the Act's content was in any way influenced adversely by Apartheid or any political considerations. Having been intimately involved with its content from its very nascence, I can state quite categorically that the motivation behind it and its content was entirely the pursuit of the best interests of creative people and the society that they serve, and in making our law of copyright conform with the best modern international norms and standards. It is true that the Act was drafted during the unhappy years of South Africa being in the unjust clutch of Apartheid. Nevertheless, it is a complete misrepresentation and misnomer to allege that the content of the Act was in any way a product of thinking informed by Apartheid principles, rather than being based on and informed by, as it was, on internationally accepted norms. The true character of the Act is revealed by the fact that it afforded the destitute family of Solomon Linda, a Black family, the opportunity of deriving considerable income from their father's tribal or ethnic song. The Act is colour blind.

The fact that the 1978 Act was adopted during the Apartheid era does not make it anymore 'Apartheid legislation' than animal cruelty or road traffic safety legislation adopted during the same period. In fact, the Act is largely based on, and derived from, British and Commonwealth copyright legislation.

Dating from 45 years ago, the 1978 Act is now in dire need of further updating but its shortcomings in this respect are in no way attributable to political considerations, as its critics and enemies are for subjective reasons wanting to suggest.

During my tenancy on the Advisory Committee, the Copyright Act was amended eight times. These amendments were all aimed at updating the Act to keep pace with developments in technology, leading cases which broached new issues, and innovations in copyright law both nationally and internationally. On each of these occasions I was the principal draftsman of the amendments largely because of the fact that I was at the coal face of all new developments in the law. This was by virtue of my active participation in the trend setting litigation and other developments in the law that took place during that period.

When computer programs became accepted as a species of work eligible for copyright, the international approach was to regard a computer program as a type or species of literary work and to apply the principles of copyright law pertinent to that category of work to them. In the Advisory Committee we felt that this was an artificial and unrealistic approach because writing a computer program was fundamentally different to writing a book.

The enforcement of copyright in a computer program as though it was a book was contrived and unrealistic. Accordingly, a subcommittee under my chairmanship adopted a new and fresh approach to copyright in computer programs. We created a separate new and distinct category of work called 'computer program' and devised a unique set of principles, in keeping with prevailing copyright principles, to be applied to it. The Act was accordingly amended in 1992 to create this new category of work and to regulate the copyright in it. This created a world first that has worked very well, and it continues to operate very successfully. This innovation was indicative of the proactive and creative approach to copyright adopted by the Advisory Committee.

FURTHER DEVELOPMENTS IN COPYRIGHT

Once the ambit of the Advisory Committee was extended to embrace the full field of IP law, the committee brought about innovations in other areas of IP as well. At an early stage a system for registration of copyright in cinematograph films was introduced and the Registration of Copyright in Cinematograph Films Act, 1978, was passed. This provided for a system of registration of copyright in films in order to streamline anti-piracy actions in that field. I drafted significant portions of the Regulations which supplemented the Act.

Dealing with counterfeit copies of films, records and other works became a severe problem by virtue of the prevalence of these ills and the difficulty in enforcing conventional IP rights to counteract this scourge. I moved the Advisory Committee to adopt dedicated legislation dealing with counterfeit goods. I conceptualised the approach that should be adopted and set up a committee under the auspices of the Advisory Committee to prepare draft customised legislation to deal with the problem of counterfeit goods. I undertook the basic drafting work. This gave rise to the Counterfeit Goods Act, 1997. This Act provided a useful tool in counteracting trading in counterfeit goods.

After 1997 there was a change of guard at the Department of Trade and Industry and a new Minister, Alec Erwin, was appointed. He made it clear to the Advisory Committee that he viewed its role differently to that which had prevailed during the past two decades when it was proactive in keeping our law in tune with developments in IP law. He basically informed the Committee that it should henceforth play a completely passive role and should only 'speak when spoken to', as it were. The result was that the serving membership of the committee, including myself, resigned or were not reappointed, and the committee for all practical purposes ceased to function as a viable and useful entity, to the detriment of IP law in the country.

Since that time (i.e. during the past 25 years) there has been only one minor amendment of the Copyright Act, which largely explains why it has become so out of date and desperately in need of being reinvigorated. There have been two ham-handed and inept attempts, both hitherto unsuccessful (thankfully, in view of the very poor quality and ineptness of the efforts) to amend the Act. More about this later.

I can only speculate as to why such a negative attitude developed in respect of IP in the government since the turn of the century. Whatever the reason might have been it has led to the significant decline in the quality of IP protection in this country, to the detriment of the welfare of the creative industries and business in general in South Africa. The country's IP legislative regime has deteriorated from being first class, state of the art by international standards, to being second rate.

My legislative role in the field of copyright came to an end at the millennium, but it did continue in other related fields about which more will be said later. Nonetheless during my 20 year stint on the Advisory Committee I learnt a lot about copyright law and my expertise and stature in the field were greatly enhanced. As all this work was done on a free *pro bono* basis, it was undertaken purely to perform a public service and to foster my own experience and comprehension of the subject matter. The valuable experience gained ultimately contributed significantly to my credentials to conduct *The Lion Sleeps Tonight* case.

CREATIVE LAWYERING – TEST CASES

Two significant events took place at Spoor & Fisher in and around 1978, some three years after I became a partner. First, the firm decided to open an offshore office to facilitate practising on the African continent. Laurie Hart, one of my valued mentors, was chosen as the person to operate the offshore office which was to be based on Jersey in the Channel Islands. This entailed him withdrawing from active practice in South Africa and relocating to Jersey which depleted the ranks of our trade mark litigators.

Next, since the size of the firm's practice had grown considerably during the past few years, it was decided to appoint a full-time managing partner to be at the helm of the firm's business. Geoff Webster was chosen to fulfil this role. This meant that my other principal mentor and the firm's front line trade mark litigator, was also withdrawn from active practice. This left me, with barely three years' experience, as the spearhead of the firm's trade mark litigation facility. I was literally thrown into the deep end. At the same time, I became responsible for servicing several of the firm's major blue chip clients, like the Rembrandt Group and major international companies like Unilever, Levi Strauss and Adidas.

The first major case that came my way after my elevation in status involved the infringement of Adidas' famous three-stripe registered trade mark as applied to sports footwear. Adidas' trade mark of three parallel stripes running from the lace ups of shoes diagonally down to the soles was world famous and their shoes were the market leader. A practice had developed for parasitic traders to manufacture and sell sports footwear similar to the Adidas product but bearing four stripes instead of three stripes. Spurious shoes of this nature were overrunning the local market, and Adidas was firmly resolved to dispose of this unwanted unfair competition. The belief was that consumers were not distinguishing between the three-stripe and four-stripe patterns and were taking the four-stripe shoes to be Adidas shoes. The spurious shoes were generally of cheap and poor quality, which was damaging the good reputation of the Adidas products. It was argued by Adidas that a four stripe device on a shoe was confusingly similar to a three stripe device and that the use of the former infringed Adidas' three-stripe trade mark.

My mandate was to bring litigation against someone, anyone, no matter how large or small, to get the court to pronounce that the use of the four stripe device infringed the three-stripe trade mark. The case was to be a test case to establish and demonstrate Adidas' rights and to make an example of one of the plethora of parasitic traders. Recovery of damages was unimportant and insignificant. The prize was to get a favourable judgment which could be waved under the noses of the other parasitic traders and act as a deterrent for their ongoing unlawful conduct. This was quite a challenge for a relative novice to trade mark litigation.

After a couple of false starts where traders to whom we sent cease and desist letters simply capitulated, we found a footwear importer (importing goods from China) that fitted the bill perfectly. This importer dug his heels in and elected to defend the case vehemently. It subsequently transpired that the consignment of spurious goods only numbered some five pairs, each worth R200, but that did not matter. The important point was that the importer decided to defend the case to the hilt which was exactly what we wanted. The case was entirely successful. The court made the finding of trade mark infringement that we were after, and the rest was a success story.

The outcome brought about the desired result of drying up the market in four stripe shoes. I had learned a very valuable lesson, namely the immense worth of conducting a successful test case where the end objective was greater than simply getting a favourable judgment against a particular trader. This was a salutary experience that I was to repeat many times in the future. It became part of my stock in trade. It also proved to be the model for the Disney case.

A band wagon developed in bringing copyright infringement proceedings where reverse engineering of industrial drawings was taking place. Suddenly copyright became an active area of practice. Although I had set the ball rolling by virtue of the article that I had published and the papers that I delivered on the subject, the pattern developed for these cases to be entrusted to patent attorneys because the nature of the copying that was taking place was akin to the infringement of patents. We trade mark attorneys were left on the sidelines. My breakthrough into this activity came about in unusual and remarkable circumstances. Was it fate/providence/coincidence/happenstance?

My brother, Peter Dean, was the Managing Director of a company manufacturing replacement exhaust systems for motor vehicles. A competitor in the field claimed that my brother's company was copying their designs through reverse engineering and instituted copyright infringement proceedings against his company. My brother turned to me to defend the case, which I did successfully. This case was the first of its kind to be successfully defended and it brought me into the limelight as a copyright litigator and opened doors for me in the field. It also broke the stranglehold of patent attorneys over reverse engineering copyright infringement cases. My brother's case was therefore an important factor in the promotion of my career as a copyright specialist. Several copyright infringement cases followed wherein I dealt with works such as textile designs, product labels and weaving patterns, and copyright law became a major preoccupation of mine.

My brother's case was the first one in which I briefed Cedric Puckrin, an advocate at the Pretoria Bar, to handle a case. He was later to become a central figure in *The Lion Sleeps Tonight* case – more about him later. We had cut our teeth in trade mark law on the same case. I was an articled clerk and he was serving a spell of pupillage at the Bar where he was attached to the Senior Counsel whom we had briefed to represent our client. It was the start of a long and fruitful association which lasted my entire career.

The instant case, which took place in Cape Town, was a trial that lasted two weeks, much longer than we had anticipated. It transpired that Cedric had to return to Pretoria on the evening preceding the last day of the hearing, in order to appear in a case there. This meant that I was essentially left to hold the fort by myself on the last day of the hearing. This did not really appear to be a problem because all that remained to be done on that day was for other side (the plaintiff) to complete their final argument in reply. There was no opportunity for our side to say anything more. Nevertheless, convention required that we should be represented by an advocate even if he simply sat there and did nothing other than bow to the judge at the appropriate times. We accordingly arranged for a local very junior counsel to sit in the appropriate seat and try to look intelligent for the remainder of the proceedings which were not expected to endure for more than an hour or so. As it happens, I knew the advocate in question because he was the kid brother of 'the girl next door' when I grew up in Camps Bay. He knew nothing whatsoever about the case and it was not expected of him that he should.

The case was complicated, particularly for a Cape Town judge because judges from that city had very little exposure to IP. During his argument on previous days Cedric had done a good job of explaining the finer points of copyright involved in the case. Nevertheless, I was a little concerned that the judge had not fully grasped the salient issue of this particular case. It was essential to our cause that he should do so, but there was no scope on the last day for us to influence him.

Overnight the judge had obviously done a lot of thinking about the case and a glimmering of understanding of the salient issue was beginning to show, having become evident from the questions that the judge put to the plaintiff's counsel once he began his argument. The counsel answered the judge's questions, putting his clients' gloss on his argument. This did not appear to satisfy the judge. He turned his attention to our stooge advocate and asked him what he had to say on the matter. Our counsel was transfixed in horror. He was like a rabbit caught in the headlights of an approaching vehicle. He did not have the slightest notion of what the case, let alone the pertinent issue, was all about and was rendered speechless. He did, however, have the presence of mind to request the judge's leave to consult with me, his attorney.

There was no way in the short time available that I was going to be able to empower the counsel to speak intelligently. As an attorney, I (at that time) did not have the right of audience before the court so I could not answer the judge. The only solution was for me to scribble written notes for the counsel to read. Then followed a somewhat comical process where our counsel would follow the script and provide an answer to the judges specific questions, whereafter the judge would ask a further question which would prompt another written answer by me. This went on for some time and by the end it was clear to me that the judge had at last fully grasped the salient issue. The hearing was concluded, and the judge provided a judgment a month or two later in which he found in our favour on basis of the very issue that was discussed. This was a close shave. It made the point that a copyright attorney has to be a man for all seasons. Developing this attribute was to stand me in good stead throughout my career and not in the least in the Disney case.

In the early 1980s the video tape market arrived in South Africa and video hire outlets where copies of movies could be obtained sprang up like wildfire all around the country. The video industry had to contend with two main problems, namely the presence in the local market of so-called parallel imports, and illegitimate or so-called 'pirate' tapes. Both of these factors threatened the commercial viability of the market.

The major American movie companies sought to appoint local licencees who would undertake local production of video versions of their films and their distribution in the market. Amongst the aspirant licencees was Gallo. The success of the proposed business model was dependent on the local licencees enjoying exclusivity in supplying the market with recorded video tapes. However, video retailers resorted to purchasing legitimately recorded video tapes in overseas markets and importing them into South Africa, i.e. dealing in so-called 'parallel imports'. Neither the movie company licensors nor the local licensee/distributors could countenance this form of alternative trading. The presence of these 'parallel imports' imperilled the market.

The situation reached such dire proportions that the local aspirant licensees took up the position that unless the availability of parallel imports could be curtailed, there would be no future in taking up production/distribution licences. The question arose whether there were legal means available to counteract trading in parallel imports. This problem was addressed by both the prospective licensees and the licensors. In particular, the American industry body, the Motion Picture Association (MPA), of which all the major American film companies were members, stepped into the picture.

I was approached by Gallo (marking my first involvement with this company) to advise whether it would be possible to prevent parallel imports from being traded in the local market, and if so, what steps should be taken to address the problem. It was clear that this was a copyright issue. I looked into the question and came to the conclusion that on a proper construction of a particular provision of the Copyright Act it would be possible to solve the parallel import problem, provided the licensing of the reproduction of films in South Africa was properly organised to take advantage of the provision in question. I advised Gallo accordingly and, based on my successful experience with the Adidas three-stripe trade mark, recommended that a test case should be brought in the most favourable circumstances.

The aim would be to establish the principle of law involved and to demonstrate to the market that the film companies were able and willing to take appropriate action to counteract trading in parallel imports.

This recommendation was passed through to the MPA and they decided to run with it.

In due course I instituted litigation on behalf of Paramount Pictures Corporation (a member of the MPA) against a prominent Johannesburg video dealer who was trading in parallel imports of the movies *Star Trek* and *Grease*. Only one tape of each film was involved, so claiming damages was a complete non-issue. This did not matter for the purposes of the test case. The prize sought was a judgment establishing the salient point of law.

The case was successful, much to the incredulity of the local dealers, who took the case on appeal, where the original decision was upheld. As was the case with the four-stripe shoes, the success of the test case brought about the prompt demise in the trade in parallel imports and opened the way for the establishment of a vibrant local video distribution business. The value and worth of the test case strategy was manifest. It was clearly a valuable weapon available to rights owners.

Later, I combined the principles of the yacht case regarding reverse engineering of drawings with the Paramount Pictures principle regarding parallel imports and conducted yet another test case on behalf of the local exclusive distribution agent of Yamaha of Japan. In this case we succeeded in establishing that parallel importation of electronic goods could be prevented on the strength of a copyright argument. This case had a significant impact on the trade in so-called 'grey goods' in the consumer goods market.

CREATIVE LAWYERING – ANTI-PIRACY

The piracy problem faced by the video industry, and indeed by a variety of different industries, required a different approach. Making and trading in unauthorised copies of video tapes clearly constituted infringement of the copyright in the subject matter recorded on the original tapes. That point did not need to be established in a test case. What was necessary, however, was to show that the copyright owners had the resolve and wherewithal to take effective counter measures.

A practical problem that had to be overcome was that of preserving the evidence and spoils of the illegal copying in order to take effective court action. Experience showed that test purchases could be made of infringing products, but by the time court proceedings could be launched, all the evidence and inventory of unlawful goods would invariably have been spirited away, which greatly detracted from the utility of taking legal action.

I became aware of a measure that recently was gaining some currency in the United Kingdom for dealing with this problem. It was known as an 'Anton Piller Order', named after the case in which it had first made its appearance in that country. Although our legal procedures had some affinities to those of the United Kingdom, ours were significantly home grown and unique to our requirements and situation. It did not necessarily follow that a UK procedure could simply be transplanted into our system.

An Anton Piller Order pertains to a situation where a plaintiff is aware that he has been the victim of unlawful conduct and wishes to enforce their rights, but has grounds to believe that, if the defendant becomes aware that court proceedings are in the offing, the incriminating evidence will be destroyed or taken out of their reach. The remedy entails the plaintiff being granted an extraordinary remedy aimed at preserving and securing that evidence so that it will be available in forthcoming litigation. In terms of this measure the plaintiff is entitled to approach the court on a confidential basis, without any notice to the defendant, and seek an order authorising an unannounced raid on the defendant's premises to seize and safeguard the evidence. Having secured the evidence, the plaintiff can then bring the court proceedings in the normal manner. It occurred to me that the situation in the video industry required the availability of such a remedy in our court procedure.

I approached an eminent senior advocate with whom I had worked closely in the past and explained the Anton Piller Order to him as he was not familiar with the measure. I asked him whether we could introduce such a procedure into our law. After consideration he opined that it may be a possibility and was worth a try. We would be breaking new ground in our law. We formulated an approach which was true to the essence of the Anton Piller Order but adapted to render it capable of being integrated into our practice. We resolved to launch a test case to aspire to our objective.

We duly found a suitable opportunity and obtained the desired order which was successfully and effectively executed. As it happened the defendant was deeply aggrieved by the execution of the order and took his displeasure out on me by punching me and giving me a black eye, an assault for which I subsequently obtained due recompense (physically assaulting lawyers while executing their duties comes at a cost). Entering into unknown territory had its perils!

The damages action that I instituted against Mr Punch yielded quite a nice return that salved my wounded eye and pride. I used the money to buy my daughter a long-desired piano. It was a case of an eye for a set of ivories! I worked out that my monetary return per punch received probably eclipsed the rate of monetary return per punch received in the ring by Mohamed Ali in his illustrious and lucrative boxing career! I nonetheless had a strong preference for a legal career despite its attendant risks.

The MPA accepted the availability of the Anton Piller Order gleefully and we widely used it to good effect in our anti-piracy litigation. The organisation had in the meantime set up a full-time agency to conduct anti-piracy action on behalf of its members in South Africa, and I was retained on an ongoing basis by that agency, which was headed by a person named Ted Askew. Ted Askew and I had many adventures going around the country obtaining and executing Anton Piller Orders.

The first occasion when a criminal prosecution involving an Anton Piller Order came before the court occurred in the then Pietersburg. The prosecutor seized with the matter was all at sea on the copyright issues, let alone on how the Anton Piller Order interacted with them. It was important that this case should be successful and set a precedent to be followed throughout the country. We did not feel that the prosecutor was up to the task. We accordingly approached the Attorney-General of the Transvaal and persuaded him that I should be temporarily deputised as a state prosecutor so I could argue the law before the court. This was a novel experience for me, and I am happy to say that it paid off and the case was successful. It once again showed that being a copyright attorney required you to be a man for all seasons.

From a criminal law enforcement perspective copyright infringement, and in particular video piracy, was allocated to the Drug Squad of the police force – a rather strange cocktail. The head of the Drug Squad at the time was a certain Colonel Basie Smit of the SA Police. He took a particular interest in video piracy and was of inestimable value to our antipiracy campaign. He much later became head of the Security Police in which role he became rather infamous.

Colonel Smit decided that the antipiracy campaign should be extended to South West Africa, a separate territory administered by South Africa under a mandate from the League of Nations (later becoming the United Nations). He consequently took Ted Askew and me on a tour of the territory in order to educate the local police and dispel the mysteries of copyright.

We spent a week in the territory actively pursuing this objective. In the evenings we socialised with the members of the local Drug Squads, who were rough diamonds to say the least. In order to gain their confidence and respect it was necessary to try to keep up with their after-hours social pursuits, particularly as they considered lawyers to be an aloof and effete breed which hampered our gaining their confidence. Many was the evening when I was cajoled into drinking alcoholic beverages while flames burned on the surface of the liquid. I survived the experience, and actually succeeded in imparting a rudimentary understanding of copyright law to the operatives. As I have said, to do my job one had to be a man for all seasons.

The use of the Anton Piller Order spread like a virulent virus into all branches of South African law and procedure, even being used in divorce proceedings! We remained conservative and circumspect in our use of it, but this was not true of all its exponents. Eventually things got out of hand and in particular the Johannesburg Supreme Court developed an aversion to it and refused to grant it, holding in a judgment that it was an alien invasion into our law and did not belong in it. This did not please the MPA as it had proved to be very valuable to them. I was requested to try and turn the tide. This fortified my own firm subjective view that the measure ought to be available in our law.

Adopting my tried and trusted formula of the test case, we contrived to take a case where an Anton Piller Order had featured to the Appellate Division of the Supreme Court with a view to getting that court to endorse it. Happily, our efforts bore fruit, and the Chief Justice personally wrote an excellent judgment in which he stamped his approval on the measure, further developing the law by laying down sensible tests, requirements and procedures for its use. It attained a proud place in our law. To put the matter entirely beyond doubt, I wrote a statutory version of it into the Counterfeit Goods Act when I drafted that legislation.

The MPA and its local agency became influential in copyright enforcement circles in South Africa, particularly in the anti-piracy field. Its anti-piracy programme was subsequently emulated by the record industry and by the computer software industry. I was retained by industry organisations seized with coordinating anti-piracy litigation in these respective fields of endeavour as well. Copyright had virtually overtaken my entire practice. I estimate that I had at that time cornered about seventy percent of the copyright practice in South Africa.

INNOVATION IN DIVERSE FIELDS

I nevertheless remained involved in practising trade mark law as well. In this area of the law, I prosecuted groundbreaking cases where, inter alia, approbation was obtained of character merchandising (using characters such as Mickey Mouse and Donald Duck as branding) as a recognised form of trading which could attract proprietary rights, and where for the first time market survey evidence was recognised and endorsed as admissible and cogent by no less an authority than the Appellate Division of the Supreme Court.

The peculiarly South African product/geographical indication 'Rooibos' was being abused internationally. Our government had taken no steps (available under international treaties) to protect the term. The principle that applied in the international milieu was that such an indication could not enjoy international protection unless and until it was protected in its home country. I published an article in which I mapped out the way in which the term could be easily and comprehensively protected in South Africa, and thus internationally as well.

There was initially no reaction on the part of the government to my article or the means of protection proposed. However, the article was picked up by the Ambassador of the European Union in South Africa, who, after holding discussions with me, intervened and succeeded in persuading the government as to the folly of not implementing my advice. This led to my proposed solution being followed by the government to the letter. It was bizarre that our government could only be moved to grant much needed protection to an important domestic industry by the intervention of a foreign ambassador!

When the new South African Constitution came before the Constitutional Court for consideration, and was subsequently approved by it, I appeared in person before that court at the hearing on behalf of the Association of Marketers and argued that intellectual property should be specifically recognised and protected as a fundamental right in the Constitution. This was not a fanciful notion on my part because IP was recognised as a fundamental right in the International Declaration of Human Rights, to which South Africa had subscribed. I was only partially successful in that regard, but the court did acknowledge that, as a form of property, IP fell withing the ambit of the property clause (section 25) of the Bill of Rights in the Constitution and was protected to that extent. This proved to be a significant concession in later years.

At about that time resistance developed to the use of the Springbok emblem by the South African national rugby team. It was said to be an Apartheid symbol, and pressure was put on the government to ban its use. I published an article in which I argued on the basis of the Constitutional Court's concession that IP constituted property, that to ban the use of the symbol, which was actually a registered trade mark, would amount to an arbitrary deprivation of property under the Bill of Rights and would be unconstitutional. The storm surrounding the use of the emblem passed over and it has retained its pride of place, becoming a national symbol of unity of purpose.

ACADEMIA

Spoor & Fisher had long held the reputation of being the leading academic law firm in the IP field. Geoff Webster wrote the standard textbook on trade mark law and another partner, Tim Burrell, wrote the standard textbook on patent law. On a good day at a fairly early stage of my incipient copyright career, Geoff Webster came into my office and advised me that Juta, the academic and legal publishers, had approached the firm with the request that we should produce a textbook on copyright law, which was felt to be in need of an authoritative work. The firm had decided that I should be delegated to undertake that project. I was flabbergasted and somewhat flattered that it should be expected of me to author such a work. However, I felt hopelessly ill equipped to do so at that stage. But a 'request' coming from Geoff Webster had the status of a directive and I had no choice but to agree to take the task on board. I pleaded for a period of grace to give effect to it.

Several years went by and I became increasingly embarrassed that I had not yet delivered on my undertaking. In the meantime, my expertise in copyright had been on the increase. I reached a point where honour required of me to produce something. I had written a series of articles on copyright for a legal journal and that gave me a starting point. I put the proposition to Juta that I should produce a compendium of all the relevant historical copyright legislation covered by a brief synopsis of the law (compiled from my series of articles). This should be done on a loose-leaf basis that could be updated and expanded with the passage of time. Juta agreed to this, and my *Handbook of South African Copyright Law* saw the light of day in 1987.

Over the years I produced fifteen updates of the work as the law evolved and my expertise grew, and it soon assumed the status of a fully-fledged textbook. It has regularly over the years been accepted and quoted as authority by the court and academic writers. In addition to writing the *Handbook* I published over a hundred articles on various aspects of IP law in South African and international legal journals.

As a student I had the vague notion that someday I would like to do a doctorate in law. When I was in the final stages of producing the *Handbook*, I decided to use one part of it, which gave a historical overview of the evolution and development of copyright law in South Africa, as the kernel of a doctoral thesis. Accordingly, simultaneously with compiling and writing the *Handbook*, I wrote my thesis on the topic of 'The Application of the Copyright Act, 1978, to Works made prior to 1979'. I was awarded a Doctor of Laws degree (LLD) on the basis of this thesis by Stellenbosch University in 1988. This thesis was later to play a decisive role in *The Lion Sleeps Tonight* case.

QUO VADIS?

By the millennium my practice was at a peak. My railroad track to somewhere had passed through many interesting and rewarding terrains. I had achieved successes and rewards beyond my wildest dreams. I was variously described in publications as 'the doyen of intellectual property in South Africa'; 'the senior statesman of IP'; 'Mr Copyright'; 'the leading IP practitioner in South Africa'. I had served a spell as the President of the South African Institute of Intellectual Property Law and was shortly to become the Chairman of Spoor & Fisher. But the end of the line, the destination to which I felt all along that the railway track was inevitably headed, was not yet in sight and remained unknown. Ten short years until my mandatory retirement from Spoor & Fisher remained. What lay in store for me? What was it that I had been preparing myself for during the past 25 years?

My involvement in intellectual property law had come about purely by happenstance, not through design. However, 25 years down the line I had made my mark in the field and my career was flourishing. Fate had set me up as a leading figure in IP. But to what end, I repeatedly asked myself.

In Tempore Leo

PART 2

VII

The Master Plan

THE PLOT

When I greeted Geoff Paynter of Gallo in reception at Spoor & Fisher on that fateful day in September 2002, I saw that he wasn't alone; he had a whole posse with him. Ivor Haarberger was a senior executive at Gallo; Hanro Friederich was the attorney who had been retained by the Linda family; Rian Malan was the author of the contentious article in *Rolling Stone*; and the final member of the team was Paul Jenkins. I knew Jenkins by reputation. For many years he had been a partner of the prominent attorneys firm, Webber Wentzel, making entertainment and media matters a specialty. I had read that he had retired from legal practice and entered the corporate environment as an executive at Johnnic Entertainment, a member of the Gallo Group. I was surprised to receive such a large delegation.

Jenkins was the spokesman. He said that, after careful consideration of my opinion and consulting all other interested parties, particularly Hanro Friederich and Rian Malan, it had been decided that all the parties would come together in a joint endeavour to further the interests of the Linda heirs in connection with *Mbube*. The way forward should be founded on the reversionary interest in *Mbube* which had passed to Solomon Linda's descendants in terms of the Dickens Clause. And they would be briefing me to take up the legal case.

Jenkins said Gallo would bear all the costs of the legal action and no expense was to be spared. I must take whatever steps were necessary to make the Linda family's rights in the song prevail. I was to achieve recognition of these rights with a view to generating income from royalties for them from the use of *Mbube* and its derivatives, particularly *The Lion Sleeps Tonight*. I could count on the support and assistance of all the interested parties. I was delighted at this turn of events, but more than a little flabbergasted by the positivity and enterprise shown by the group, particularly after a hiatus of two years since I had delivered my opinion.

After brainstorming the matter, we concluded that the best way of achieving the objective of demonstrating the existence of the family's rights to the world at large would be to conduct a test case in which a definitive court ruling would be sought. It should state that the Linda family owned the copyright in *Mbube* and was thus entitled to control the use of *The Lion Sleeps Tonight*. The purpose of the test case was, in keeping with its nature, to use an actual dispute as a means of getting a court ruling that recognised and established the reversionary interest principle, and its applicability to *Mbube/The Lion Sleeps Tonight* situation. In effect we would be emulating the approach adopted successfully inter alia in the Adidas and Paramount Pictures cases, which had proved to be very worthwhile and effective endeavours.

In the final analysis our view was thus that the interests of the family would be best served by conducting a prominent copyright infringement case, as a test case, against a high profile defendant who was using *The Lion Sleeps Tonight* without the authority of the family in a country where it owned the copyright in *Mbube* – in other words, a country that was a former member of the British Empire or Commonwealth. The higher the profile of the target the better because we wanted the case to attract publicity and make a strong impact.

The object of the exercise was to make a forceful statement that the family had the power to control the use of *The Lion Sleeps Tonight* and would henceforth be in a position to act against all infringers of the copyright in *Mbube*.

Assuming that we would be successful, a platform for future action would be created and the way would be paved to go forward in the future to institute damages claims against users of the song whether in performances or in producing records. That would be phase two of the campaign. Once the validity of the cause of action had been established, the job would in the main be done and then pursuing damages claims against infringers would be essentially a much simpler sort of debt collecting exercise.

Another option that would be open to the family would be for the copyright in *Mbube* to be sold and assigned to a third party, for instance a music publisher or an investor, who would be prepared to pay a lump sum commensurate with the value of future royalties to be collected for the use of the song. The endorsement of the validity of the family's copyright claim would establish the viability of this opportunity. This is not an uncommon practice in the music industry and had previously been followed in the United Kingdom by beneficiaries of the reversionary interest. Indeed, it was put into effect in the case of the Dickens family following the adoption of the Dickens Clause in legislation.

A good high profile example of the approach of selling off the right to collect royalties is the sale of the rights to the Beatles' song repertoire to a third party to be used for that party's gain. In the circumstances of the daughters this approach would have the advantage of realising a sizeable lump sum in the short term and would absolve them from the chore of chasing royalties around the world.

Both these options would become available and viable if we were to succeed in obtaining a suitable judgment in the envisaged test case. The test case was the key.

Although damages might be claimed in the test case, and later pursuing claims in that regard would be a card that could be played at an appropriate time, they would be incidental to the main purpose of the test litigation.

LEGAL FRAMEWORK

In South Africa damages in civil law cases, particularly in intellectual property matters, are very difficult to prove and claims in that regard are problematic. The departure point is that the plaintiff is entitled to claim as their damages the amount that they are actually out of pocket on account of the defendant's unlawful conduct. This could take the form of revenue that was forfeited through loss of sales or the forfeiting of royalties for the exploitation of the product. The plaintiff must quantify their damages in a specific amount of Rands and cents. One cannot simply make sweeping claims that damages have been suffered. That is insufficient. The precise amount of damages experienced by the plaintiff must be proved by means of appropriate evidence.

The facts as to the magnitude and extent of the unlawful conduct that gave rise to damages are invariably peculiarly within the knowledge of the defendant, e.g., how many infringing copies have been produced and sold and at what price? The classic argument is that those sales have been lost by the plaintiff and the profits that he would have made from selling them equal his damages. That amount represents the value of the extent he is out of pocket. But it is not as simple as that because a variety of factors can come into the equation which detract from this premise. For instance, the infringing copies might have been sold at a lower price (the normal situation), which enables the defendant to argue that the public was willing to purchase their product at the lower price but would not have bought the product at the higher price. I once had a case where the defendant successfully argued that the plaintiff could not possibly themselves have made the contentious sales because they were out production at the time and therefore had no available stock.

In an attempt to alleviate this problem, the Copyright Act was amended at the instigation of the Advisory Committee to introduce, as an alternative to paying damages, a remedy for copyright infringement whereby a plaintiff could claim payment of a reasonable royalty in respect of the dealings in infringing copies. But even this remedy required the plaintiff to prove the number of articles sold by the defendant, although the price at which they were sold was not necessarily relevant, because the level of the royalties to be paid could be established by showing what objectively would have been the going rate for royalties in the circumstances.

The upshot of this is that there has only been one reported case where damages have been awarded in a South African copyright infringement case, and then only for a trifling sum.

In South Africa it has become the standard practice in copyright and other IP infringement cases for the proceedings to be divided into two distinct phases. In the first phase the question of whether infringement has occurred is determined. Assuming that this is established, the case then goes over to a second phase, in practice referred to as an 'enquiry into damages', namely the determination of the quantum of the damages that has been suffered. The plaintiff is then largely reliant on information provided by the defendant to obtain the facts that they require in order to compute the amount of the damages that they have suffered. This virtually amounts to a separate trial. It is a very cumbersome and expensive process and there is generally a strong incentive at this stage to negotiate a settlement of the damages claim. The rationale for this dual procedure is that there is no point in going to the trouble and expense of conducting an enquiry into damages unless and until the infringement has been established. Then, and only then, the quantum of the damages becomes relevant. There is little point in pursuing the enquiry if the costs of doing so significantly outweigh the likely damages award.

A similar two-pronged approach is adopted in copyright damages claims in the United Kingdom.

THE TARGET

The choice of a target for the test case narrowed down to Walt Disney, which was then producing the musical show, *The Lion King*, incorporating the song *The Lion Sleeps Tonight* in London. Disney and the way it used *The Lion Sleeps Tonight* made it a very suitable candidate for a test case. It was difficult to contemplate a higher profile target than Disney.

The case would be brought by means of a procedure that allowed for evidence to be produced by way of affidavits, which obviated witnesses having to appear in court to present live evidence at a trial. Apart from the costs involved in conducting a lengthy trial, it was felt that the Linda daughters were not well suited for appearing at a trial in the United Kingdom and being cross-examined by skilled barristers. This meant that we would be unable to make a formal claim for damages as this form of procedure did not allow for processing such a claim. For the purposes of a test case this was not really a material consideration.

Since *The Lion King* stage show had been performed in the UK for a lengthy period already, there would in principle be scope to recover a significant amount of damages or lost royalties from Disney. The claim would cover only uses of the song made by Disney alone and not by the vast variety of other parties who had also used it in one form or another. Those other manners of use could not be laid at Disney's door as they had no connection with Disney. So, there was the possibility that we could informally throw in a claim for damages at an opportune moment as the case progressed, possibly as part of a settlement. In any event a formal damages claims could follow later as a separate proceeding. I was instructed to institute copyright infringement litigation against Walt Disney in the United Kingdom on the proposed basis.

As a legal practitioner this was a marvellous opportunity for me. I was given *carte blanche* to bring a major copyright infringement case on viable grounds, in a legal forum that was literally on the world stage. It had all the makings of being the high point of my legal career and I was excited at the prospect.

DEVELOPING A CASE

My first thought was that Gallo should be the claimant or plaintiff. This would require them to take assignment of the family's rights in the song. But Jenkins was adamant that Gallo wanted to remain in the background and not be the protagonist in the case. The family must be the plaintiff. But there was a problem because Regina Linda and the Linda children had signed away all their rights to the song in the past.

I explained to Jenkins and the other members of the delegation the bones of the problem. I advised that the nature of copyright, as an asset, is unusual because under copyright law you can enter into a present day assignment of future copyright. This means the author of a prospective work can assign his copyright in that work to, for instance, a publisher, even before pen is put to paper. When the work comes into existence, the copyright is immediately transferred to the assignee, or in our example, the publisher.

The same principle applies where someone enters into a present assignment of copyright that they don't currently hold but may acquire in the future. In this situation, as soon as that person acquires the copyright, his assignment is activated, and the copyright automatically passes to his assignee. I explained that this is what happened in the case of Regina and the Linda children with their assignments to Folkways and that it would be fatal for them at any stage to acquire ownership of the copyright. This would scupper the entire enterprise. As soon as the ownership of the copyright devolved on any of them, it would automatically and immediately pass to Folkways through activation of the past assignments and the Dickens Clause could not be used to assist them.

We talked loosely of the 'author's heirs' becoming the recipient of the reversionary interest in the copyright in *Mbube*. But that was an oversimplification, and it wasn't what the relevant section of the Imperial Copyright Act actually said. What it said was that the reverted copyright would pass to the deceased's 'legal personal representative *as part of his estate*' (emphasis added). The text of the section can be viewed in Appendix II on page A2.

This provision had never been interpreted by any court, but I took it to mean that the reverted copyright would pass to the Executor in the deceased author's estate. What the law then contemplates is that in due course the Executor will transfer the copyright to the heirs or some other party they nominate. This latter proposition made good sense because it meant that the Executor could sell off the reversionary interest to another party, for instance a music publisher, and derive immediate financial benefit for the estate instead of waiting 25 years for the copyright to vest and for the benefit to materialise. Using this interpretation we decided to proceed on the assumption that the Executor of Solomon Linda's Estate was the holder of the transferred copyright, and that the proceedings should be instituted by that Executor in his representative capacity.

Although I was confident about my interpretation of the provision regarding the identity of the recipient of the reversionary interest, I nevertheless thought it prudent to consult an expert in the field of the law of succession in order to get an authoritative view on the question. Hanro brought along Prof JC Sonnekus of the University of Johannesburg to give us an opinion. He expressed an entirely different view, and adamantly advised that in terms of the relevant provision the copyright had devolved directly on the Linda heirs and not on the Executor of the Estate. Rather arrogantly, he – as one versed in the law of succession – told me that I did not understand copyright law. His advice caused me some consternation as it would have meant that we had no case because the copyright in the song would have then automatically flowed to Folkways in terms of the assignments that the heirs had executed. I was not, however, prepared to abide by his view, and I sought a second opinion from Prof Marius de Waal of Stellenbosch University, who endorsed my view completely. I found the second opinion more compelling and was prepared to regard it as correct and to proceed on that assumption. Nonetheless, Prof Sonnekus' opinion did introduce some element of uncertainty into our case which was to emerge at a later stage.

Of course, our acceptance of the view endorsed by Prof De Waal gave us the go-ahead to proceed with the case. It meant we would have to have Solomon Linda's Estate re-opened and get an Executor appointed in the Estate. We would then instruct British solicitors to prepare a copyright infringement case in the name of the Executor against Walt Disney in the UK High Court. This would be a tricky brief for me to prepare, because I was required to tell a British lawyer how to interpret an archaic and obsolete provision of British copyright law when the success or otherwise of the case turned on the meaning and effect of that provision.

On the whole I was comforted that I would be able to call on the support of Hanro Friederich and Rian Malan who had a close relationship with the Linda heirs and a good knowledge of the factual background. They could provide valuable information pertinent to the facts of the case, and could liaise with the daughters in order to secure their co-operation and act as a go-between whenever this was necessary. We promised to stay in close contact.

All this was easier said than done because it meant appointing an Executor in the estate of a Black person who had died intestate in poverty in 1962, some 40 years earlier! This appeared to be a daunting prospect, given the status of Black persons at that time.

Nevertheless, I was excited. This case would effectively make new law both in South Africa and internationally. Although there had been a handful of cases in the United Kingdom dealing with the interpretation of the relevant provision of the Imperial Copyright Act, none of those cases had approached the matter from the same angle that we were going to adopt. I was gratified that Gallo was at last taking up the challenge to redress past wrongs in a responsible manner.

VIII

Mastering the Plan

SETTING THE BALL ROLLING

The year following that meeting – the one that gave me the go-ahead to prepare a case against Walt Disney in the United Kingdom – was a long and frustrating one fraught with problems in preparing the groundwork for the case.

I lined up Clive Thorne of the British solicitors firm, Denton Wilde Sapte, to act on behalf of the Executor of the Linda Estate in bringing the court case. I knew him to be a competent and knowledgeable solicitor, particularly in UK copyright and entertainment law matters. I outlined the cause of action to him, and he agreed with my view of the law and the approach I proposed to adopt. He was poised to prepare the papers to start proceedings. Retaining his services had been the easy part.

The major difficulty came in appointing an Executor, and the case couldn't get off the ground until this appointment had been made. Absent an Executor, there was no plaintiff to bring the proceedings. In the circumstances that I have already outlined there was no practical alternative to the Executor being the plaintiff. We had to conjure up one from somewhere.

But before we could appoint an Executor, we first had to establish a formal deceased estate. This was the first step. I called on the assistance of my colleague, Herman Blignaut, to look after this aspect of the project.

Solomon Linda lived and died in Johannesburg. This brought him within the jurisdiction of the Transvaal Provincial Division of the Supreme Court. The Master of this division of the court is responsible for winding up estates in the jurisdiction of the court. We told him we needed to appoint an Executor to deal with a previously unknown asset of an estate dating from 1962 and asked his advice on how to proceed.

He said at that time the estates of Black people living in Johannesburg were the responsibility of the Magistrate of Johannesburg, so Solomon Linda's Estate would have been wound up under his jurisdiction. Before we could do anything else, we needed to trace the file dealing with that estate. The matter was complicated because the legislation that had existed in 1962 relating to the estates of Black South Africans, being considered Apartheid legislation, had since been repealed and new legislation had been put in place.

Herman paid a visit to the Magistrate in Johannesburg and outlined the circumstances of the case. The matter was foreign to the official because jurisdiction for winding up estates had long since been removed from magistrates. Nevertheless, he promised to search the records at his office to see if he could find a file relating to Solomon Linda's Estate.

He found no trace of any such file, but suggested it was possible that files dating from 1962 had been transferred to the State Archives. Herman examined the records at the State Archives and, to our pleasant surprise, found a file dealing with Solomon Linda's Estate. It showed Linda had died intestate in1962, and the sum total of his assets at the time of his death was a bank account with R145. This had been passed to his heirs, the Estate had been wound up and the file closed.

We took the Linda Estate file to the Magistrate of Johannesburg, who begrudgingly accepted that it was his task to appoint an Executor under the old legislation to deal with the newly discovered asset and oversee its proper disposal. These early steps in the process of establishing the Linda family's rights involved highly esoteric and unfamiliar obsolete law for everyone concerned. Time would show that it was absolutely crucial that we got it right.

These were complications that we had not anticipated, but we were undeterred by them. Would less dedicated lawyers have been willing to persevere? This process took many months but eventually Hugh Melamdowitz, a partner of Spoor & Fisher, was formally appointed as Executor. This meant that he would serve as the plaintiff in the court proceedings, which had the advantage that the individual occupying the position would have a good understanding of what the matter was all about.

In the meantime, I met with the three surviving Linda children, Elizabeth, Fildah and Delphi, to explain what was taking place and to hear what they had to say about the case as they knew it. One of the four children, Adelaide, had recently died of Aids, at least partially brought about by their impoverishment.

Since the Executor essentially acts on behalf of the heirs, although Gallo was the actual client, it was important to meet with them and to bring them into the matter. It would be highly unusual and irregular for an executor's team to refrain from having contact with the heirs of the Estate that he was administering. We wanted to play strictly by the book in view of the magnifying glass that would doubtless be applied to all our activities. As it happened, precisely this would in due course come to pass.

I also wanted to get a feel for what sort of witnesses they would make if it became necessary for then to give evidence in support of our case.

My meeting with them was arranged by Hanro Friederich through his close relationship with them, and he accompanied me on the visit, acting as a go-between. They listened blankly to what I had to say. This was understandable because of the complexity of what I had to say. They heard me out with obvious skepticism because many similar promises of gaining an income for them from the use of *Mbube* had been made in the past, including by lawyers, and all had come to naught. Their expectations had been raised on several occasions, only to be dashed. They had no reason to believe my project would have any better prospects, and that I would be any different to the others who had come along with unfulfilled promises. I assured them that this time things would indeed be different. I was to meet with them once again on a second occasion as a follow up.

For reassurance that we were on the right track about the law of succession, in particular relating to Black people, I consulted with experts in the law of succession under traditional African laws. Nothing I learned from them changed my view.

THE BOMBSHELL

Now that we were at last in a state of readiness to move forward with launching the case in the name of the Executor, I arranged another consultation with Paul Jenkins. This was 22 April 2004. The aim was to bring him up to date with all that had been achieved during the past several months and get his go-ahead and actually launch the litigation in the United Kingdom.

I was sitting across the table from him, in the company of Hanro Friederich and Rian Malan, when he dropped a bombshell. Gallo had decided to drop the project, to withdraw from it completely. They were willing to provide funding to cover all costs to date, but as far as they were concerned, the matter should be shelved, and they would have no further part of it.

I was completely shattered. I had been working on this matter for more than three years and just when we were ready to put our carefully laid plan into action, Gallo aborted it.

Jenkins explained that the group of companies of which Gallo was a part, particularly Nu Metro, were the South African licensees of Walt Disney. From a business point of view, they couldn't be involved in an adversarial situation with their own licensor. He didn't explain why this hadn't been an issue those many months before when he was party to the decision that Walt Disney should be the target for the test case.

What should have been a triumphant meeting – because at last we had appointed an Executor and opened the way for our plan to be put into action – was now a debacle. My earlier suspicion returned. Had Gallo intended this matter should ever go to litigation or had they banked all along on it not being feasible to reopen the Estate and appoint an Executor? Whatever the case, the project appeared doomed to be consigned to the scrap heap.

But I wasn't prepared to have it end here. Too much effort, money and emotional capital had been invested for me just to simply drop it. Mindful of the promise I had made to the Linda daughters, I told Jenkins I was going ahead with the project, with or without Gallo. I would hopefully find someone else to fund the costs of the litigation, and we would pursue the project to its conclusion. This was said more in bravado and hope than with conviction.

I took stock. It simply wasn't going to be possible to go ahead with litigation against Walt Disney in the United Kingdom; the cost burden would be too heavy. The theatre of action would have to move to South Africa where we could better manage costs and where I hoped key role players such as the advocates could be persuaded to act *pro bono*.

I told Jenkins that I now proposed to bring copyright infringement proceedings against Walt Disney in South Africa, before the Transvaal Provincial Division of the Supreme Court, but that other parties would have to be added as co-defendants. Unlike in the United Kingdom – where Walt Disney was actually undertaking the production of the stage show and thus directly perpetrating infringing conduct – in South Africa they had at best collaborated with other parties that made unauthorised use of *The Lion Sleeps Tonight*. Disney's conduct had taken the form of authorising or licensing others to distribute the film version of *The Lion King* in the home entertainment market and in cinemas. In other words, Walt Disney were causing others to infringe and were thus a contributory infringer collaborating with those who were responsible for actually reproducing and distributing copies of the film or otherwise exploiting the sound track of *The Lion King* in South Africa.

He assured me that the project's continuation would enjoy the tacit and moral support of Gallo, even though they would no longer play an active role. This was important, because one of the co-defendants would have to be their company, Nu Metro, as the distributor of *The Lion King* movie in South Africa. I was told that I could look to Gallo for information and documentation if necessary. He understood why Nu Metro had to be added as a formal defendant in the proceedings, whereas in fact Walt Disney would be the true defendant, and promised to explain the situation to Nu Metro and get their buy-in.

Nu Metro's involvement would be purely nominal and for purposes of form. He told me there would be no problem with this. As the case unfolded all these assurances would prove to be meaningless and worthless.

IMPLEMENTING PLAN B

I had to think carefully how I should proceed in the light of this shattering development. I was on my own, out on a limb, along with Hanro

Friederich. I didn't really even have a client since the Linda children had played no active role at all and Hanro Friederich and Rian Malan had been mainly interested bystanders. Gallo, my client who had been paying my bills up till then, had jumped ship with the result that the source of funding had run dry. But I was determined not to dash the hopes of the Linda children yet again if I could possibly help it. Besides, it was far too early to give up on the mission. Righteous causes cannot die that easily!

Forced to abandon Plan A but determined to persevere with the project, I now had to implement Plan B. The departure point was that Walt Disney would be sued for copyright infringement in South Africa, as what is known as a 'contributory infringer', essentially an accessory. Nu Metro – and possibly others – would be joined in the proceedings as the theoretical principal infringers – they were the ones who were actually exploiting the song in South Africa, though their involvement in the case would be somewhat nominal. The real target was Disney, and the activities of the others were simply the pretext for suing Disney. This was the first time in my experience that the actual target in a copyright infringement case was a mere contributory infringer, in other words a supporting actor. This was turning out to be a case of several firsts.

Since Walt Disney Enterprises, the American company in question, had no presence in South Africa and wasn't actually trading here, I had no choice but to proceed against South African-based entities which were trading in South Africa and had used the song, *The Lion Sleeps Tonight*, in the sense that it was part of a film, videos and music CDs they had been exploiting. You can't really have a contributory infringer without a principal infringer. The argument was that Disney were causing the others to infringe in South Africa. This argument, which was crucial to the case, subsequently came under the spotlight and will be discussed below in due course.

At the outset there were three major problems in putting together Plan B. In the first place, we needed funding for the litigation; without it, it wouldn't be practical to continue. The second problem was that the South African court doesn't have automatic jurisdiction over a foreign-based corporation that has no presence in South Africa and is not itself trading here. Although Walt Disney had acted through licensees and agents in this country, this didn't give the South African court jurisdiction over it.

The third problem was that I no longer had an instructing client. Although the Linda family would be the beneficiaries of successful litigation, they weren't my clients; Gallo was, or rather, had been. Moreover, the daughters had not the slightest conception of what the case was all about (besides the desired outcome, and as it turned out, they didn't really even understand that) and they were in no position to give me any sensible instructions.

We tackled this problem by enhancing the role of Hanro Friederich, the family's attorney, from that of being an interested bystander and assistant to the status of the client to the end beneficiaries' representative or attorney. He had at the very outset of his being involved in the matter obtained a formal power of attorney from them to act on their behalf.

As the Executor was to be the plaintiff, he could be the figurehead and ostensible client, but his role was really confined to fulfilling the administrative role of winding up the Estate and being the nominal principal player. But all this would be more form than substance. In practice, I would in reality be instructing myself. I was in fact the person driving the entire endeavour. This placed me in a vulnerable and stressful situation.

There was a way around the jurisdictional problem. The law provided that the South African court could obtain jurisdiction against a foreign corporation in a monetary claim if that corporation had property based in South Africa and that property was 'attached' to provide security for the execution of any monetary and/or costs award made against them.

Attachment involves obtaining a sort of pledge or lien over the property in question. It is necessary to apply to the court for an order that specified property be attached for the purposes of founding jurisdiction against its owner. While being a theoretically sound approach, its utilisation in the present instance presupposed that Walt Disney owned some property rooted in South Africa.

A search in the Register of Trademarks showed that Walt Disney owned around 250 registered trade marks in South Africa, including marks such as Donald Duck, Mickey Mouse and Disney itself. As previously explained trade marks are considered to be property in South Africa. Moreover, the Trade Marks Act makes provision for trade marks to be attached as security, so the way forward was to apply to court asking for the attachment of all of Walt Disney's registered trade marks in South Africa. If the order was granted, the jurisdictional problem would be solved. Attaching trade marks in order to found jurisdiction over a foreign entity had never been done before in South Africa. If we were able to accomplish this, we would be breaking new ground. It was a daring but essential ploy. It matched relying on the Dickens Clause for the cause of action in audacity. It was living on the edge.

The change of the theatre of action from London to Pretoria for the litigation had no effect on the nature of the court case. It remained a test case where the endorsement by the court of the validity of our cause of action based on the Dickens Clause was the prize. However, whereas in the UK we would use a form of proceedings where evidence would be in the form of affidavits, and the matter would not go to a trial with no damages being capable of being awarded, the situation in South Africa would be different.

Founding jurisdiction against a foreign based party by means of an attachment of property located in South Africa was only feasible if the claim sounded in money, i.e., in the present case, required the payment of damages. This is an essential requirement of the law relating to attachment of property for jurisdictional purposes. In other words, we were obliged to include a claim for damages in a specific amount in our case. This meant that we would have to utilise a form of procedure where damages could be awarded. The upshot of this is that we would have to institute an action that would lead to a trial with oral evidence. This was not ideal as it meant the witnesses, i.e. at least one of the daughters, would have to get into the witness box and face cross-examination. We had reservations about this prospect, but we had no choice in the matter. We would have to cross this bridge when we came to it.

In the premises, our claim against Disney and the other defendants would have to be in respect of a specific sum of money as damages. Notwithstanding this, the case remained a test case and the prize was a finding of copyright infringement in favour of the Executor. We would resort to the standard practice of stating a specific amount of damages and requesting in our pleadings that the damages issue be referred to an enquiry to be held at some future stage. That would be phase two and would probably never be pursued on account of the paltry sum that would at best be awarded, which sum would be far exceeded by the cost of conducting the enquiry. There was a prospect that a settlement making some provision for a measure of damages could intervene, but that would be a bonus or bonanza.

It must be appreciated that I was following the formula for test cases successfully used in the past in the Adidas and Paramount Pictures cases and others. The former case involved trading in five pairs of cheap shoes, while the latter case was in respect of hiring out two video tapes. The amounts of the damages claimable in those cases were miniscule, yet they were highly successful test cases and handsomely achieved their objectives, namely establishing very important and telling principles of law which were valuable precedents and trend setters. The Disney case was intended and designed to emulate this line of cases.

Repeating the success of the previous cases would open up the opportunity of future suits for real damages on a widespread scale and relatively straight-forward basis. That was the long term objective but not the present and short term goal of the Disney case.

The damages claim in the Disney case was in reality a ploy to enable us to meet the jurisdictional requirements. However, it fulfilled the secondary purpose of adding spice to our case, moving Disney to defend the case in court (which was critical for the test case), and promoting media interest in the case, which was an important element of our strategy.

Being a test case, the damages issue was in reality a façade, as it had been in the Adidas and other test cases in the past. However, as in those previous cases, it was essential in this test case that the defendant should actually contest the case in court because a successful court judgment was the goal. Accordingly, we had to choose a measure of damages that would cause Disney to take umbrage and decide to defend the case in court. Giving them the opportunity of simply paying off what they would consider a trifling amount in order to make the case go away (an easy and practical solution for them) would defeat the object of the exercise. We decided on the figure of R15 million. This was an arbitrary and grossly inflated amount in the circumstances, but we considered that it would be suitable to accomplish our objective. As the question of the amount of damages due to the Linda family in the litigation later became a contentious issue, I will deal with it in some detail in due course.

The solution to the funding problem was less obvious. The most likely source of funding would be a major South African corporation that would see the cause as worthwhile and, largely for reasons of altruism or charity, be prepared to put up the money needed. Doing so might also have public relations benefits to them. I earmarked certain of Spoor & Fisher's major corporate clients as possible benefactors.

I reasoned that we'd have a better prospect of finding a funder if I could approach possible candidates with something concrete – in other words, a project that was already in existence and underway – rather than with what might appear to be a speculative idea to be implemented in the future, all going well. I decided to launch the proceedings against Walt Disney first and only then, armed with an actual court case in progress, approach possible funders.

This was a bold and risky venture because once litigation began there was a potential liability for payment of the other side's legal costs if the litigation was aborted or unsuccessful. I would, of course, be acting on behalf of the Executor of an estate which had no assets (other than those to be realised by the outcome of the litigation) and the Executor would be acting in a representative capacity and therefore strictly speaking not personally liable for paying the other side's costs. Since the daughters would not be parties in the litigation there was absolutely no risk of payment of any costs or other financial penalty being required from them. They only stood to gain from the litigation and not to lose financially in any way. There was thus ostensibly no party against whom Disney could obtain a viable order that its costs be paid.

Nevertheless, there was always the risk that a powerful and successful defendant like Disney could find some way to get satisfaction of its claim for costs by holding actors or participants involved in the litigation, such as the Executor or the attorneys (i.e., me or my firm), personally liable for the costs. I was therefore taking a serious gamble. I was also putting my professional reputation on the line.

ASSEMBLING THE TEAM

In the changed circumstances, I considered it inappropriate for a partner of Spoor & Fisher to act as Executor and decided to change to an independent outsider. I approached Stephanus (Fanie) Griesel, a chartered accountant who had done auditing work for Spoor & Fisher in the past but was no longer the firm's formal accountant. Like myself, he accepted the appointment despite the risks and the prospect that he might never receive payment for his services. He was influenced in doing so by altruistic considerations and out of loyalty to me.

Next, I needed to secure the services of advocates to act for the Executor. In view of the ground breaking and extremely complex legal issues involved, which could result in the making of new law, it was necessary to appoint Senior and Junior counsel. I approached Cedric Puckrin SC (to whom I have previously referred), who had handled most of my litigation for many years, and Reinhard Michau, who had been my articled clerk and assistant at Spoor & Fisher before going to the bar and became an advocate. I explained the case and asked if they would be willing to act *gratis*, or at least on a contingency basis (which is permissible in terms of the Bar rules). They agreed to a contingency arrangement, which meant that they would charge no fees unless and until the matter was successful, in which case they would be paid out of the proceeds of the court case; if there were no proceeds, or insufficient damages were realised they would receive no payment for their contributions. The measure of the payment to be made out of the damages awarded would in terms of the bar rules be an amount equal to double their normal charges. If this came to pass it could place a financial burden on the funder and/or the Estate, but I had no choice. I had to field counsel in the fray and if this was the only way of doing it, then so be it. Hanro Friederich, as the daughters' attorney, was aware that this was the basis on which counsels' services had been enlisted, and he concurred with the arrangement. There wasn't any alternative!

It is generally recognised that it is unreasonable to expect advocates, who are sole practitioners and earn a living by selling their time, acting on a *pro bono* basis to devote many hours (usually for the benefit of indigent or disadvantaged clients) at no charge, to gain no reward when their action fails – as it often does – but at the same time have no hope of recompense should they succeed. Allowing contingency fees at least gives them the prospect of obtaining some recompense if they should hit the jackpot for their clients. In this eventuality clients paying the contingency fees do not have to dip into their own pocket to reward the advocate; they merely have to be content with gaining a reduced prize from the litigation. This scenario has the benefit for the public of increasing the possibility that advocates will be willing to act on a *pro bono* basis.

In the case in point, at the time when I approached Puckrin and Michau their prospects of gaining any benefit from their contingency arrangements were realistically extremely remote. They were well aware that the test case was unlikely to realise any significant damages, if any at all. They were also under no illusions about the perhaps precarious basis of our cause of action. They were really reconciled to acting for free, and were willing to do so, to their credit.

Cedric Puckrin and I walked a long professional road together. It commenced in the early 1970s when we were both fledgling IP practitioners and it had passed through his becoming a celebrated Senior Counsel and I being regarded as one of the leading IP attorneys. Although Cedric had a vast and successful general practice, IP was his forte. He was generally considered as being probably the leading IP counsel in South Africa. I reckon he handled about seventy-five percent of my litigation, and was my first choice of counsel. We worked well and successfully in cohorts. We had been through thick and thin together. We also enjoyed working with each other and experienced good times in the process. I could relate a myriad of anecdotes about our cases. There is one that springs immediately to mind for no other reason than because it is rather amusing.

We were acting in a trade mark case. The trade mark in issue was Eezi Blo Bloons. The product in question was a children's party trick consisting of a thick soapy-like solution, which, by means of blowing into it through a straw, created a stream of ephemeral balloons. The argument was about whether the trade mark was simply descriptive and thus a generic term, albeit corrupted. Our client was absolutely insistent that the manner of use of the product should be demonstrated in court. This entailed eminent counsel, i.e., Cedric, using the product to blow bubbles from the bar in the direction of the judge on the bench, a most unusual occurrence in court.

Unfortunately, despite prior instruction by the client and concerted practice, Cedric's bubble/balloon blowing skills left a lot to be desired and did not match the quality of his oratory. Much to the irritation of the judge he struggled at length to produce any bubbles of significance. Eventually he produced a couple of feeble ones at which the judge snorted dismissively. The judge was singularly unimpressed by his performance and having to be subjected to it. Cedric understandably experienced a state of acute embarrassment. For the first and only time in all my dealings with him over some 40 years, he was at a loss for words. However, he soon recovered his composure and delivered his usual outstanding argument that won the day. Although I cannot say for sure, possibly the judge decided that the trade mark was not purely descriptive on account of Cedric's struggles to produce any balloons/bubbles!

We had developed a close bond and this, together with his formidable talents (besides balloon blowing), made him an ideal person to bring into the case as senior counsel who would be prepared to act with scant prospect of any financial reward.

In addition to our personal relationships and their loyalty to me, Cedric and Reinard were also motivated by a sense of altruism and a desire to see moral justice being done.

I was most grateful and encouraged that I could enlist the assistance and support of two of the leading advocates in the country in the intellectual property field in pursuing my perhaps somewhat Quixotic cause.

In the final analysis, therefore, at the outset of the case none of the professionals involved had any firm expectation of obtaining any remuneration for their efforts. We were taking on the case in spite of our having little prospect of being remunerated, and not because we would be paid for our services. Our motivation was to right a social wrong stemming from Solomon Linda being taken advantage of through his inexperience and ignorance and being exploited unduly by the music/ entertainment industry.

Against this background we marched into battle against the mighty, heavily resourced Walt Disney adversary. Our team, lacking any financial resources, consisted of Cedric Puckrin, Reinard Michau, Hanro Friederich and me, with Fanie Griesel in the background. After initially showing some interest in, and support for our venture, once we got under way Rian Malan retired from the fray and played no part in the court case that ensued, nor did he show any marked interest in it, save that he ultimately did make a cameo appearance in the sunset of the case. He seemingly considered that his job had been done by raising awareness of the plight of the daughters and facilitating the taking of some positive action. But perhaps, having considered what we planned to do and the enormity of the task and risks we were taking on, he considered the whole plan to be too hairbrained in nature and wanted no part of it. Whatever the case may be, he is nevertheless to be commended for setting the ball rolling in the first place.

As far as the hands-on running of the case and the decision making were concerned, we were down to two people, namely Hanro and me. Although to all outward appearances and for formal purposes Spoor & Fisher was running the case, in fact I had not really involved the firm in the case, and I was performing in a solo capacity in the firm's name.

IX

The Lion and the Mouse

TAKING MICKEY HOSTAGE

We put Plan B into action and commenced the litigation by bringing an application before the court for an order attaching Walt Disney's registered trade marks. This kind of application required us to disclose all the circumstances of the case and to make out a *prima facie*, or provisional, case that the claim would be successful. In the event that the order was granted, we would issue a summons, accompanied by the particulars of the claim, setting out the executor's entire case.

We had prepared the particulars of our claim for launching the action and it was attached to the application. An application of this nature is brought *ex parte* – in other words, no notice is given to the potential defendant(s). The defendants in the action would be Disney Enterprises Inc, David Gresham Entertainment Group/David Gresham Records (Disney's South African agents relating to the commercial exploitation of their works) and Nu Metro Home Entertainment (the exclusive distributors of their films, and thus the animated *Lion King* movie in South Africa).

In our papers we outlined in detail how Griesel came to be the current owner of the copyright in *Mbube*. We also showed that Gresham and Nu Metro had commercially exploited *The Lion Sleeps Tonight* in South Africa without appropriate authority. We claimed that Disney caused, or aided and abetted, Gresham and Nu Metro to perpetrate copyright infringement by licensing and causing them to conduct commercial activities featuring the song. This unlawful conduct had caused the plaintiff to suffer damages in the amount of R15 million. A copy of our particulars of claim can be viewed in Appendix III to be found at page A3. See paragraphs 24 and 25 at page A19.

The attachment order was granted on 29 July 2004, and we thereafter served the documents on Walt Disney in Los Angeles. The die had been cast. At the time I couldn't help thinking of Mark Antony's speech at the funeral of Julius Caesar in Shakespeare's play of that name in which he said, 'Now let it work. Mischief, thou art afoot, take thou what course thou wilt.'

At this point I had expended around 60 hours of billable time since embarking on Plan B which would have translated into a fee of in the region of R240 000. Counsels' fees covering consulting with me, settling the papers that I drafted and appearing in court to move the application would have been in the region of R100 000. Spoor & Fisher's disbursements in respect of having the papers served on Disney in Los Angeles would have been in the region of R15 000.

DISNEY EMPIRE STRIKES BACK

Retribution came quickly and viciously. A few days later I attended a routine meeting of the board of the South African Federation Against Copyright Theft (SAFACT), the South African representative of the United States based Motion Picture Association (MPA), the name by which the MPAA had now become known. I was immediately asked to leave the meeting because my directorship of SAFACT and all relations with the MPA had been summarily terminated. Members of Nu Metro, a company in the Gallo group, led the charge. When the Chairman of the Board and of the meeting, Roger Lecomber, with whom I had worked for many years from the outset of my involvement in dealing with the piracy of movies, and who had clearly not been told what was to transpire at the meeting, raised objections to this high handed action, he too was summarily dismissed from his position and sent packing.

Disney, an influential and a leading member of the MPA, was a powerful enemy to cross. I also became *persona non grata* with Nu Metro. It was apparent that Gallo and their group had changed their allegiance, possibly to make amends after being roasted by Disney for their treason in becoming involved in a planned court action against them. The fact that Gallo were now in the other camp posed a potential problem for our litigation as they possessed inside information on our legal situation, our possible weaknesses and our strategies.

I tried to explain to the MPA that my firm wasn't Disney's attorneys because, although we had acted for them in the distant past, they had terminated relations with us some years earlier. Indeed, I had previously acted against them in certain trade mark matters. I had no doubt there was no conflict of interest in my acting against Disney; we had no confidential information about them that was relevant to this case or compromised us. This case had nothing to do with video piracy, which was my area of involvement with the MPA and its members, so there was no ethical reason why I couldn't act against Disney. Anyway, Disney was just one of several members of the MPA and the case didn't involve this organisation. It was to no avail. The guillotine had fallen!

In the case of Nu Metro, I pointed out that adding it as a defendant had been done in consultation with Paul Jenkins, who had promised the group's moral support. I suggested they discuss the matter with him so it might be seen in its proper perspective; it was not in essence an unfriendly act. I don't know if it was ever discussed with Jenkins, or if it was, what he said, but my pleas had no effect. My banishment to the wilderness was complete. I felt deeply betrayed.

Despite these setbacks I was undeterred. I had confidence in our case. I believed it was sound in law and pursued a noble cause. Over the years I have found in conducting intellectual property litigation that it is important to maintain the moral high ground. You must try to get the court to want, subjectively, to find in your client's favour. It then becomes a matter of theorising and rationalising the legal principles that can justify a largely subjective viewpoint on the part of the judge. I had no doubt that we had the moral high ground, particularly before a South African court. This confidence gave me fortitude in dealing with the problems that beset me.

This confidence was soon to be tested to the limit by what was about to unfold.

FIGHTING ON TWO FRONTS

The moral virtues of our case, which gave us the high ground in the South African litigation, were a powerful weapon. I was convinced the battle against Disney should be fought on two fronts, the legal front and the propaganda front. There was a good prospect of making headway in the battle on the propaganda front, which entailed creating bad publicity for Disney (with its wholesome family image) because they could be said to be gaining a fortune at the expense of a poverty-stricken African family by exploiting a work that was properly owned by the African family. I decided that while the legal case was the foundation of our attack, propaganda was probably the best battle ground.

So, I embarked on a concerted publicity campaign, not only in South Africa, but internationally. It turned out to be very successful and the story of the case spread like wildfire in the local and international media. *The Times* of London took up the cause, as did various American newspapers. It was featured on the CNN and BBC World television programmes. In South Africa I conducted numerous press, television and radio interviews. Disney was portrayed in an unfavourable light.

Ironically, the attachment of Disney's registered trade marks was what the media seized on as particularly newsworthy. This was epitomised by a cartoon that appeared in an American newspaper; it showed Mickey Mouse behind bars in the tower of a castle resembling the Disneyland castle, with a by-line to the effect that Mickey was being held hostage in South Africa.

The propaganda assault achieved considerable momentum and success. The fact that Mickey Mouse, Donald Duck and their friends had been taken hostage in South Africa caught the media's and the public's imagination around the world. Indeed, an important factor in Disney being an attractive target for our test case was their susceptibility to publicity and their aversion to bad PR. We reasoned that our propaganda campaign would cause them embarrassment and motivate them to dispose of the case as soon as possible, which would augur well for the prospects of achieving a suitable outcome.

In setting the propaganda campaign in motion and conducting it in the initial stages I spent approximately 15 hours of my time, which would have given rise to a debit of around R60 000.

FINDING A FUNDER

With the case underway, it was essential to resolve the funding issue – and speedily. We were out on a limb and playing a risky game. I put out feelers to some of Spoor & Fisher's major corporate clients. While they expressed interest and appreciation for the cause, there were no signs that funding was likely to be forthcoming.

Then Hanro Friederich told me he'd had a chance encounter with the Minister of Arts and Culture, Dr Pallo Jordan, at an airport and briefly mentioned the case to him. Minister Jordan had shown some interest, in the context of his portfolio. We decided to take the bull by the horns. I had dealt with senior officials at the Department of Arts and Culture in the past. Through them and my contacts in entertainment and cultural circles, we got an appointment with the Director-General of Arts and Culture and his advisers.

Hanro and I met with them and told them all about the case. We gave them copies of the court papers and suggested there was a case to be made for the Department to fund the litigation. We argued that the outcome would be beneficial to a very needy South African family whose forebear was a South African cultural icon. It would result in the South African roots of *The Lion Sleeps Tonight* being made public knowledge throughout the world, which would be a boost for South African culture. It would show that the law provided redress for disadvantaged South African authors, composers, artists and the like, who had been held back in the dark days of political oppression by their poor bargaining position against powerful companies in the entertainment and cultural spheres. It would demonstrate that copyright could be a powerful weapon in the cultural milieu and could benefit all, including the severely disadvantaged.

We gave them an estimation of what we thought the litigation was likely to cost going forward. It came as an enormous relief when the Department agreed to fund the litigation to the tune of the projected amount. From that time onwards I submitted regular reports and fully detailed and motivated invoices for our services in respect of the case, calculated in accordance with Spoor & Fisher's standard practices. In a sense the Department became a sort of co-client, although a passive one in regard to the conduct of the case.

This reporting and billing procedure did not encompass the services that had already been performed prior to the decision to fund the litigation. In the meantime, I had provided yet further services, which, if they had been covered by billing, would have amounted to around an additional R50 000, being the charge for an additional 13 or so hours of my time. These services covered my efforts to find a funder including preparing for and attending the meeting with officials from Arts and Culture, as well as serving the court documents on Nu Metro and the other defendants, and processing the Notices to Defend the action filed by all the defendants.

In summary, between implementing Plan B and launching the case, and Arts and Culture taking on its funding, I performed services for the benefit of the daughters to the approximate value of R370 000. These services were not charged out to anyone, so their monetary value in effect constituted a donation on the part of Spoor & Fisher to the cause of the daughters' welfare.

During this passage of time and until Arts and Culture stepped into the picture, I of course did not know whether we would ever receive any remuneration for conducting the entire case. For all I knew I would be pouring the monetary value of all my services performed over the entire duration of the case into a bottomless pit. Counsel also did not know whether the monetary value of the services that they had already donated, and of all the services that they would be providing for the duration of the remainder of the case, would ever be anything but a donation to the daughters on their part. Yet, we were all prepared to put our best endeavours into the case irrespective.

Could this selfless attitude on the part of the legal team ever be labelled as being money grabbing? Methinks not.

COUNTERATTACK

My sense of accomplishment at the launching of the case and securing funding for it was soon dispelled by a telephone call from an unsettled Fanie Griesel, who advised that an urgent court application made by Walt Disney Enterprises had been served on him in his capacity as the Executor and the plaintiff in the action. He forwarded the court papers to me, and I studied them without delay.

In their court application Disney sought to strike a quick blow which would destroy our case without any further ado and without the matter going to trial. If successful, this attack would be an unmitigated disaster. I had not anticipated a counterattack of this nature when giving our estimate of the likely costs of the litigation, or at all. We were all out on a limb.

A new chapter in the saga was about to unfold.

X

The Empire Strikes Back

OPERATION HOSTAGE RELEASE

It was cold and barely light when I got out of bed in our chalet at the Madikwe Game Reserve on 7 September 2004. The daily dawn bird chorus was starting up. My wife, Dana, and I were about to go on an early morning game drive provided by the lodge in which we had hired accommodation for a few days of well-earned rest and recuperation after the rigours and stress caused by conducting the Disney litigation.

A few months had passed since Walt Disney, in defence of their empire, had launched their court counterapplication. We had prepared and filed our papers in defence of the application. The matter had been heard in court, and we were waiting for judgment. It had been a physically and mentally taxing time, and I had withdrawn to the bush to recharge my batteries and regain my equilibrium. There is no better way to do this than to commune with nature.

Walt Disney, through their attorneys, Adams & Adams – Spoor & Fisher's main competitor for being heralded the leading intellectual property attorneys in the country – had brought a High Court application against the Executor seeking to set aside the attachment of their trade marks. It had also applied to compel Spoor & Fisher to pay their costs of the proceedings out of our own pockets, on a so-called Attorney and Own Client basis, an unconventional and extreme punitive measure intended to censure a firm of attorneys or their clients for bringing frivolous or vexatious litigation. The fight was becoming personal.

If Disney were successful in their counterapplication and the court was to have granted this costs order, we, Spoor & Fisher, would have been liable to pay Disney the best part of a million Rands out of our own pockets. I would not have been popular with my partners, to put it mildly, for causing this loss to the firm. This was yet another of the risks to which I had exposed myself and my firm through taking on this case.

This wasn't the first time in my career that Adams & Adams had been guilty of playing the man and not the ball when we were opposing each other in litigation. Once, when I brought a copyright infringement action against a prominent academic, alleging that he had plagiarised a textbook, Adams & Adams, on behalf of their defendant client, had launched a defamation action against me personally. It was on the grounds that as the attorney I had drafted the founding affidavit in the copyright infringement case in which it had been alleged that their client had deliberately copied or plagiarised an earlier work. (I might mention that this is an essential and standard statement in making out a copyright infringement claim.)

So much for collegiality in the intellectual property legal profession! But I suppose that, as the saying goes, all is fair in love and war. Be it as it may, as a lawyer this was not my way of doing things and I took umbrage at it. However, it did not weaken my resolve to press on with the case – quite the contrary. Nevertheless, it upped the ante on the personal risks that I was taking as the attorney.

Now Walt Disney and their attorneys had gone on the offensive. *The Lion King* had bared its fangs and claws in no uncertain terms and had come out growling, spitting and scratching.

There followed a hectic period of drafting and exchanging affidavits, preparing for the hearing and ultimately having the matter heard in the High Court. A procedure that normally takes three to six months to complete was compressed into a few short weeks.

The objective in having the court set aside the attachment of the trade marks was to remove the basis on which the court could exercise jurisdiction over Disney. If the application was successful, it would have spelled the end of the matter in the court. The court would simply have decided that it could not hear the case.

To succeed, Disney had to persuade the court that, for reasons outlined in its application, the order granting the attachment of the trade marks was wrongly made. The thrust of their case was that the Executor did not have a valid cause of action against them. In other words, no infringement of copyright belonging to the Executor had occurred. That being so, the attachment order had been wrongly granted.

Disney's application was based on three main points. First, that Griesel, claiming to act as the Executor of Solomon Linda's Estate, had no legal standing to bring the copyright infringement case; second, that the Executor had made incomplete disclosure of all the relevant facts and circumstances in his affidavit supporting the attachment application; and third, that Disney had not caused, authorised or aided and abetted the alleged infringement by Gresham and Nu Metro and was therefore not a contributory infringer.

It was interesting that no challenge was made to the claim that the reverted copyright had vested broadly speaking in Linda's heirs or that the conduct of Gresham and Nu Metro was indeed an infringement of copyright. These two issues were the real meat of the principal case.

Once I got over the initial shock of Disney's counterapplication, I realised it was for the best because it meant the legal dispute between the parties would be resolved almost immediately, without having to go through the time-consuming and expensive process of a trial, which would probably only have taken place some two or so years hence. The crux of the matter was whether the Executor had a valid copyright infringement claim against Disney or not. A positive answer to this question was really what we were after.

GOING HEAD-TO-HEAD

I was prepared to meet Disney's challenge head on. The wording of section 5(3) of the Imperial Copyright Act stated that the reversionary interest passed to the 'personal representative' of the deceased author. This was, of course, British legislation that had been adopted holus-bolus into our law and it needed to be interpreted in conformity with our law in general. As previously mentioned, I concluded that the term 'personal representative' of the deceased meant in the South African context the 'executor' of a South African deceased estate. Disney challenged this interpretation and argued that Griesel ought in any event to have been appointed by the Master of the Supreme Court, not the Magistrate of Johannesburg.

We countered that the British legislation must be adapted to suit South African circumstances and that the Executor of the Estate was the envisaged role player. Griesel's appointment as Executor by the Magistrate of Johannesburg was valid because we followed directions from the Master of the Supreme Court and this could be justified on the basis of a proper analysis of the applicable law, which we presented to the court. The situation was complicated because the legislation that was pertinent to the question, being 'Apartheid law', had been repealed in the meantime and there were complicated constitutional issues involved.

Disney's point about incomplete disclosure of all the relevant facts referred to our failure to deal with the assignments of copyright that Regina and the Linda children had entered into in 1983 and 1992, respectively. It was perfectly true that we made no mention of these assignments – for the simple reason that they were irrelevant. Since Solomon had assigned away his right in his 1952 agreement the 1983 and 1992 assignments were worthless in respect of the original copyright. They could not apply to the reverted copyright because it had vested in the Executor and could only have belonged to either Regina or the daughters when and if it was transferred to them by the Executor – and this could only occur after the Executor wound up the Estate, which hadn't happened yet. In effect they were relying on Prof Sonnekus' argument that the reverted copyright had vested directly in the heirs in 1987.

We refuted Disney's arguments that they hadn't authorised or aided and abetted, i.e., caused, Gresham's and Nu Metro's infringing conduct by analysing the licence agreements Disney had entered into with these companies. They contained clauses relating to specifications for advertising, quality of product, and so forth, which Disney insisted licensees must observe, as well as clauses laying down performance standards. On the strength of these agreements, we argued, it was clear that Disney had played an active role in aiding and abetting, thus causing, the infringing conduct.

The matter was argued in court for a full day before Judge F. Daniels, a competent and experienced judge. Senior and junior counsel were briefed by both parties, in our case Advocates Puckrin and Michau, on the strength of the contingency agreement that I had entered into with them. Based on the impression that I had gained of the judge's attitude at the hearing I was optimistic that we would succeed, and the order Disney sought would be refused. But, on the strength of many years of experience with High Court litigation, I knew that impressions count for nothing; the court's attitude could only be learnt from the judgment when it was handed down, and not until then.

OUT ON A LIMB

This had been a very hectic and pressurised time for me. I had to draft affidavit evidence for Giesel to sign in his capacity as Executor and prepare the case in answer to Disney's claim under severe time constraints. Since Adams & Adams and Disney had brought the application on an urgent basis with drastically shortened periods for filing documents, I had to drop everything I was doing and devote all my time to putting up our case. I was in dire straits. I had put my reputation and career on the line in going ahead with this case. There was the risk that the court may make the punitive costs award that Disney sought against my firm. This would compound the financial prejudice to the firm caused by my being fired by two major clients through taking on the case.

It was not surprising, then, that I had opted to get away from it all and sought to commune with nature by heading for the bush.

THE CALL IN THE WILD

So, there we were on a game drive at Madikwe. We came across a pack of wild dogs hunting an impala. The dogs drove the impala into a thicket and although we could see nothing, the impala's screams and the dogs' howls left us in no doubt about the outcome. I had considerable sympathy for the impala; I knew exactly how it felt.

Then my cell phone buzzed as a text message came in: judgment had been handed down in the Disney case. Disney's application, including the demand that Spoor & Fisher must pay the costs of the application, had been dismissed. It was significant that the court had issued a specific ruling dismissing the claim for costs against the firm. By contrast it had decreed that the general costs award relating to these proceedings should stand over to be determined in the trial which was to follow. This distinction indicated that the court considered that the order sought by Disney against the firm was entirely unfounded and it treated it with disdain. This was a cause for relief and satisfaction for me. The text of the court's judgment is to be found in Appendix IV at page A22.

The court effectively found that our case against Disney was sound in law and accepted all the arguments we had advanced to counter the points that Disney had made in their application. In particular, it found that Griesel had validly been appointed as the Executor by the Magistrate of Johannesburg and that the 1983 and 1992 assignments had no relevance to the present case for the reasons we had advanced. It did not subscribe to the views propounded by Prof Sonnekus regarding the initial vesting of the reversionary interest.

The judgment was a complete vindication of all the fundamental issues on which our infringement case against Disney was based. Having found that our case was sound in law the court had endorsed the validity of our cause of action based on the Dickens Clause. This was the goal that we had set out to achieve by means of the test case. Indeed, the objective of our test case had been reached. We had established the recognition of the reversionary interest and its applicability to the facts of the Disney case. We could actually have packed up all our things and gone home because our mission had been completed. However, procedurally we could not unilaterally withdraw the main action without incurring an adverse costs order. Any discontinuation of the main action had to be done in terms of an agreed settlement and the case was not yet ripe for that. 'Round one' to us, but there were other rounds to come.

The result came as an absolute tonic to me, and I prepared myself mentally to re-enter the fray and deliver what I hoped would be a knock-out blow or at least a victory on points.

XI

Downing the Giant

BREAKING THE NEWS

Eighteen months later the battle with Disney was over. We had won and we were holding a press conference on 15 February 2006 to make this announcement and give the media brief details of the settlement that had been reached with Walt Disney. David had downed Goliath with his sling shot.

I was ecstatic at the outcome of the case. I had gambled with my career, reputation and self-esteem at stake, and won. The case had caused a sword of Damocles to hang over me for six long years. The case had satisfied all the requirements of a good test case. My interpretation of the law regarding the reversionary interest (scorned by some) had proved to be correct and had won the day. Above all, however, I was delighted to have brought some joy into the lives of the daughters and had been able to place them in a position where their future was relatively financially secure. This had come about through an unexpected, but very welcome financial bonanza, the securement of which had not been originally expected.

What had especially gratified me was that the railway track that I had been following for virtually my whole life had reached a sought after destination that was fulfilling in that I had been able to achieve the power of good and to use my talents and abilities to make a difference in the service of social justice. Also, as a proud South African, I was happy to have benefitted the country's cultural heritage and standing by obtaining international recognition of Solomon Linda and his song as being truly South African.

I must confess to having a feeling of gleeful satisfaction at having put one over the high and mighty Walt Disney Enterprises, particularly in view of their nasty and vindictive attitude towards me personally. We laid a trap for them, and they walked right into it. We wanted a defended court action in the form of a test case so that we could get a judgment. We had to offer sufficient bait for them to want to defend the case because it would not have suited our purposes to have a no contest. If, for instance, we had claimed the amount of the realistic actual damages that the Linda Estate had probably suffered, say R5 000, i.e., US$350, the chances are that they would have regarded the matter as trivial and in all likelihood would simply have paid the amount claimed to get rid of the matter expeditiously, or ignored the claim altogether. It is unlikely that they would have contested the action over such a trifling amount. However, we set the bait at the right level, and they entered into the fray lock stock and barrel, which is exactly what we wanted. Our plan came together.

As it is, after the case had commenced and the matter had become topical in the international media, I received an email from a proverbial American man in the street. In it he told me that he was following the case with interest but couldn't understand why Disney had decided to incur the trouble and expense of defending it. He pointed out that their disputing the claim had caused them an enormous amount of bad press. He said they would have been far better advised to have made a public show of being magnanimous, caring and public spirited. This could have been achieved by calling a press conference to announce and herald their decision to pay a destitute African family their just desserts for inadvertently abusing of their rights, and by paying for the daughters to visit the United States in order to appear at the press conference so that a show could be made of them receiving the money. This whole exercise would have cost less than a one-minute advertisement at an American Super Bowl event and would have generated far better publicity for them. They could have turned the whole affair into a positive public relations exercise, rather than expose themselves to public opprobrium as was happening as a result of the attention being given to the court case.

It seemed to me that there was some merit in this thinking, but I was pleased that Disney had chosen to opt for the aggressive bullying approach as it suited our purposes admirably and played right into our hands. They certainly would have got off far more lightly if they had followed the suggested approach rather than what was provided for in the settlement, save of course that in the final analysis Abilene was footing the bill for the settlement, and not them. More about this later.

The media conference was our moment of glory. Hanro Friederich and the Linda daughters were present, but Rian Malan passed up attending. I had asked the Department of Arts and Culture to send a representative in view of their significant contribution to the litigation, but at the eleventh hour they declined and also asked me to withhold all information about the identity of the funder of the litigation. I found this puzzling. Their initial reaction to my invitation had been that they were only too happy to announce to the world their role in this notable victory. However, by the nature of this very strange case and what had gone before, I had learned not to be surprised about anything, and I simply accepted their wishes. It was not for me to reason why. As a result we had to be circumspect in what we told the media about the funding of the litigation. We issued a media release at the conference describing the outcome of the case.

CLINCHING THE VICTORY

The outcome of Disney's application to set aside the attachment, i.e., Disney's counterapplication, which established to validity of our claim, had really been the climax of the whole matter. After that, we and the defendants had gone through the motions of following the procedure for the damages action which was to follow. We had exchanged pleadings, made discovery of all relevant documentation, prepared for the hearing of the case, and attended the mandatory pre-trial conference between the parties a few weeks before the trial was due to begin.

Not unexpectedly, when the lawyers met for the pre-trial conference, the question of a settlement was broached. This was done at the instigation of the Disney team. Indeed, the case cried out for a settlement. Disney was hurting due to the adverse PR it was experiencing and had been set back on their heels by the blow experienced in the counterapplication. We had been dropping hints with the other side during the course of the conflict that this case was merely the forerunner of similar cases to be instituted in due course throughout the former British Empire – which was of course nothing but a bluff, but they were not to know that. This must have been an unpleasant and unwanted prospect for them. They must have been thinking that the matter was not worth the candle.

On our side, due to the unexpected counterapplication and the costs that it incurred, the funding granted by the Department of Arts and Culture had been used up and no further funding was forthcoming. Moreover, our objective of establishing the soundness of our cause of action and claim had been established – we had achieved our desired successful test case result which could serve as the launching platform for further substantial damages claims against other infringers in the future. Then there was always the risk of losing the case and forfeiting the benefits of the success in the counterapplication – the bird in the hand was worth two in the bush! Finally, at best all that could be gained by pursuing the action to its final conclusion was to secure payment of probably a paltry couple of thousand Rands at the end of a long drawn out expensive trial and enquiry into damages. It was a no- brainer that a reasonable settlement was the best outcome for the family. After negotiations lasting a few days, a settlement agreement was signed.

Before going on to set out and discuss the terms of the settlement that was reached, it is expedient to explain certain issues against the background of which the agreement was reached. They have a strong bearing on the desirability and worth of the settlement.

INFLUENTIAL FACTORS

A noteworthy point had arisen during the exchange of pleadings: Disney were claiming that *Mbube* was not an original work, but rather a traditional song that Solomon Linda had simply adopted – it was thus in the public domain; as such it enjoyed no copyright. If this was factually correct it would have provided a complete defence to our copyright infringement claim and our case would collapse in a heap. This was obviously a crucial issue. We had considered it at the outset but had satisfied ourselves that we could probably overcome it. But there was always an element of doubt.

The crux of the matter was whether the song was indeed a traditional Zulu song. It had been described in some of the documentation as being 'traditional'. This claim had also been made in the litigation between Folkways and Abilene in the United States. It had to be investigated and addressed. Obviously, Solomon Linda was not available to deal with the originality of his work! I decided to seek out and consult with an authoritative Zulu musicologist who could give expert evidence on the point.

I located the pre-eminent sage on traditional Zulu music and culture. He advised that *Mbube* was not a traditional song and had indeed been composed by Solomon Linda. What had happened was that the popularity and success of the song had spawned a new genre of music among the Zulu people and many other similar songs were subsequently composed. This genre of music became known as 'mbube' music. The original song thus created a 'tradition' and not the other way around. The musicologist had agreed to give expert evidence to this effect at the trial. This was reassuring, but it begged the question of what contradictory evidence the other side might come up with.

What typically happens in this situation is that the one side enlists an expert witness who says that the matter is red, whereupon the other side produces an expert witness who says that it is blue. The court must then decide which expert is to be believed. There was a fine line between the song becoming traditional before or after Solomon Linda first exposed it to the light of day. This was thus a potentially fatal defect in our case, and it impacted on its possible outcome. It was a cause for concern, perhaps a proverbial skeleton in the closet. The settlement would, however, make it moot and of no practical relevance. Nevertheless, it weighed with us in deciding whether or not to go for the settlement on offer.

During the course of the settlement negotiations, it emerged that Disney had approached and obtained a licence from a company in the United States called Abilene to use the song *The Lion Sleeps Tonight* in

The Lion King production. Abilene is the alter ego of George Weiss, one of the purported composers of *The Lion Sleeps Tonight*. As previously explained, *The Lion Sleeps Tonight,* is a work enjoying copyright in its own right, despite being a derivative of *Mbube*. Abilene owns the copyright in, and controls the use of, *The Lion Sleeps Tonight* as a stand-alone work.

In granting a licence to Disney to use the song, Abilene had declared that it held the necessary rights to the song and had given an indemnity to Disney for any claims that might be made against it by third parties arising out of the use of the song. This meant that any damages that we might be awarded in the litigation, and which were paid by Disney, could be reclaimed by them from Abilene. Disney were thus in reality a front or go-between for Abilene. Abilene could not have been a defendant in the proceedings in the first place because there was no basis for the South African court to have jurisdiction over them. Furthermore, we only became fully aware of the relationship between Disney and Abilene in the final stages of the dispute and prior to that there was no evidence available as to the role played by Abilene in the infringement.

In effect the real defendant in the copyright infringement claim, despite their not being a party to the ligation, was thus Abilene. Disney was simply its surrogate. Since the financial liabilities arising out of the infringement claim would be laid at the door of Abilene, Disney brought Abilene into the settlement negotiations. They were made a party to the settlement agreement, and it was therefore Abilene instead of Disney that bore the brunt of the obligations placed on the defendant under the settlement. This situation was to have far- reaching consequences in the settlement that was reached.

I had some sympathy for Disney because it had probably acted in good faith in incorporating *The Lion Sleeps Tonight* in *The Lion King* and had done everything that could reasonably have been expected of them in getting all the necessary authorisations to use it in the production. They were not to know that their licensor didn't in fact hold the necessary rights to licence it. My sympathy was, however, tempered by the arrogant and vindictive manner in which they went about conducting the case, and by their attitude in general.

ENTITLEMENT TO DAMAGES

It must at this juncture be reiterated and clarified exactly what the executor's damages claim entailed. I have already broached this subject earlier and what follows here is to some extent a recap as well as an elaboration of the question.

The damages claim was actually a side issue. The *raison d'etre* and objective of the damages claim was, as previously explained, primarily to enable the South African court to have jurisdiction over Disney, a foreign company without any place of business or physical presence in South Africa. The whole purpose and goal of the litigation was to establish the principle that the Linda Estate was the copyright owner of *Mbube* and was entitled to control the use of the song and its derivatives in South Africa. It would follow that, if the case was successful, a precedent would be created for implementation in other countries in the former British Empire. It was to be a test case on this issue.

In a claim for damages before a South African court, the court can only award damages actually proven to have been suffered in South Africa, i.e., through conduct perpetrated in this country. Damages suffered in other countries are irrelevant. Although the family, or more correctly the Executor, owned the copyright in some 50 countries – and potentially had a damages claim in all of those countries – our litigation could only deal with the South African damages.

The measure of damages recoverable in our action was the royalties that ought to have been paid for the use of the song *The Lion Sleeps Tonight* in the soundtrack of the animated movie or the stage show *The Lion King* when it was commercially exploited in South Africa and when such version of the song was sold as a record or played in public. All other uses of the song by others in South Africa, of which there were a myriad, were irrelevant to the case on hand because Disney had no involvement in them. In an optimistic estimate those damages would have amounted to no more than a couple of thousand Rand.

Our damages argument was that the family ought to have received royalties in respect of every occasion that the film or stage show sound track version of *The Lion Sleeps Tonight* was aired in South Africa or reproduced on a record, tape or the like in South Africa. The onus of proof of the facts in this regard lay with the Executor. The necessary information could only be obtained from the defendants. The sources would have to be Nu Metro as far as video versions were concerned, David Gresham with regard to audio recordings, and Nu Metro and possibly other cinema operators in respect of screenings in cinemas. Gathering this material would have proved to be an exceedingly difficult and a monumental task for the Executor. Our opponents held the key to all the relevant information. This material would have to be dredged out of them by court procedures such as discovery and/or by means of cross examination of witnesses, all of which would be time consuming and costly, with no-one to foot the bill.

Having arrived at the extent of the exploitation of the sound track version of the song, the royalty rates that would have been charged by the copyright owner if licences had been sought in such instances of exploitation and the revenues they would have yielded must be calculated and proved. In this situation account would have to be taken of the fact that *The Lion Sleeps Tonight* was but one of around 20 songs comprised in the soundtrack of the movie or the stage show. This would have been an accounting and evidential nightmare. Suitably qualified witnesses such as accountants and music industry cognoscenti would have to be fielded, their fees would have to be paid and the time taken up by their testimonies being presented would have to be added to the potential counsels' fees.

In my view the sum total of these royalties, assuming they could have been proved by admissible evidence, would probably have amounted to no more than a few thousand Rands. On the other hand, the cost of assembling the evidence and presenting it at an enquiry into damages would have run into many hundreds of thousands of Rands. Going that route was obviously not remotely viable. The only practical route was to arrive at an agreed figure by way of a settlement, a scenario I had successfully managed many times before in my career.

As previously mentioned , in order to make Disney sit up and take notice of our case, and not dismiss it as trivial, we felt that we had to trump up the damages and claim a larger figure in our court papers, without being absurd. We settled on an amount of R15 million, as a total thumb-suck. This amount bore no relation to reality, being stated entirely for effect. It was totally out of the question that we could ever get anywhere near proving damages in that amount in the court case, but the claim added significant gravamen to it. In retrospect this strategy was clearly misunderstood by other non-legal role players who took the amount seriously.

THE SUM OF THE PARTS

It is commonly said that copyright operates worldwide. In other words, when a work is made in South Africa copyright subsists in it throughout the world. This is true to a point, but it is not as simple as this statement suggests. International copyright is governed by the Berne Convention, the membership of which embraces virtually all the countries in the world. The cornerstone of this convention is so-called 'national treatment'. In terms of this principle all member countries are required to protect works emanating from other member countries as though they were works of their own nationals. Their national legislation is applied to foreign works in exactly the same way as if they were domestic works. This means that, for instance, a South African work is protected in, say the UK, under domestic law as if it was a work of British origin. Conversely, a work of British origin would be protected in South Africa as if it was a work of South African origin. In each country a work enjoys a separate copyright under the laws of that country. Assuming there are 170 member countries of the Berne Convention, every original work will enjoy 170 separate copyrights.

Consequently, if the copyright owner of a work made by a South African is infringed in the UK, that person must sue for infringement of the British copyright in that work in the UK in accordance with British copyright law. If damages are claimed, they are limited to the damages which occurred in the British market. In accordance with this principle when copyright infringement is claimed in South Africa, the damages that can be claimed are restricted to the damages incurred in the South African market. It is on this basis that the damages claimable in the instant case only amount to the losses incurred in the South African market. The fact that the royalties flowing from unauthorised use of the song *The Lion Sleeps Tonight* might have amounted to millions of Rand in the UK and elsewhere is irrelevant to copyright infringement in South Africa.

If the Estate of Solomon Linda wished to claim damages in respect of infringement of the work in other countries, it would have to institute separate and fresh lawsuits in each and every one of those countries in terms of the copyright subsisting in it, and in the courts of each of those countries. This issue has been greatly misunderstood in the popular narrative regarding the instant litigation. A settlement that could embrace multiple countries would have major advantages.

The South African case was the one shot we had to achieve the goal of putting in place the groundwork for getting meaningful income for the Linda family from the exploitation of *The Lion Sleeps Tonight* not only in South Africa but also internationally.

THE SETTLEMENT

It was of enormous significance that Abilene was brought into the settlement because all its terms were made binding on them as well as on Disney. Abilene held the worldwide copyright in *The Lion Sleeps Tonight* and could control its exploitation throughout the world by all and sundry and could reap rewards for its use on this basis. In the result, by virtue of the settlement, the copyright in *Mbube* was brought to bear and effectively enforced against Abilene with effect not only in South Africa but also internationally without their ever having been a party to the litigation. The principal infringer, and indeed in effect the true defendant, was thus swept up into the net. We killed two birds with one stone! The legal implications of this were profound. On the other hand, if the litigation took its course and resulted in a successful judgment the obligation placed on the defendants would not have applied to Abilene and one of the birds would have flown.

The basis of the settlement was that the Executor would withdraw the action, thus aborting the litigation, and each party would be responsible for its own costs. Disney and Abilene formally recognised that Solomon Linda was the original composer of what became *The Lion Sleeps Tonight* and he would be acknowledged as a co-composer in all further notifications in respect the song. The Executor granted a full licence to Abilene and its licensees to use *The Lion Sleeps Tonight*, subject to the payment of royalties. Abilene was required to make a substantial lump-sum payment to the Executor to cover past unauthorised uses of the song in lieu of damages. They also assumed the obligation to pay industry standard royalties for all future uses (i.e., not only uses in *The Lion King*, but by whomsoever and in whatever manners) of *The Lion Sleeps Tonight* for a period of ten years.

At Disney's insistence a trust was to be established to take up ownership of the copyright in *Mbube* and to receive all payments and to distribute the funds to the heirs. Also at Disney's insistence, the obligation was placed on all parties to keep the details of the financial arrangements, and in particular the amount of the lump sum payment, confidential on pain of the agreement being subject to summary cancellation if this obligation was breached. The terms of the settlement were embodied in a written agreement signed by the Executor, the Linda daughters, Disney and Abilene, as well as the other nominal defendants. The settlement took place in 2007, some seven years after I first began working on the case.

The acknowledgement of the derivation of *The Lion Sleeps Tonight* from *Mbube* was an important element of the settlement. The Department of Arts and Culture were prepared to finance the litigation *inter alia* because they considered it important that the world at large should be apprised of this fact so that the song would be recognised as a significant piece of South Arican culture. It had been previously accepted that the song was of American origin. Furthermore, Solomon Linda would be accorded due fame for his contribution to the field of music. Their decision to fund the case would thus be vindicated.

BOUNTEOUS PAYMENTS

The lump sum payment to the Estate by Disney/Abilene was a significantly large sum by any standards. It was by far in excess by many multiples of the amount of damages that would have been awarded if the case had gone the distance, and the outcome had been successful. To this extent the lump sum payment was a resounding success.

In addition, to their aforesaid contribution to damages Abilene/ Disney agreed to pay ongoing royalties for future uses of *The Lion Sleeps Tonight* on a worldwide basis – not only in South Africa or even in former British Empire countries (which was the geographical limit of the rights held by the Estate). The agreed territory thus included, *inter alia*, the whole of Europe, the USA and the Far East in which the Estate held no rights whatsoever and had no entitlement to receive any royalties under copyright. This was astonishing and truly marvellous. What an outcome for a test case on a legal principle where damages were not even a priority!

But it got even better. The term of the copyright in *Mbube* lasted until 50 years after Solomon Linda's death in South Africa and in all but a few countries of the world. As Solomon died in 1962 this meant that the copyright expired in 2012. Thereafter the work fell into the public domain and could be freely reproduced and performed without any consent and free of the payment of royalties. However, the settlement provided that the royalty payments would be made for a period of ten years after the date of the settlement, i.e., until 2017. In other words, the Estate was being granted a bonus period of five years for the payment of royalties despite their rights having already expired. Overall, this was an absolutely amazing deal.

CONSEQUENCES OF THE SETTLEMENT

All the members of the legal team were overjoyed at the degree of success that had been achieved by the settlement. This result to the litigation by far exceeded our wildest dreams. The settlement put the lid on the favourable decision in Disney's counterclaim which already achieved our primary goal with the litigation, which was establishing the soundness of the Estate's legal claim. Now there was an amazing financial bonanza on top of it. The alternative would have been to carry on with the court action which would probably last for another year or so and incur additional costs for which there was no funding. Also, there would be the prospect of future appeals against a favourable judgment. Our adversary had deep pockets, whereas ours were empty. In particular to obtain favourable judgments in all the countries of the former British Empire in order to achieve the same outcomes as the settlement, would involve bringing around 50 separate copyright infringement cases around the world. This was simply never going to happen. Moreover, absent the settlement the future damage payments would fall away in five years' time when the copyright expired. As far as we were concerned it was an absolute no-brainer that the settlement should be concluded with alacrity, and we subscribed to it unhesitatingly.

It was necessary to make provision for the money due to the Estate from the settlement to be properly managed. Perhaps surprisingly Disney insisted that a formal trust should be established, with the daughters as the beneficiaries, and that the monies flowing from the settlement should be paid into that Trust and it should manage all such funds on behalf of the daughters. Disney appeared to have some concerns that the money that they were bestowing on the family should not be squandered and this arrangement would be the best way of ensuring that this did not happen. Perhaps they felt that if the monies were not used in an appropriate manner to improve the financial lot of the daughters any public fallout would be placed at their doorstep.

Whatever their reasoning and motivation might have been, this measure coincided with our own viewpoint. Apart from any considerations regarding proper management of the spoils of the litigation, there was another strong point in favour of the trust proposition. For reasons already explained the daughters should never become the owners of the copyright in *Mbube* because the copyright assignment they had executed would cause the copyright to immediately flow to Folkways. The owner of the copyright and the managers of the funds that it produced under the settlement must be someone else and should be one and the same. The copyright owner was the obvious person to administer and enforce the copyright and collect and administer the funds it produced. A trust could fulfil this role admirably. It was therefore common cause that a trust should be created and registered and the copyright should in due course be assigned to it and the available funds paid out to it by the Executor when the distribution of the Estate took place in due course.

I have often wondered what caused Disney to make quite such a generous settlement proposal. I have been unable to come to any conclusion. I can only speculate. It was very apparent that Disney was not enjoying the unfavourable and critical attention and comment that it was enduring on account of what the public construed as dishonourable conduct. They were doubtless anxious to curtail it, and this could not happen while the litigation was pending and in the public eye. Furthermore, they were incensed that a third party had interfered with their precious trade marks and had indeed acquired a lien over them which could restrict their manner of dealing with them. Obviously, they were anxious to put an end to this imposition on their property. Then there was the prospect of further ligation which would prolong their agony. As previously mentioned, we had hinted that a campaign of international litigation was in the offing once the legal correctness of the Estate's claim to copyright in the song had been given judicial endorsement. They would be facing similar claims all around the world for years to come. They were not necessarily to know that this was largely a bluff on our part. All these factors probably played a role in their wanting to make the whole matter go away, and quickly. The only way out of their predicament was to make the Estate an offer that it could not refuse, which was what their offer was.

The amount of money that was at issue, although being extravagant from the perspective of the Estate, was inconsequential to Disney. Added to this was the fact that Disney stood to recover all the money they expended from Abilene in terms of the indemnity that they held. Abilene would be footing the bill, and Disney had them over a barrel. Disney could afford to be generous with someone else's money! There was thus not necessarily any downside to Disney getting rid of the litigation by paying out some money in what would have been publicly perceived as a very generous settlement.

GLAD TIDINGS

While the legal team and the Executor had not the slightest doubt that an incredibly advantageous outcome for the family had been achieved, we considered it appropriate to consult the daughters on their views. The problem that we faced was that the daughters had absolutely no understanding of the matter. It was complex by anyone's standards and the task of explaining it to them, given their background, was daunting. We decided that the best approach was to have Hanro and Rian Malan undertake this task because they had the closest connections and relationships with them, and we believed that the daughters trusted them. I had consulted with the daughters on a few occasions and had twice visited them at their house in Soweto during build up to the court case. Some of them had also attended a meeting of the legal team. I had endeavoured to explain to them what we were about, but it was apparent to me that what I had to say to them went clear over the top of their heads. They appeared to view me as some stranger who claimed to be advancing their cause and somewhat reluctantly were prepared to give me the benefit of the doubt.

Hanro had good insight into all the ramifications of the case and was well equipped to enlighten them. Moreover, he was their duly appointed attorney of some years standing by that time. I had distinct reservations of Rian Malan's grasp of the finer points – he had not been involved with the team from the time that Gallo withdrew from the matter and had no legal background, but I thought that the combination of the two of them could do the job. Their mandate was to make the daughters comfortable with the settlement and secure their required signatures to the settlement agreement. They reported that they had accomplished their task, and they delivered the signed agreement.

THE ESTATE AND THE TRUST

The settlement was consummated, and the case was wound up. Fanie Griesel set up and registered the Trust. As the Executor he completed the formalities of winding up the Estate. This included sorting out and paying the estate duty for which the Estate was liable to the fiscus arising from the lump sum payable by Abilene. This was a significant amount of money, and a sizeable slice of that payment went towards the payment of the estate duty. Estate duty was levied at a rate of 35 percent of the proceeds of the payment made by Disney/Abilene.

In addition, Griesel paid counsels' fees for their services in regard to the court proceedings as well as his prescribed standard executor's fees. Counsel had, of course, at the outset entered into a formal contingency fees agreement with Spoor & Fisher in accordance with the precepts of the Bar Council. This entitled them to charge double their normal fees if the case was successful, which it indeed was. Consonant with standard procedures, counsel billed Spoor & Fisher, who paid them, and then in turn billed the Executor.

Spoor & Fisher's own charges (i.e., my fees), compiled in terms of our standard charge out rates, had been debited to, and paid for by, the Department of Arts and Culture out of the funds that they made available for the litigation, which funds had been depleted. These funds were for paying the strict litigation costs. The arrangement did not extend to remunerating Hanro Friederich, who had his own financial arrangements with the daughters.

Hanro was at all material times the daughters' personal attorney and held a formal power of attorney from them. His representation of the daughters and financial arrangements with them had been concluded before I entered the picture and the commencement of the litigation (he had been acting for them as their attorney for at least two years prior to my meeting him). Those arrangements covered his services from his introduction to the family, which was brought about by Rian Malan, until his mandate from them was concluded. I surmise that Hanro's financial arrangements with the daughters had probably been brokered by Rian. I had no insight into the nature or quantum of his remuneration as this was a private matter.

The counsel who acted in the case, Spoor & Fisher (including me personally – all my services were performed and charged on behalf of the firm) and the Executor derived no other remuneration from the case and its proceeds, besides the aforegoing. All these parties derived remuneration strictly in accordance with standard procedures and rates, and no form of commission or gratuity or other financial benefit was obtained by them out of the proceeds of the case.

Hanro and I selected and arranged the appointment of the trustees who managed the Trust that had been registered. I was adamant that Spoor & Fisher, and I in particular, should not play any role in the management of the Trust. We were the litigation attorneys who handled the court case and once it was concluded we were *functus officio* – our role was complete. We are intellectual property specialists and practised solely as such; we were not involved in the management of trusts and had no expertise or interest in that area of practice. I wanted to avoid there being any suggestion that we were motivated by self-interest in any way in the management of the spoils of the case.

I felt that Hanro and Rian Malan should be trustees in view of their fairly long-standing association and affinity with the daughters. Hanro agreed but to my surprise and dismay Rian wanted nothing of it. Despite my best efforts he could not be persuaded to become involved. I felt that the Trust was the poorer for his obduracy and non-participation. Perhaps many of the troubles that later eventuated could have been avoided if Rian had served as a trustee.

In selecting additional trustees, we were guided by the function that the Trust would be performing. We chose individuals with relevant expertise. We secured the participation of Nick Motsatse, the CEO of the South African Musical Rights Organisation (SAMRO), the entity seized with collecting and distributing royalties for public performances of music, and an individual who was a senior member of one of the major record companies. They would act as trustees in their personal capacities and divorced from their companies.

It was considered essential to have someone with accounting expertise on board in order to administer the Rands and cents. I contacted several people I knew who had the relevant expertise but drew a blank. Eventually, as a last resort, I recruited Glen Dean (no relative of mine), who was employed as Spoor & Fisher's Financial Manager. It was made very clear to everyone involved or interested that he would be acting purely in his personal capacity and not as any form of a representative or agent of Spoor & Fisher. He had the merit that he had previously been employed by the SABC and therefore had some experience in the entertainment industry.

All the trustees took on the job and were motivated by a desire to assist the daughters to improve their lot in life and to benefit to the greatest extent possible from the windfall that had befallen them. Furthermore, I arranged for them to obtain counselling by a professional service which provided assistance and succour to people who had acquired large sums of money and were unaccustomed to dealing with it. This came about through my acting for Uthingo, the first company to which the management of the National Lottery had been entrusted. They operated such a service for winners of lottery draws. They agreed to take up the daughters into their programme at no cost. An altruistic spirit of helping the daughters to make the most of their good fortune also prevailed amongst them, as well as all of us.

I caused the assignment of the copyright into the Trust to be drawn up and executed. I advised the Trust that as the copyright owner there were opportunities available to them to obtain further remuneration from the exploitation of the song and its derivatives. Indeed, the copyright could even be sold by them to someone who would see it as an investment to be used for extracting royalties for future uses of the song. I pointed out that this may be the preferable option for them. It would be a quick and clean opportunity and would obviate administrative hassles in the future.

All uses of *The Lion Sleeps Tonight* authorised by Abilene were out of the picture in view of the licence granted to them by the settlement but uses by all other parties without Abilene's authority constituted infringement of their copyright in addition to infringement of the copyright in *Mbube*. This opportunity existed in all countries which were part of the former British Empire but would expire in 2012 when the copyright expired in all but for a few countries like the UK, Australia and Canada where the term of the copyright would endure until 70 years after Solomon Linda's death, i.e., until 2032. In particular Folkways and other users of the song *Wimoweh* were prime targets as this song had not been affected in any way by the settlement and the licence granted to Abilene. I pointed the trustees in the direction of taking action against Folkways. I had already broached the subject of their liability with Folkways by way of setting the ball in motion.

It must be appreciated that the conclusion of the case was not considered to be the end of the matter. It was only the end of the beginning. In the classical test case scenario, the first objective was to establish the legal foundation for future claims. This had been achieved. The next phase involved using the platform that had been established in order to mount a campaign of enforcement of damages claims against all unauthorised users of the song. The matter was now on the threshold of this phase.

SPREADING THE GOOD NEWS

At the press conference held on 15 February 2006 to mark the end of the case, there was considerable interest from the media, both national and international. The media had followed developments closely and given prominence to them all along. I have no doubt that the amount of publicity the case generated worldwide – and the adverse nature of this publicity – had probably been the single most important consideration prompting Disney to settle.

The press conference went off well even though the media were disappointed that I couldn't disclose the amount of the settlement paid by Disney/Abilene for past infringements. I also had to tell them that the funder of the litigation wanted to remain anonymous (the Department of Arts and Culture later relented and itself made the announcement publicly in parliament). News of the settlement spread worldwide, and it was reported in both the national and international media. It was heralded as a welcome success for the Linda family.

I discussed the case widely in the press, on radio and in television interviews both in South Africa and internationally. On one occasion Elizabeth, the most articulate of the daughters, and I appeared together on a television chat show at which there was a consensus that a remarkable benefit had accrued to the family for which they should be grateful. In discussing the case and its implications in public I explained that the precedent had been set, other authors who had been deprived of their birth rights, so to speak, by being led into making unfavourable dispositions of their copyright works while Apartheid held sway during the twentieth century could perhaps now sleep more easily in their graves. The precedent of the Linda case could be followed by their heirs as well, and their copyrights could be reclaimed and exploited for their benefits. This of course applied not only to songs and musical works, but also to artistic and literary works. The case brought far wider benefits than for the family alone.

I was contacted by lawyers from several countries (including in Europe, to which the Estate's rights did not extend) offering to bring cases for the family on a similar basis in their countries. These were largely misguided due to insufficient attention being given to the details of the original claim and the settlement. A lawyer practising in the West Indies, in which the Imperial Copyright Act also held sway, enquired of me whether the Linda example could be followed in the case of the songs of Bob Marley. On being informed on the facts regarding his songs and his death, I expressed the view that there seemed to be a parallel case for his heirs. I have no knowledge as to whether this opportunity was ever taken up.

PUTTING THE CASE TO BED

I was gratified by the outcome of the case and proud of the result that had been achieved. It had been a long and exacting journey, lasting six years, and the road had many ups and downs. I regarded the case as probably the most noteworthy achievement of my career.

The press conference marked the end of what was really a rags-to-riches fairy tale. The Linda family would be receiving ongoing payments of considerable sums of money. The lion had been aroused from its long hibernation and shown its true South African colours. But it was time to move on. I closed my file.

In the meantime, a new taxing challenge had arrived like a bank of clouds rolling in from the Atlantic Ocean over the Cape Peninsula. It engulfed my practice for the remaining three years until my mandatory retirement in 2010. The Linda case was eclipsed like the sun being blocked out by the advancing bank of clouds. A new season was upon me. My practice that had to some extent been put on hold by the Disney case was about to take off in a different and all-embracing direction which was already brewing.

Phase two of *The Lion Sleeps Tonight* project should be undertaken by a new team in a new venture. The hard work had already been done. My job had come to an end. The 2010 Soccer World Cup was beckoning me.

Post Leo

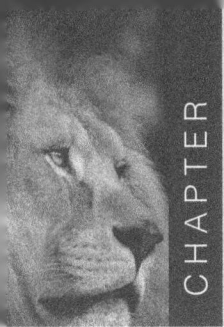

PART 3

XII

Ambush

BACK TO THE FUTURE

I silenced the shrill ringing sound of the telephone by answering it. I was sitting at my desk in my office at the Law Faculty at Stellenbosch University. The voice at the other end said, 'Hello Owen, this is Rian Malan.'

This was a blast from the past. Some seven years had passed since *The Lion Sleeps Tonight* case had been concluded. It was now 2014. I had not heard from or seen hide or hair of Rian Malan since that time. A lot of water had passed under the bridge in the meantime. I had moved on and had no connection with the Disney case or any of its *dramatis personae* in the meantime.

I took a moment to recover from my surprise at hearing Rian Malan at the other end of the telephone. I answered, 'Hello Rian, how nice to hear from you again after all these years since we last spoke. How are you and what are you doing with yourself these days? The last I heard about you was that you were singing in a country music/pop band at country festivals.' He responded, 'Yes, I have been doing that from time to time. I moved away from Cape Town and relocated to Gauteng. I found the weather in Muizenberg unpleasant, and I headed for better climes. But tell me about yourself. I gather you are now an academic at Stellenbosch University. How did that come about?' 'Yes,' I replied. 'It took place in stages. First, I relocated to Spoor & Fisher's Cape Town office in 2007 and then, after I retired from the firm in 2010, I became a professor at Stellenbosch University.'

'That's all very interesting,' he responded. 'Tell me more'. 'Okay, you asked for it, here goes,' I replied. 'It's a long story!' It was indeed, so

I confined myself to giving him a truncated version of the following full story.

AMBUSH MARKETING

Subsequent to the conclusion of the Disney case in 2006, my legal practice had undergone a significant change of direction which had carried through to my retirement from Spoor & Fisher and active legal practice in 2010, some four years later. It came about in a curious way which was interwoven with the Disney case. The new direction had its beginnings and had occupied my 'idle' moments during the Disney case.

A prelude to it all had its beginnings way back in 1994, while I was serving on the Statutory Intellectual Property Law Advisory Committee. At that time we were approached by a prominent Johannesburg attorneys' firm with a novel proposal. The 1995 Rugby World Cup to be staged in South Africa was imminent. Both the South African and international rugby authorities organising the tournament were concerned about a modern commercial phenomenon known as 'ambush marketing'. The attorneys, who represented the rugby authorities, had come to the Advisory Committee with a proposed measure that was aimed at preventing and counteracting ambush marketing from taking place at the forthcoming Rugby World Cup. Ambush marketing was considered to be a threat to the viability of major events like the Rugby World Cup.

Major sporting extravaganzas like the Rugby, Soccer and Cricket World Cups and the Olympic Games are dependent to a large extent on commercial sponsorships to finance their endeavours. Large commercial ventures, like sports goods, clothing and alcoholic beverages suppliers, airline companies, hotel groups and the like, advance vast sums of money to the organisers of the events in return for the right to advertise their wares at the event, and to use the event as an advertising platform or vehicle for the promotion of their products. The latter form of benefit generally takes the form of using the logos and other advertising properties created for the event by the organisers as branding for their products. Each of these sponsors is given the monopoly of using the event and its identifying symbols for the purposes of marketing their products in their own sector of the market. For instance, a beer producer who becomes a sponsor is given the right to be the only beer producer in the world who may ride on the back of the event for marketing purposes. In other words, the sponsor is given the exclusive right in their field to use the event for promotional and marketing purposes. This is a valuable and desirable tool for a marketer, for which an exorbitant fee is paid, by way of a sponsorship, to the event organiser.

The success of this form of venture is heavily dependent on the sponsor actually being able to exercise the exclusive right granted to it by the event organiser. A sponsor who pays a vast sponsorship fee for obtaining an exclusive marketing right will be aggrieved if his competitors assume to themselves the unauthorised opportunity to ride on the back of the event in competition with him, without having to pay sponsorship fees. The whole value of a sponsorship is drastically undermined and damaged if the sponsor's competitors cannot be, and are not, closed out. It is a straightforward equation; if a sponsor cannot obtain the exclusivity for which he pays, and thus obtain the valuable edge over his competitors, he will not pay a sponsorship fee. Without the income from sponsorship fees, major events are unviable and cannot be staged.

In the cutthroat environment of international marketing, the competitors of event sponsors have no scruples in not respecting the rights of sponsors and the practice has developed and become pervasive for them to use any and all means to take advantage of the promotional opportunities provided by major events. The competitors assume to themselves the right to use the event for promotional purposes in exactly the same way as do the sponsors. This brazen conduct on the part of non-sponsors amounts to ambush marketing.

Ambush marketing, in simple terms, takes place when non-sponsors of an event conduct themselves as though they are sponsors and assume to themselves the benefits of sponsorships without paying for the privilege. Event organisers seek to curtail ambush marketing in various ways. The obvious solution is to invoke the law, provided of course the law has mechanisms to render ambush marketing unlawful. Therein lies the rub.

In South Africa, as in most countries in the world, the common law provides a remedy known as 'passing off', or sometimes as 'unlawful competition'. This remedy enables a trader (the brand owner), who has through extensive public exposure of his brand or trade mark caused that mark or sign to develop a reputation as being a badge of origin of his goods or services to derive certain rights. The brand owner is empowered to prevent another from using that mark, or a confusingly similar mark, in relation to their goods or services where that manner of use is likely to cause those goods or services to be thought to originate from the brand owner, or to be connected in the course of trade with them. In other words, a member of the public is deceived into thinking that the other person's goods or services are those of the brand owner. This remedy can play a role in the major event situation if a non-sponsor, for instance, uses the event logo in relation to his goods or services. The public will be deceived into thinking that the trader in question is a sponsor. In this situation the unauthorised use of the logo will amount to passing off and be unlawful. The event organiser would be able to obtain an interdict or injunction preventing that unlawful conduct.

The remedy of passing off is, however, of no assistance to the event organiser or to a sponsor, where the non-sponsor does not mislead others into thinking that their goods are those of a sponsor but rather uses their own trade mark in a manner that brings it into association with the event in such a way that the renown of the event rubs off onto his goods. For instance, the non-sponsor might place an advertisement for their product prominently across the road from a stadium where the event is staged, or might cause a section of the crowd attending the events to wear tee shirts prominently featuring their brand so as to catch the public eye. These are activities that are the preserve of sponsors. This form of ambush marketing is generally not unlawful in terms of the common law, and special measures are required to render it unlawful.

AMBUSHING WORLD CUPS

The proposal placed before the Advisory Committee referred to above was aimed at preventing ambush marketing from taking place at the forthcoming Rugby World Cup. It entailed a complicated and convoluted form of registration of sponsorships. While the Advisory Committee was sympathetic towards the objectives of the proposal, it considered it to be practically unworkable and therefore unacceptable. Because the Advisory Committee could see the need for measures to control ambush marketing, it decided that a couple of its members should be deputised to meet with the attorneys and to explain to them that their objective was not without merit, but that another approach should be devised. I was one of those delegated to this task. The outcome of the meeting was that I undertook to try and come up with a theory for a measure that would achieve the objective.

After much deliberation I devised a theory based on the principle of abuse of rights, which is an accepted form of actionable conduct under the common law. My departure point was that an owner of land who uses his property in a manner that causes an unjustifiable nuisance to his neighbour can in law be prevented from doing so (for instance, a tree on his property drops leaves on the neighbour's property causing the blockage of his drains resulting in flooding). The prejudiced land owner can restrain his neighbour from causing a nuisance to him. The remedy in respect of 'nuisance' is recognised in the common law in South Africa and is well known.

A parallel could be drawn where a non-sponsor uses his own trade mark to encroach upon the exclusive rights in respect to an event granted to a sponsor by the event organiser. This conduct by the non-sponsor amounts to using their trade mark where it is not welcome and creates a 'nuisance' for the sponsor, and for that matter the event organiser. This manner of creating a nuisance at the event ought to be capable of being prevented at the instance of those to whom prejudice is being caused, in the same way as a land owner can prevent leaves from his neighbour's trees from causing a nuisance by blocking his drains. In both instances the property of one person is being used in such a way, and in a circumstance that it is unreasonably causing prejudice or damage to another person.

However, if this nuisance theory in respect of ambush marketing was to be given effect, it would have to take the form of a legislative measure. I felt that this could be achieved by a small amendment to the Merchandise Marks Act, a statute which outlawed various forms of trading practices, particularly those entailing the use of marks of one form or another.

I conveyed my views to the attorneys representing the rugby authorities and suggested to them that they put together a proposal along these lines. In the end nothing came of this interchange, whether because the short time before the Rugby World Cup did not allow for Parliament to pass legislation, or for some other reason, I know not. However, I decided to publish an article on my solution to the ambush marketing problem in a legal journal. In my published article I outlined the problem and drew attention to the two forms that ambush marketing could take. I called the passing off form of ambush marketing by 'association,' and the 'nuisance' form of ambush marketing by 'intrusion.' I outlined the amendments to the Merchandise Marks Act that could give effect to my theory. The article caused some interest in legal circles, but the issue was not taken any further. The Rugby World Cup had already been and gone.

The years rolled by and the Cricket World Cup to be staged in South Africa in 2007 loomed on the horizon. On a good day in 2006 out of the blue I received a visit from the official at the Department of Trade and Industry responsible for intellectual property legislation and policy, one MacDonald Netshitenzhe. He informed me that the international and South African cricket authorities had required that, as a condition to South Africa having been awarded the privilege of staging the Cricket World Cup in South Africa, the country must adopt adequate and effective measures to prevent ambush marketing from taking place in connection with the 2007 tournament. He asked whether I could assist in achieving this outcome.

I referred him to what had transpired at the time of the Rugby World Cup some 12 years previously and to the article that I had published. I expressed my willingness to implement that proposal if that met with his approval. He agreed and I drafted the required amendments to the Merchandise Marks Act and some subordinate legislation. These enactments were rushed through Parliament and the other official channels. Unfortunately, the time available was not altogether adequate and the measures only came into effect towards the end of the tournament. They therefore did not play a major role in the tournament. The important point was, however, that they became law.

The Merchandise Marks Act is a criminal statute, and the amendments made to it effectively rendered ambush marketing a criminal offence. This was an important factor in its enforcement and in counteracting the wrongful conduct because it could be enforced by the police. This was extremely useful in making the measures practicable because action could be taken immediately and on the spot.

Normally with civil law wrongs one would have to bring civil court proceedings to obtain appropriate relief. Such court proceedings are long winded and could take several months to conclude. As major sporting events such as World Cups are over and done within in a matter of a few weeks from beginning to end, going the civil law route would not achieve the objective properly because the relevant event would be long gone before a matter could come to court and relief obtained. It would be a case of shutting the door after the horse had bolted. What was necessary was a measure that could produce results in a matter of days. Access to criminal proceedings could achieve this at least as far as putting a stop to the unlawful activity was concerned. Arrests could be made and unlawful goods could be confiscated on the spot. The cases could be concluded later but the immediate objective could be achieved expeditiously.

In the final result the amendments to the Merchandise Marks Act effectively outlawed ambush marketing by both 'association' and 'intrusion', making them both criminal offences. Any criminal action taken could be supplemented by follow-up civil law proceedings for damages. The civil law cause of action would be common-law unlawful competition, i.e., trading and competing in contravention of criminal law. In some quarters the measures were labelled as being draconian, but they did the job. The measures also had an important deterrent effect, because they caused potential ambush marketers to run the risk of becoming criminals and therefore to think twice before embarking on ambush marketing activities.

Offences under the Merchandise Marks Act can give rise to severe penalties. In the case of a first conviction a fine of up to R5 000 per infringing article or up to three years imprisonment could be imposed by the court. In the case of a second or further conviction the level of the sanctions could be increased to a fine of R10 000 or five years imprisonment, respectively. Naturally, a criminal record was also the consequence of a conviction. This was a notable censure in the case of directors of major trading companies, which were the most prone to indulging in ambush marketing.

2010 SOCCER WORLD CUP

South Africa decided to bid to host the 2010 Soccer World Cup tournament. Bidding countries were required to submit information, *inter alia*, on the extent to which their laws and legal system qualified them to successfully host the tournament. The capability of their legal machinery to combat ambush marketing was an important element of this enquiry. The South African bidding team were able to point to our recently adopted legislation specifically aimed at preventing and penalising ambush marketing. The point was correctly made that our law rendering ambush marketing by specifically intrusion and association unlawful which was unique and unequalled anywhere in the world. History shows that South Africa's bid was successful, and our country was appointed by the Federation Internationale de Football Association (FIFA) as the venue for the 2010 tournament. This opened a new chapter in my legal career.

I had an association with FIFA commencing in 1994. That was when the World Cup Soccer tournament was held in the USA. A South African trader used the brand World Cup to sell its wares in South Africa. On FIFA's instructions I instituted a court case founded on passing off in order to restrain the trader from using the mark and thus riding on the back of the tournament taking place in the USA. The court accepted that FIFA's World Cup trade mark enjoyed a repute in South Africa despite the fact that they had never traded in the country, upheld the claim and issued an order restraining its use by the local trader. Subsequently

Spoor & Fisher obtained registration of certain of FIFA's trade marks in South Africa.

When South Africa was appointed as the host for the 2010 World Cup I saw an opportunity to become involved in the intellectual property aspects of the tournament. I visited FIFA's offices in Zurich in 2007, and relying on our firm's past association with them, offered our assistance in dealing with their intellectual property issues regarding the forthcoming tournament. I drew their attention to the work that I had done in respect of ambush marketing. My efforts bore fruit, and I was designated as the lawyer responsible for FIFA's intellectual property with respect to the 2010 tournament. As a result, from 2007 onwards I became involved with FIFA's intellectual property on virtually a full time basis. This was the time that coincided with the end and aftermath of *The Lion Sleeps Tonight* case.

In terms of Spoor & Fisher's retirement policy, I was due to retire as a partner and from active practice in 2010 and this meant that the remainder of my career was effectively taken up on a virtually full time basis with the FIFA 2010 World Cup soccer tournament. *The Lion Sleeps Tonight* case receded into oblivion.

Another factor came into play. Being by origin, and dyed in the wool in spirit, a Capetonian I had absolutely no doubt whatsoever that I would return to my roots upon retirement. This conviction was all the more present in my wife, Dana, who had migrated to Pretoria in our early days under sufferance. At the turn of the century Spoor & Fisher had opened a satellite office in Cape Town. In 2007, although being Chairman of the firm, I negotiated a transfer to the Cape Town office, which then became my professional home until my retirement three years later. Since at that stage I was working virtually full time for FIFA, I reasoned that I could carry on my practice as easily in Cape Town as in Pretoria. I could work remotely from there with my back-up team in Pretoria as well as if I was based in the latter city. I became the forerunner of all those who in later years took to working from home during the Covid pandemic. I accordingly relocated to the Western Cape and took up residence in Stellenbosch in the latter part of 2007.

I developed a concerted plan of action for FIFA to navigate the battle fields of the Soccer World Cup in the intellectual property and ambush marketing field. This commenced with an extensive programme to register all their logos, brands and other *indicia* as trade marks in every conceivable category, and as designs. I also undertook the necessary spade work to rely on the benefits of the amended Merchandise Marks Act for purposes of combatting ambush marketing, and to enable copyright infringement claims to be mounted where appropriate.

As the remedies available under the amended Merchandise Marks Act were virgin territory, I advocated, and FIFA agreed, that it was necessary to bring a test case to demonstrate the efficacy of the remedies available for us to combat ambush marketing. In this respect I was following my tried and tested recipe that had been effective in many situations in the past, and most notably in *The Lion Sleeps Tonight* case. The successful outcome of the recent *The Lion Sleeps Tonight* case encouraged FIFA to go down the test case route.

The strategy was to find someone, anyone, to sue at the earliest possible opportunity, preferably well in advance of the commencement of the tournament, so that by the time the tournament got under way the efficacy of the remedies would already have been approved by the court and demonstrated to potential ambush marketers. As was the case with Disney, the target should ideally be as large and as prominent a party as possible so that the test case could have maximum publicity and effect. But if the worst came to the worst, we would sue the first possible victim that came along, no matter how significant or insignificant they may be. The paramount requirement was that we should have a contested case. A successful court judgment was the prize, and all other considerations faded into insignificance. This was the classic test case formula.

The problem we encountered was that in the early days leading up to the tournament the big hitters were not yet active, and we had to resort to attacking relatively small fry. The first few parties we took on capitulated immediately, which frustrated our endeavours. Eventually we came up against a relatively small producer of snack foods who resisted. They were perpetrating both ambush marketing by intrusion and by association, which suited our purposes admirably. The case was entirely successful and the desired favourable judgment, upholding all our arguments and claims, was obtained. The test case result that we sought had been attained. The size of the other party and the small amount of produce on the market were irrelevant.

The objective of demonstrating how the ambush marketing legislation worked, and that FIFA had a viable and effective cause of action against ambush marketing, had been attained. All the preparatory steps for conducting an anti-ambush marketing campaign had been put in place timeously before the Soccer World Cup commenced and we could rely on the platform that had been established in order to act expeditiously against any ambush marketers.

At the previous Soccer World Cup in Germany in 1996 the Dutch beer brewing company, Bavaria, had conducted extensive ambush marketing activities effectively with impunity. FIFA believed that they would attempt to adopt similar measures at this World Cup. We expected that true to form Bavaria would target the matches played by their own home team, the Netherlands. When the first match to be played by the Netherlands team was imminent, we made preparations and put a plan of action in place. The day dawned and sure enough it happened.

A group of around 50 attractive young blond-haired women dressed in normal clothing arrived at the match. They took up seats in a block. At a prearranged time, they all stripped off their outer clothing to reveal brief orange coloured (the colours of the Dutch national team) dresses bearing the registered logo of Bavaria. This combination of factors brought their conduct squarely within the compass of the ambush marketing provision of the Merchandise Marks Act that I had drafted. It amounted to a classic case of ambush marketing by intrusion.

They were thus perpetrating a criminal offence. Armed with the favourable judgment in our test case endorsing the principle of the unlawfulness of ambush marketing by intrusion, we were in a position to request the police force present at the game to take appropriate action. They complied and arrested the full contingent of offending women. They removed them from the ground and imprisoned them. The ambush marketing was curtailed.

The episode caused a storm of controversy. The Dutch government lodged a complaint with the South African government. This was all to no avail because the women had clearly been involved in unlawful conduct as had been verified in the test case. However, FIFA had no intention of pressing charges against the women. They were models who had been hired for the purpose, and they had no conception of the implications of what they had been requested to do. They were soon released. Bavaria, the puppet masters, were, however, a different proposition.

We were geared to launch a criminal complaint against them and to institute urgent civil proceedings against them for an interdict restraining their unlawful conduct and for stated damages coupled to an enquiry into damages. Similarly to the Disney case, Bavaria was a foreign based company, and it would be necessary to attach their South African registered trade marks in order to found jurisdiction in the South African court in respect to them. We had made all the preparations for doing so.

However, Bavaria immediately capitulated and came forward with a settlement request. A settlement was achieved on very favourable terms for FIFA. The crux of the settlement was that Bavaria undertook to cease and refrain from all ambush marketing activities not only for the duration of the tournament but also for future World Cup competitions. In the circumstances it was not necessary to institute any of the proposed legal actions. The exercise was a resounding success. It turned out that FIFA were not required to take any anti-ambush marketing enforcement steps for the remainder of the tournament.

That completed the story that I gave Rian over the telephone, but some comments on it are warranted and insightful.

There is a salutary lesson to be learned from this episode. It was a near perfect implementation of the test case formula. In the first place FIFA bought into my proposed plan of action and trusted that I knew what I was doing. A test case was brought in which nominal damages were claimed, but with the prime and major objective of establishing and demonstrating the effect and implementation of a particular principle of law. Once that objective had been attained the issue of claiming damages in the test case became unimportant, if not irrelevant. The platform established by the prior test case was subsequently used and put to good effect in the Bavaria case.

Bavaria's attitude to the action we took against them was the archetypical reaction expected from a defendant in such a case. On account of the successful test case they immediately realised that the game was up. The case illustrated and epitomised the advantage of already having an established platform in place due to having a successful test case under the belt. The ability to rely in this way on a test case was the trump card. This is exactly what had been envisaged to be achieved in the Disney case, but unfortunately there was the issue of damages arising out of the test case (where they were inconsequential), instead of being viewed as a wonderful bonus, subsumed everything and the real significance and value of that case were obscured into oblivion. The attitude of the daughters and the misinformation disseminated in Cullman's film took care of that.

FIFA astutely appreciated that, armed with an appropriate test case, they may in future be able to obtain compensation for damages suffered without having to rely on carrying through litigation. The rationale of the test case strategy is really not that difficult to understand if one approaches it without preconceived prejudices. Moreover, it has been shown to have worked in the past and to bring about good results.

Unlike in the Disney case, FIFA did not delude themselves that in a case against Bavaria in South Africa they could claim damages arising from ambush marketing that had taken place in Germany and other countries, or from all and sundry other ambush marketers with whom Bavaria had no connection and who had not been involved in Bavaria's offending conduct. This realisation is not rocket science.

Fortunately, and wisely, the legal team acting in the Bavaria case, essentially the same personnel who were involved in the Disney case, were not accused of furthering their own interests at the expense of those of the beneficiaries of the litigation because they earned some fees for their efforts. In the Bavaria case there was no suggestion that the team should not be entitled to be remunerated.

During the build up to the tournament, and the tournament itself, I attended all FIFA's regular meetings on legal and administrative matters so that there could be a comprehensive exchange of information between me, the FIFA officers and other persons and bodies involved in the relevant aspects of organising and running the tournament. Carrying out my FIFA mandate was an all-embracing and time-consuming endeavour.

I took to conducting an extensive publicity campaign explaining the law on ambush marketing and the consequences of being brought to book. This entailed doing interviews on television and radio and in the media generally as well as conducting workshops and the like. The objective was to dissuade would be ambush marketers from chancing their arms. This campaign was largely successful.

All this activity carried me through to the conclusion of the World Cup tournament and to my retirement from Spoor & Fisher and active legal practice in July 2010.

After July 2010 I entered an entirely new chapter in my life. My future would unfold in ways that I did not expect.

XIII

Twilight Time

CHANGE OF IDENTITY

'So, you had an interesting and stimulating conclusion to your career as a practising attorney. You must be very satisfied with the way your career went,' said Rian, continuing our telephone conversation. 'Yes, I had a rewarding and fulfilling run as an attorney and retired on a high note,' I replied.

'But how did you become involved with Stellenbosch University and then pursue an academic career?' Rian enquired. 'Like in my entire legal career, happenstance, fate, call it what you will, played a significant role. I will elucidate. It was the beginning of my twilight time,' I responded.

What follows below is an elaboration of the information that I conveyed to Rian.

TAKING A FRONT SEAT

My retirement from Spoor & Fisher after some 40 years of active legal practice was a major milestone in my life. The sun was setting on my career, but it turned out that several rays of sunlight were yet to be seen before the sun dipped below the horizon. The tranquillity which characterised sunset was not yet upon me. This was due to a variety of factors, some good and some not.

After the publication of my *Handbook of South African Copyright Law* in 1988, I received requests to present lectures giving instruction on copyright from various quarters including business organisations, seminar presenters and South African universities. I took to lecturing on the subject on a fairly regular basis. In particular, I acceded to requests to present lectures at Stellenbosch, Cape Town, Rand Afrikaans and

Witwatersrand Universities. In effect I became a part time university lecturer. This situation endured for a few years and then stopped mainly because the universities had appointed permanent lecturing staff to present the subject.

Shortly after I retired from Spoor & Fisher, I gave a lecture on copyright to a group of film makers in Cape Town. After the lecture I was approached by an individual, Sadulla Karjiker, who informed me that he had been appointed to lecture, *inter alia*, IP at the Law Faculty of Stellenbosch University. He enquired of me whether I would be willing to lecture to some of his classes. I replied in the affirmative as I was now a gentleman of leisure. In order to set up the arrangement he made an appointment for me to meet with the Dean of the Law Faculty, Professor Gerhard Lubbe, some days hence.

Before my meeting with Professor Lubbe could take place, I had a chance encounter with Dr Frederick Mostert, a senior legal official in the Rembrandt/Richemont group, whom I knew well and from whom I took instructions when acting for that group over a period of many years.

Mostert advised me that his boss and the head of the group, Dr Johan Rupert, was desirous of establishing a Chair of Intellectual Property Law at a suitable South African university and he sought my view as to which university would be the most suitable candidate. I informed him that I was about to commence lecturing at Stellenbosch and that I thought that this university would be most suitable. He liked this idea whereupon I advised him that I was about to meet with the Dean of the Law Faculty and if he wished I could raise with him the question of whether he was interested in establishing the envisaged Chair. To cut a long story short, the Chair was set up at Stellenbosch and I was appointed as the incumbent in the capacity of a full professor, a position for which I qualified by virtue of my doctor's degree and track record in academic writing, as well as my previous lecturing experience. The appointment was for a period of three years, but it was subsequently extended for a further two years.

I was given carte blanche to set up the Chair as I thought fit and I was provided with supporting staff. I immediately set up a course for a Masters degree in IP (LLM degree) as well as a postgraduate diploma in the subject catering for non-lawyers. I set out to make the Chair the custodian of IP in the country as I considered that the performance of the Department of Trade and Industry was sadly lacking in that respect. I also had the goal of popularising IP, i.e., bringing it to the attention of the general public and familiarising them with what it entailed. I wanted them to become aware of how, perhaps unbeknown to them, it permeated their very day-to-day existence, whether in the form of the brands of the products that they bought and used, the books and newspapers they read, the letters they wrote, the computers they used, the music they listened to, the television they watched, the cars they drove, the appliances they used, etcetera, etcetera. To this end I arranged public lectures, set up a laymen's education programme and copiously published articles in the media and/or a blog that I set up on a website established for the Chair, called IPSTELL. These articles featured IP topics, in particular in relation to current affairs.

Frederick Mostert is the son of Judge Anton Mostert, the judge who blew the lid off the Information Scandal involving Eschel Rhoodie in the 1970s. Mostert caused the IP Chair to be named the Anton Mostert Chair of Intellectual Property Law after his father. I had misgiving about this title as Judge Mostert had little or nothing to do with IP, but it was not for me to reason why.

I believed that the Chair ought to have been called the Anton Rupert Chair because Dr Rupert had in building his business empire believed in, and utilised, branding, i.e., trade marks, as an important means to achieve success. He was a staunch believer in the value of trade marks and the intellectual property system that protected them. He was indeed a champion of intellectual property, and this eminently qualified him to have the Chair named after him. Moreover, the group of companies founded by him was financing the Chair.

When the launch of the Chair was presented to the media, I was asked to explain why it had been named after Anton Mostert. I did not believe that nepotism was a satisfactory response, so I had to come up with some other explanation. After some creative thinking I said that Anton Mostert had achieved renown because he had fearlessly and forthrightly discharged his civil duty in exposing bad practice in the Information Scandal by revealing the truth; a principal objective of the Chair was to act as the custodian of IP and to speak out forthrightly against governmental bad practice in the IP field resulting in prejudice to the law and those whom it was supposed to protect. In this respect the Chair would be emulating the praiseworthy conduct of, and following the good example set by, Anton Mostert. This warranted the Chair being named after him. This explanation found favour. Nevertheless, my view that the Chair should be named after Anton Rupert remains steadfast.

I retired from the University at the end of my five year stint in 2015 and I was replaced as the incumbent of the Chair by Sadulla Karjiker, who I had in the meantime shepherded through to a doctorate in copyright law and to a professorship. The Chair continues to flourish under his capable stewardship and fulfils the objectives I set for it.

During my time at the Chair, in conjunction with my former Spoor & Fisher partner, Alison Dyer, I compiled and edited *Introduction to Intellectual Property Law*, a student's textbook, which was published by Oxford University Press, and which is prescribed by most of the major South African Universities. I have continued all along to be associated with Spoor & Fisher in the capacity of a consultant, mainly doing opinion work.

That explanation brought Rian Malan up to date on what I had been doing and how I had been spending my time in the aftermath of the Disney case. This was later to become relevant when it was suggested that I had irresponsibly forsaken the welfare of the Linda daughters instead of remaining involved with their lot in life. I plead not guilty to this charge. Apart from any other considerations, my hands were more than full in dealing with the other pursuits that I have outlined as well as in other legal pursuits to which I will refer in due course.

REEMERGENCE OF THE LINDA FAMILY

It transpired that the real purpose of Rian Malan's phone call to me was to convey to me the disenchantment of the Linda daughters with the financial benefits that they were experiencing from the outcome of *The*

Lion Sleeps Tonight case. They seemed to believe that they were being cheated out of the money that was due to them. What annoyed me was that Rian seemed to side with them on this score and to cast aspersions on the integrity of the trustees of the Trust that had been appointed to administer to the proceeds of the song and even the legal team who had handled the case.

I advised Rian that I had not been involved at all with the Trust or the matter in general for the past eight years but that I had the utmost confidence in the trustees to properly and fairly manage the finances of the Trust.

Bearing in mind that Rian had summarily turned down my pleas that he should become one of the trustees, I took exception to his criticism and seemingly instinctive mistrust of the trustees. I had carefully chosen the trustees, all of whom I held in considerable esteem, and I considered it unlikely in the extreme that they were guilty of any dishonesty or mismanagement. Nonetheless, I undertook to contact the trustees and to arrange for him to have complete access to all the books of account and other materials relating to the operation of the Trust so that he could investigate the daughters' accusations and satisfy himself as to the true state of affairs.

I duly spoke to Glen Dean, who was still in the employment of Spoor & Fisher, and made the necessary arrangements. Rian subsequently conducted a full inspection of the affairs of the Trust and found nothing untoward, as I had anticipated.

Glen Dean (who I previously pointed out had no family connection to me) related a sad and disappointing tale to me, which I summarise below.

He roundly rejected the daughters' accusations. He told me that the trustees had found carrying out their duties to be an extremely onerous, unpleasant and frustrating experience. So much so that two of them had resigned in disgust at the conduct of the daughters. They experienced that their efforts to remunerate the daughters on an organised and reasonable basis were spurned out of hand and that the daughters pestered them day and night for more and more money. They suspected that payouts to at least one of the daughters were squandered on personal indulgences.

The daughters showed no appreciation for their efforts and treated them with severe rudeness. Acting as a trustee was a thankless task. Both he and Hanro, the only two survivors of the original group, did not believe that they could carry on much longer in the function, for which they were not being remunerated. A family member of the daughters had been added to the trustees, and he was acting fast and loose with the funds.

I was most dismayed to hear all this. I could not help but wonder whether all my efforts, the risks that I took, and the stress I endured to achieve success in the case had been worthwhile. I consoled myself that I had given my best shot in conducting the case and achieving what was generally accepted to be an amazing outcome. How the daughters chose to conduct themselves with regard to the spoils of the case was out of my hands. I had given them an opportunity to come good in their lives and it was up to them to make the most of it. They held their fate in their own hands. I had hoped that they would invest the monies that came to them wisely so as to provide for a comfortable and secure future. However, it turned out to be wishful thinking on my part. What went wrong? I answered my own question; perhaps a lack of education, ignorance and resultant misunderstandings!

It seemed to me that the root of the problem was that they had not become recipients of the multitudinous millions of dollars that they fondly believed was due to them. The expectations of what monies they would be getting were unrealistic and way over the top. Their assessment of what they actually received was weighed against their mythical expectations. When it turned out that they received less money than they fancied they ought to be getting, they turned to biting the hands that were feeding them.

It was difficult to understand why they were so misguided about the amount of money that they would be receiving. Hanro Friederich and Rian Malan were delegated to explain the terms of the settlement to the daughters and secure their signatures to the document. The daughters were required to sign the agreement, which they did. The financial details of the settlement were spelled out in the agreement, including the amount of the lump sum payment, which the parties were required to keep confidential. If there were any concerns about the amount of the compensation that the Estate would be receiving, they could have been raised then.

It is possible that Rian might not have understood the niceties of the financial arrangements, because he had somewhat lost track of what was going on, but Hanro certainly had a clear understanding of the nature of our actual damages claim and all that the settlement entailed. He could have addressed any queries that might be raised about the amounts involved coming from the daughters or from Rian. I am not aware that any reservations were voiced at that stage, and none were ever conveyed to me.

Some while subsequent to my telephone conversation with Rian Malan a further spectre arose. I received unwelcome correspondence from a firm of attorneys acting for the daughters. In these letters the attorneys threatened to sue Spoor & Fisher for misappropriation of moneys due to the daughters. I advised the attorneys that Spoor & Fisher had been the litigation attorneys and that their role in the matter had ceased when the litigation was finalised. We had billed the Department of Arts and Culture for our services and had derived no further remuneration from the case.

It is possible that the attorneys might have been misled by the fact that, although Spoor & Fisher's charges had been paid by Arts and Culture, there was nevertheless a record of a substantial payment made to the firm by the Executor. This represented the reimbursement of the firm's disbursement in respect of counsels' fees. The executor's payment of counsels' fees perhaps featured in his books as an unqualified payment to Spoor & Fisher. It may thus have appeared as though an undue payment had been made to Spoor & Fisher. In other words, they were perhaps under the misapprehension that Spoor & Fisher had been paid twice, i.e., first by Arts and Culture and then again by the Executor. However, the daughters' attorneys, by the nature of their profession, must have been well aware of the standard practices followed in the attorneys' profession in regard to billing for fees and disbursements arising out of litigation. They would have known full well that when an attorney briefs an advocate, the attorney is the contractual principal in the arrangement and is responsible for paying the advocates fees. The advocate has no contractual relationship with the attorney's client. The attorney pays the advocates' fees and then in turn recovers his costs in that regard from the client.

In terms of this *modus operandi*, Spoor & Fisher paid the fees of Puckrin and Michau and then billed the Executor with our disbursements in respect of counsels' fees. In any event a simple enquiry could have clarified the matter, but this never happened.

Spoor & Fisher had absolutely nothing to do with the further administration of the funds due to the daughters in terms of the settlement. I referred the daughters' attorneys to the trustees. At the same time, I advised them that according to my information the funds due to the daughters had been properly managed by the trustees and that no misappropriation of any funds had taken place. I suggested to them that they make a thorough study of the case and in particular the of the settlement agreement, and that they reassess their clients' position.

The letters from the attorneys did not immediately dry up and the same allegations and claims were made over and over again. I ignored the further letters and eventually they stopped coming.

It was obvious that the attorneys, like their clients, the daughters, had adopted an extremely uninformed, naïve and unrealistic approach to their estimation of what ought to have been due to the daughters out of the settlement, and this was the foundation of their misguided belief that part of the money must have gone missing.

I was nonplussed and aggrieved by the fact that the daughters and their attorneys had adopted such a negative view of the outcome of the case and that they had decided that Spoor & Fisher and the rest of the legal team were guilty of dishonourable conduct. I viewed the unfounded accusations of the daughters' attorneys as an aberration not to be taken seriously and elected to ignore the whole episode. I did not let them interfere with the success story of what had been achieved by the lawyers acting on their behalf in conquering the mountain and reaching the summit, something that at the outset appeared to be an impossible quest. But, alas, it was to prove not to be the end of the matter.

This whole episode left a very bad taste in my mouth, and I reminded myself that the daughters had at no stage even had the good grace to thank me for my efforts on their behalf and for going out on a limb, at considerable cost to myself in terms of stress endured and prejudice suffered, to improve their lot. Their ingratitude was extremely disillusioning.

INTROSPECTION

Experiencing a sunset often gives rise to contemplation and introspection. So it was with me in this twilight time. I embarked on some soul searching and self-analysis.

Towards the end of my time at the Chair, prompted by the episode that I had with Rian Malan regarding the discontent of the Linda daughters, which caused me to wonder why I had ever persevered with the case against all odds, I decided to write a novel on another subject to explore and analyse the personal characteristic which induces someone to doggedly persevere with a project when all the odds appear to be stacked against them.

The novel had that personal characteristic (which I had identified in myself, and which had played a significant role in my conducting and persevering with *The Lion Sleeps Tonight* case) as its central theme. I called this personal characteristic 'the top of the mountain syndrome'.

This personal characteristic ingrained in me had in fact emerged and manifested itself in an earlier court case that I had conducted but I had not previously put a finger on it or conceptualised it. I decided to use that court case as the basis and the vehicle for expounding the top of the mountain syndrome.

The court case in question took place in the late 1980s. I brought a copyright infringement case for an academic publishing company and two authors against a competitor academic publishing company and their author. At issue was the unauthorised reproduction of significant parts of the plaintiffs' legal textbook by the defendants. At first blush it seemed to be an open and shut case because substantial parts of the plaintiffs' book had been copied virtually verbatim in the defendants' book. However, this proved to be an illusion and what eventuated was by far the most bizarre and convoluted case I ever handled. There were instances of forged evidence, planted evidential materials intended to be exposed by a spurious Anton Piller Order, threats of physical violence and even death, invasions of privacy, counterclaims for defamation (against me personally), perjury, aggression against the judge, to mention but a few of the aberrations that took place. The outcome was that my clients lost the case. I was incensed by this result and was convinced that the defendants had gotten away with proverbial murder. I was determined not to let the matter rest there and to leave no stone unturned in getting the truth and justice to prevail, whatever it may take. We appealed against the judgment.

In order to get around the defendants' dishonesty and deceit that had won the day for them I sought new evidence. My quest was successful, and I unearthed two witnesses who had not hitherto been known. In the one instance this entailed my travelling to Greece to track down and interview one of the witnesses. This further evidence proved conclusively that the defendant had indeed falsified evidence and lied when giving testimony.

Normally it is not possible to introduce new evidence in an appeal but in this instance, we applied to the appeal court for leave to adduce the fresh evidence. We were confident that the new evidence would be admitted and that this would cause the appeal to be successful. However, shortly before the appeal was due to be heard, my publisher client, without consulting me or the authors who were co-plaintiffs, decided to settle the case, much to our chagrin. That was the end of the matter, and the new evidence was never heard. As a result, the defendants got off scot-free and prospered handsomely from their dishonesty.

I was devastated by this outcome and felt cheated and frustrated that I had been unable to ensure that justice was done. This was compounded some ten years later when I had a chance encounter with a certain individual. This occurred at a workshop in Pretoria in which I participated. A stranger came up to me and enquired whether I was the attorney who had conducted the legal textbook case. When I replied in the affirmative, he told me that I had read the situation in the case completely correctly and that the defendants had indeed falsified evidence and lied in court. He could say this on good authority because he had personally assisted the defendants in perpetrating their nefarious conduct. He told me this in a gloating manner which infuriated me. I attempted to take steps to resuscitate the case, but this was in vain. Too much time had passed, and it was not considered feasible or even desirable to rake up the old bones. I resolved there and then that someday I would write a book about the case disclosing the fresh incriminating evidence that was never presented in court.

After I had retired from Stellenbosch University, I completed the book. However, I decided on a prudent approach and wrote the book as a fiction novel, with names and places being changed. The book was entitled *The Summit Syndrome*. The defendant author in the court case had in the meantime become a prominent academic and I had no appetite for possibly facing a defamation claim.

My alter ego in the novel was named Alan Benedict. Benedict explained why he was so persistent and had persevered in driving the case against all odds towards a successful conclusion and spared no effort in doing so, albeit that he was ultimately not rewarded with success. He attributed his attitude to what he called 'the top of the mountain syndrome' or put differently, 'the summit syndrome'.

My fictional character, Alan Benedict, describes the 'summit/top of the mountain syndrome' as follows:

> *I am possessed by what I call the 'top of the mountain syndrome'. It represents my personal credo and has two aspects. In the broad sense, it entails striving tirelessly to overcome all adversity; in the narrower and perhaps more literal sense, it means that when you take on a project or a journey, it is like being confronted with a mountain. You carry on climbing until you get to the top of it. You do not give up, and you do not turn around until you have reached the summit, and your objective has been achieved. If you do not accomplish this, you will never be fulfilled of feel satisfied.*

In this passage Alan Benedict describes a personal characteristic of his own, but also of his alter ego, me. Reaching 'top of the mountain' does not equate to attaining success or fame. It denotes the courage and perseverance not to give up until you take something through to its final conclusion or destination, come what may, even if defeat awaits you there. But the syndrome is inherently underpinned by the hopeful sentiment that the endeavour will be successful.

The summit syndrome played a significant role in my conducting and persevering with *The Lion Sleeps Tonight* case despite all the pitfalls, disappointments and setbacks that I encountered along the way. In particular it tipped the balance in making me decide to carry on with the case despite its abandonment by Gallo. My logic and reason told me to walk away from the case and relinquish it as a lost cause, but my spirit wouldn't allow me to do that even though the hopeful sentiment of success was at a very low ebb. Logic, reason, and even common sense, were propelled into the back seat. Experience has taught me that sometimes the summit syndrome can be a curse rather than a blessing.

Writing a book about the textbook case caused me to realise that I was possessed by the summit syndrome. It had actually permeated my life for as long as I could remember. The textbook case was merely a manifestation of it but using it as a theme in a book raised it to the level of consciousness. It was like coming to the realisation that I had a previously unrecognised allergy. Previous manifestations of it included my doing a doctorate in law and the saga of the Anton Piller Order where it became an obsession with me to strive for excellence and success irrespective of the outcome.

In the case of the doctorate there was no financial or obvious professional advantage to be derived from obtaining that qualification. It did not materially influence my situation as a practitioner in any way. It was of monumental insignificance to my career. My peers in the profession felt no need or urge to embark on such an undertaking. It was not as if I had spare time on my hands and was looking for some way to occupy myself. On the contrary it came at a time when I was at my busiest and most pressurised, and I had to make time to accomplish the task. It was simply something that I felt that I had to do. I had to take my legal expertise to a zenith. It had to strive to reach the summit.

Despite my efforts to adopt a somewhat cavalier attitude to the interventions of Rian Malan and the daughters' attorneys regarding the proceeds of the legal settlement, I had to concede to myself that the episode upset and troubled me. I felt aggrieved that what I had regarded as something of an altruistic crusade should have backfired on me and that my integrity and motives had been called into question. I was annoyed by the ingratitude that was being displayed and that my virtue was being transformed into a vice. I asked myself how and why I had allowed myself to get into this unhappy situation. I took the whole case into review and put my feelings about it and its ramifications under the microscope.

In my introspection I reasoned that there had been good cause for me to take on the case in the first place. It was an interesting and challenging legal project and another opportunity to make new law. I had what appeared to be a client with deep pockets that was fully committed to the cause. There was every prospect of earning good fees. Indeed, the case excited me. However, all this changed when Gallo decided to abandon the case. It then became an entirely different ball game.

I could, or perhaps should, at that stage have heaved a sigh of professional regret, closed my file, walked away and moved on to the next case which would certainly have come my way. My services were in considerable demand. That would have been the normal, logical and prudent thing to do. But I did not do that. Instead, I embarked on a hazardous and risky (some said insane) venture which could (and did) have a serious impact on my career. Why did I do this? I was but a few years from retirement and I was riding the crest of a wave professionally. I could have coasted comfortably into retirement with a successful career behind me. What possessed me to take on this immense and daunting challenge on behalf of strangers that I did not know and to whom I had no prior obligation. It was not as if I had advised Solomon to execute the assignment of copyright in *Mbube*!

To begin with, what did not motivate me was money. An attorney basically derives income from selling his time. I was entering into a situation where at the outset I did not have any funding for the forthcoming case so I would be deriving no income. Moreover, I would be expending many hours which I could otherwise have been selling to the next client and thereby earning the income due to a very senior legal practitioner. Not only would I be earning no income but also, I would be forfeiting the opportunity of earning fees from another source. At the time of launching the case I had no guarantee that I would ever obtain funding for the litigation. Accordingly, I had to face the prospect of conducting a fully-fledged court case from which not only would I derive no income but also, I would be missing out on other fee-making activities.

Furthermore, there were likely to be expenses associated with the litigation that I would have to bear myself. Since the case was to be a test case with scant realistic possibility of obtaining any meaningful recompense from Disney, there was unlikely to be any pot of gold at the end of the rainbow even if I was successful. While I had some hope that I might eventually be lucky enough to find someone to fund the litigation, I had at the outset proceeded on the assumption that no funding would be forthcoming, and I would be left entirely to my own devices. If I could not come to terms with this situation, I must leave the matter well alone. This was the risk that I must be willing to take.

The basis on which I would be acting was that I would withhold from charging any fees for my services unless and until there were any funds available to defray my standard charges.

I had perforce to brief counsel to act on my behalf as in those days attorneys were not permitted to appeal in the High Court, and in any event, I had no practical experience in actually conducting a trial and leading and cross-examining witnesses. In the absence of having any funding I had to persuade them (a senior and a junior advocate) to act without any remuneration. I would have to call up past favours or credits in order to achieve this. Cedric Puckrin and Reinard Michau, my longstanding advocates of choice, agreed to do so out of loyalty to me. They, who basically also sold their time in order to derive income, would be in the same position as me with regard to making financial sacrifices.

The advocates acted on an approved contingency basis. Their only prospect of getting any remuneration would be if, in addition to the case being successful, there were funds available from sufficient spoils of the litigation in the form of damages. Bearing in mind that this was a test case, the prospects of this coming to pass were in principle minimal.

In the final analysis the prospects of both counsel and me getting any remuneration from the litigation were meagre. Yet we were all willing to conduct the case. What was the motivation and driving force? In the case of counsel, it was largely out of solidarity with me. But what about me?

I was moved to take on the case, warts and all, with its attendant risks, on basically three accounts. First, the 'top of the mountain syndrome' had set in, and to be true to myself I had to take this case through to its conclusion. There were no two ways about it. Second, I had this instinctive and compelling conviction that it was my destiny all along to handle a case such as this; this was the destination to which my train track had been irreversibly headed. I had reached the end of the line. There was no logic in this belief – it was purely a matter of gut feel. Finally, I had enormous empathy for the lot of the daughters. I felt that justice and fairness demanded that their poverty stricken existence should be alleviated by the fruits of the talents of their father, of which he had been deprived through lack of education and awareness of the true value of intellectual property and what it should have achieved. His naivety had been abused by those who ought to have been more honourable. Here was an opportunity to rectify the situation. I believe that this sentiment was also shared by counsel, and it influenced their willingness to become involved.

There was actually another reason why I decided to go ahead with the case off my own bat when Gallo abandoned it. I will discuss it presently when it is opportune to do so.

When I took the outcome of the case into review, I was filled with a sense of pride, achievement and satisfaction. I had reached the summit in no uncertain terms. I had successfully climbed Mount Everest. The case had been the highlight of my career. I had made new law and placed the daughters in a good position to change the trajectory of their lives and live in a degree of comfort and security which was hitherto unknown to them. I'd achieved all my objectives. It had been a case of high risk and high reward, in a non-material sense. My sense of accomplishment at what the case achieved in terms of justice was ample reward.

TAKING STOCK

After spending the twilight gazing at the setting sun, once the sun disappears below the horizon a sense of completion pervades. The time of closure comes about. After my spell of introspection had concluded it was time to take stock of the matter and lay it to rest.

When viewed from my perspective the matter had a highly successful outcome. In the end the lawyers got their just due rewards and received reasonable remuneration for the work they put into achieving a successful result at considerable risk to themselves. I had earned my standard fees for the work I had done through billing the Department of Arts and Culture, which were paid to Spoor & Fisher, and counsel had been appropriately rewarded for their selfless efforts. Full effect could be given to their contingency agreement by paying their fees from the proceeds of the successful case, as required by the standard procedure. Despite their entitlement to double their normal fees, their bills were not excessive by virtue of the fact that their role had essentially been confined to advising me from time to time, settling the court papers that had been drafted by me, and appearing in court to defend the application brought by Disney to set aside the attachment of their trade marks.

In all the circumstances of the case none of the lawyers believed that they had overreached themselves in obtaining the measure of remuneration that they received. Our charges had been computed on a standard and approved basis and we felt justified in charging those fees on account of the magnitude of the monies that the daughters were receiving in terms of the settlement, especially since we had all embarked on the case having reconciled ourselves to the fact that we would probably be receiving no remuneration at all and had been prepared to take that risk.

Neither Spoor & Fisher nor counsel had taken a cut of the proceeds of the case, which is standard practice in contingency litigation in the United States of America. In that country contingency arrangements could bring lawyers an income of 45 percent of the monies recovered. In the present instance the advocates would have earned multiples of their remuneration in this case if that system prevailed in South Africa.

The State had done well out of the case because the amount expended by Arts and Culture on covering our fees was adequately compensated by the estate duty levied on, and paid to, the fiscus in respect of, the windfall that had accrued to the Linda Estate. The daughters had received generous rewards. The test case had achieved its objective in that it had been demonstrated that the reversionary interest had caused the ownership of the copyright in *Mbube* come back home.

As mentioned, Hanro Friederich had made his own financial arrangements with the daughters, which were confidential to him and them. He had first been consulted by them, in conjunction with Rian Malan, as far back as around 2000, and they had appointed him as their lawyer. He and Rian conducted extensive investigations as to what, if anything, could be done to obtain some remuneration from the use of *The Lion Sleeps Tonight*. In this connection he had met with the attorneys who had obtained the assignments of copyright in respect of *Mbube* from Regina and the daughters in respectively 1983 and 1992. He and Rian had investigated whether those assignments could be challenged. All these services provided by him were unconnected with the Disney litigation (which was not even in contemplation yet) and any remuneration obtained by him from in that respect was unconnected with the case.

Upon my entry into the picture in 2002 Hanro worked with me in the capacity of the daughters' attorney, and I engaged with him on that basis. I understood that decisions he made concerning the Disney case were taken in that capacity, acting in terms of the mandate that he held from them. We were two attorneys with separate functions and roles collaborating in pursuit of a similar objective.

When I launched the action against Disney his role changed slightly in that in a sense he stepped into the role of the daughters' instructing attorney, still pursuing his existing mandate from them. He was not handling the litigation, as I was, but rather he was overseeing the daughters' interests in it. In that role he consulted with me on the decisions and steps I was taking in pursuing the litigation. He provided me with valuable assistance and counsel. But his status in the matter never changed. He remained the daughters' private attorney and he did not, as it were, descend into the arena of the actual litigation. He was on the sidelines. His services on behalf of the daughters remained a separate issue from the conducting of the litigation. This situation was reflected in, and consonant with, the fact that he looked to the daughters themselves for his remuneration for his services, as he had done from the outset of his relationship with them. In the result his remuneration in connection with the litigation was not part of the litigation costs and was not the responsibility of, or paid by, the Executor or the Trust.

I later learned from viewing Cullman's film that the daughters had at the outset agreed to pay Hanro 20% of any monies that accrued to them through his efforts. The daughters obviously thought that to be an appropriate level of remuneration in the circumstances of the matter and there has been no suggestion of which I am unaware that this is not the case. I assume that this arrangement was entered into with the blessing of Rian Malan since he introduced Hanro to them and worked with him in the early days of assisting the daughters. In these circumstances there can be no suggestion that Hanro was not entitled to receive the remuneration that was due to him and was presumably paid by the daughters directly. Hanro's remuneration thus falls outside the debate regarding the proceeds of the litigation that was received by the daughters.

I have no doubt that he had given the daughters good service and value for money in helping them both directly, and indirectly through his association with the litigation. To the best of my knowledge when Hanro subsequently assumed the role of a trustee of the Trust, like the other trustees, he fulfilled this role *pro bono*.

The outcome of the case was widely regarded as a remarkable success story – a rags to riches fairy tale – by the international media that had followed the case. There was widespread public joy and approbation that the daughters had been blessed by the favourable outcome of the case. I would like to think that Solomon Linda would have been pleased that his family gained substantial rewards from the use of his song despite the fact that he had divested himself of all rights to it by means of the copyright assignment that he executed. His family had in effect been fortunate enough to have been given a second chance, which doesn't frequently come about in life.

XIV

Copyright on the Rack

DISCIPLE OF INTELLECTUAL PROPERTY

Shortly after Rian Malan's intervention, my contract at the Chair of Intellectual Property Law ended, and I retired from the University of Stellenbosch at the end of 2015, some nine years after the conclusion of the Disney case.

I nevertheless continued to be involved with the Chair as a fellow and later as an Emeritus Professor. I also retained my position as a consultant to Spoor & Fisher. Aside from these associations I became a free agent with few formal obligations. I looked forward to a relatively quiet and leisurely life. It was, however, not to be. I could not shake off my career-long connection with copyright and my activism for the cause, and unbeknown to me a huge storm, which would engulf me, was brewing on the horizon.

Together with other likeminded IP practitioners, academics, business people and persons who were disciples of the doctrine of intellectual property, I was concerned that the new government that came into power in the mid 1990s would not have the same respect for intellectual property as had previously been the case in South Africa and in keeping with the approach of the western world in general.

Intellectual property as a whole, and copyright in particular, is essentially a very pure form of capitalism. It is underpinned by a philosophy which is aptly given expression in Article 1 section 8 Clause 8 of the Constitution of the United States of America. This provision empowers Congress 'to promote the progress of science and useful arts, by securing for limited times to authors and inventors the exclusive right to their respective writings and discoveries.'

This simple clause sums up in a few words the underlying principles of copyright law and intellectual property law in general. Copyright law seeks to create a system whereby the creators of original works are afforded a qualified monopoly in the use and commercial exploitation of their works in order, firstly to compensate and reward them for the effort, creativity and talent expended and utilised in the creation of the works, and, secondly, to act as an incentive for them to use their talents and efforts to create more and better works in the future. The reward and incentive is constituted by affording them the opportunity to gather all the commercial fruits of their works for a limited period, after which the works fall into the public domain, i.e., they become unrestricted public property, and can be freely used and reproduced by others.

A balance is thus struck between the interests of the individual and the public interest. The rationale behind this philosophy is the establishment of a profit incentive for the creators of original works. In striving to create works primarily for their own benefit, creatives ultimately benefit society as a whole by contributing to its general welfare. A sort of compact is struck up between creatives and the state. In return for the state granting an opportunity for creatives to profit, indeed make a living, from creating new works, creatives in due course bestow their works on the public for their unlimited use indefinitely into the future. The works pass into the public domain.

The effectiveness of the profit motive is dependent on the degree to which creatives are able to maintain and enforce their qualified monopoly. If the law is not effective in achieving this outcome the whole system falls down. It is thus essential that the law should be fit for purpose. The erosion of the quality of the law and its enforcement is thus prejudicial to the efficacy of the whole system.

This mindset prompted the attempt to have intellectual property specifically designated as a fundamental right in the Bill of Rights in the Constitution of South Africa adopted in 1994. This was not a fanciful proposition because it enjoys this status in the Universal Declaration of Human Rights to which South Africa subscribes. As previously mentioned, the efforts in this regard were not crowned with success.

Our worst fears began to materialise as the millennium approached. The Statutory Advisory Committee was emasculated and keeping the law up to date went onto the back burner. The hitherto regular updating of the Copyright Act fell into disuse. Beginning with Alec Erwin, each and every Minister of Trade and Industry consecutively appointed was a card-carrying member of the South African Communist Party, individuals whose political persuasions were not in harmony with the philosophy of intellectual property. In figurative terms it amounted to putting the wolf in charge of minding the sheep. Officials appointed in the Department of Trade and Industry to manage the intellectual property system had no experience, expertise or even insight into the subject matter. To put it bluntly, in general they had little or no understanding or knowledge of the law and what it was all about. The efficiency of the patent and trade mark registries declined markedly. Worst of all, outlandish notions of future changes to the laws began to surface.

The officials in the Department developed an antagonistic attitude to the specialist IP practitioners who had previously enjoyed a healthy and co-operative relationship with the officialdom. The new officialdom was generally not willing to heed any advice on the law coming from the specialist practitioners. At one stage the South African Institute of Intellectual Property Law even prepared a High Court application against the Minister to compel him and his officials to provide better service to the practitioners and the public at the Patent and Trade Mark Office. Thereafter the situation improved slightly. An unhappy and worrisome state of affairs prevailed.

I was mindful of the parlous state into which intellectual property law had fallen when I created the Chair at Stellenbosch University. It caused me to set acting as the custodian of IP law as one of the goals and functions of the Chair. This marked an effort on my part to wrest the decline into which IP was falling, a campaign that I had commenced while still in active practice as an attorney. I published many articles on the declining fortunes and state of IP in pursuing this objective. The critical views that I voiced did not make me popular with the officialdom. Nonetheless, paradoxically, as previously related, they turned to me for salvation when the chips were down, and urgent measures later became necessary to combat ambush marketing.

MISGUIDED LEGISLATION – IPLAB

The Department's sullying of IP came to a head shortly after the Soccer World Cup of 2010 when it introduced into parliament the Intellectual Property Laws Amendment Bill (IPLAB), a singularly remarkable and misguided piece of legislation which was fundamentally flawed and technically inept. It was poorly drafted and was riddled with anachronisms and inconsistencies and was a heresy to IP. It sought to amend the standard IP statutes, but principally the Copyright Act, by the introduction of protection for traditional or indigenous works. These works included folklore, rock paintings and all forms of works and processes handed down from generation to generation, often only existing in an unwritten or intangible form. These types of works defied the basic tenets of international and South African IP law.

Over the years there had developed something of a consensus in worldwide IP circles that traditional knowledge/indigenous works warranted some form of protection. This issue was taken up by the World Intellectual Property Organization (WIPO) and it had long grappled with finding an appropriate theoretical basis for such a form of protection. It was a longstanding work in progress. There was general acceptance of the notion that the normal principles of IP could not be applied to this form of protection. The reason for this is that such protection would operate in the reverse direction to that of IP.

IP protection is postulated on the premise that a fresh new/original work was created upon which is conferred a qualified monopoly in favour of known and identified creatives to enable exploitation and the garnering of financial reward by these creators for a limited period of time, whereafter the work passes into the public domain and becomes common property.

On the other hand, and conversely, protection for traditional knowledge (TK) entails plucking works which might have been in existence for centuries, the authorship of which is generally unknown, out of the public domain, creating property rights in them which will probably exist in perpetuity and give rise to the payment of fees for their use.

The rules regulating rights in IP as enshrined in copyright and other forms of IP law, cannot possibly be used, even with some adaptation, to protect works based on such a diametrically opposed scenario. A new formula is required albeit with some degree of kinship to IP.

IPLAB set out to achieve precisely the impossible. It creates a new species of copyright work that is protected in perpetuity, cutting across the existing species of literary, artistic and musical works, and applies the existing tenets of IP to this category. In so doing it rides roughshod over, and undermines the cardinal principles of, copyright such as originality, existence in a material form, authorship, limited term of protection, and public domain. It caused an outcry in IP circles and was widely criticised and condemned. I joined this chorus and in so doing appeared on several occasions before the parliamentary Trade and Industry Portfolio Committee that was seized with the consideration of the Bill. I argued that there was merit in providing for a measure of protection of TK, but that it should be accomplished in new legislation that was customised to fit the special character and requirements of this type of work – so called *'sui generis'* (constituting a class alone) legislation. As it became clear to me that the committee members had little understanding or conception of what I was talking about, I hastily prepared a draft *sui generis* bill illustrating my point to assist them in understanding it. This model bill eventually gave rise to the private members bill proposed by the Democratic Alliance (DA), the principal opposition party.

The DA bill was rejected by parliament as the African National Congress (ANC) had a commanding majority in parliament and it was clearly hell bent on passing the IPLAB. I wondered whether IPLAB was in fact a political ploy by the ANC to curry favour with voters and particularly tribal authorities in the rural areas for the forthcoming 2014 general election. One of the effects to the Bill would be to create an income stream for the tribal authorities who would become the owners of TK works in terms of the Bill.

Parliament paid scant regard to all the criticisms of IPLAB, and to the unfavourable independent economic impact assessment of it, and it was passed and signed by President Zuma in 2013. It was not, however, brought into operation and up to the time of writing, some eleven years later, it has still not been brought into operation. Thus, although it is in theory on the statute book it has fortunately and thankfully to date not become part of our law.

While the controversy around IPLAB was raging I received an approach from senior officials at the Department of Arts and Culture. This contact was undoubtedly prompted by the involvement that the Department had with *The Lion Sleeps Tonight* case. I had collaborated with them at that time when they were financing the case and more particularly when I was reporting to them, and they were paying Spoor & Fisher's fees. I had developed a good working relationship with them. I was informed that the Department was of the view that the Department of Trade and Industry were not doing a proper job in administering copyright and in particular were failing to promote the wellbeing of authors, artists and other creatives, who were indeed Arts and Culture's constituency. They accordingly wanted to put in a bid to government to take over responsibility for copyright from Trade and Industry. They enquired of me whether I would be willing to support their cause. I had no hesitation in replying in the affirmative because I considered that the lot of copyright would be considerably enhanced by removing it from the clutches of Trade and Industry. I felt that Arts and Culture would do a much better job and would bring far more interest and passion to bear on promoting the wellbeing of copyright. Indeed, any change from Trade and Industry would be beneficial. It is not without significance that shortly after this communication Solomon Linda was posthumously awarded a state medal for his contribution to South Africa's cultural heritage.

I never heard anything more about this matter and no debate on it ever emerged in public. I surmise that a turf war probably ensued within the ranks of government and that Trade and Industry, which was a more senior ministry, no doubt defended the shrinkage of their empire vehemently and ultimately won the day. I remain of the view to this day that copyright ought rather to be housed in Arts and Culture and nothing has happened in the interim to cause me to have second thoughts. On the contrary, the ongoing conduct of Trade and Industry in regard to copyright has fortified my view. This is something that the new government of national unity (which came into being through the elections in 2024) ought to consider now that the winds of change are to some extent wafting through government with previous opposition parties now included in the government.

Another development that took place in or around 2018 was the intervention of the Department of Science and Technology. This Department followed and accepted the arguments that any protection of TK must take place through the adoption of *sui generis* legislation. It held the Trade and Industry's Intellectual Property Laws Amendment Act, 2013, (IPLAA) in a measure of contempt and accordingly decided to prepare its own legislation to achieve this end. It constituted an expert advisory committee to assist with the drafting of this legislation. I was asked to join this committee along with an IP professor from the University of Cape Town (who incidentally had been a schoolmate of mine at Sea Point for a while), an IP professor from a university in India and a specialist IP practitioner from Argentina who worked with the international United Nations body, WIPO, in drafting IP legislation.

The Department of Science and Technology, assisted by the committee of experts, duly produced the Protection, Development, and Management of Indigenous Knowledge Systems Bill, 2019 (the Systems Act). This Bill passed through the parliamentary process swiftly, the Systems Act was passed and came into operation in 2019.

The departmental draftsman listened to the views of the committee of experts but did not always accept them. The result was that the Act, while being acceptable, is not ideal. Its great merit is that it grants a measure of protection to TK, including works in the nature of copyright like subject matter, in *sui generis* legislation which created a new form of quasi IP. To that extent it is a vast improvement on the IPLAA abomination. Significantly, it protects the identical subject matter to that covered by IPLAA, but on an entirely different basis with the result that Systems Act and IPLAA could award the ownership of the proprietary rights in a particular item to different persons. This would create a completely untenable situation and would cause chaos if applied in practise. The upshot is that the two statutes are incompatible and cannot exist side by side.

Since the Systems Act has overtaken the IPLAA, the latter has become redundant. The committee of experts advised that the IPLAA should be repealed and drafted a clause for insertion in the Systems Act effecting such a repeal. The Department accepted this recommendation, but the clause was later removed on the grounds that government policy did not allow for one department's (the Department of Trade and Industry) legislation to be repealed by another department (the Department of Science and Technology). This meant that the inevitable repeal of the IPLAA will have to be accomplished at some stage by Trade and Industry, something which has apparently not been considered to date. The IPLAA is thus perforce a dead letter.

MISGUIDED LEGISLATION – CAB

The Department of Trade and Industry's next contribution to the tarnishing of copyright and the protection of creatives, which followed in 2017, was to produce the Copyright Amendment Bill (CAB). This Bill first saw the light of day in 2015. It was roundly condemned as being defective and unacceptable by the responsible copyright community and was replaced by a changed Bill in 2017. It too could not pass muster and was condemned by the copyright community. The criticism of this Bill was severe, and the Trade and Industry Portfolio Committee decided that it could not be carried forward. This Committee thereupon took to rewriting it themselves. With respect, a portfolio committee which is comprised of politicians with little or no legal background, and in particular no grounding in copyright law, is ill-suited to undertake the drafting of what is a complex legal technical statute with both local and international implications.

The parliamentary legal adviser, who too was without any particular expertise in copyright or intellectual property law, shouldered the major drafting burden. Admittedly a panel of advisers was consulted but the members of this panel consisted almost exclusively of persons who held a jaundiced view of copyright and felt that the existing law was antagonistic to the interests of users of copyright material. Their objective was to water down the protection conferred on creatives in respect of their works and to open the way for users to make free use of copyright works at the expense of the rights of copyright owners.

Two distinct camps with opposite views on the nature and purpose of copyright came to the fore. The one group was broadly in favour of creatives having strong proprietary rights to control the uses of their works in keeping with the fundamental purpose of copyright, while the other group preached a doctrine that the purpose of the legislation was to grant users of works extensive rights to reproduce and otherwise use the works of others for their own benefit and without having to seek the concurrence of copyright owners. The pro-copyright lobby (the creatives) consisted primarily of originators of new works and those who derived rights from them and wished to be in a position to derive financial benefit from the use of their works.

Examples of the members of the creatives group are authors, artists, composers, film producers, record producers and publishers. The anti-copyright lobby (the copyists), on the other hand, comprised proponents of freedom of expression and untrammelled access to information, and persons who wanted to be in a position to reproduce works with the minimum of constraints and not be beholden to copyright owners to seek permission to use their works nor to pay for the right to use works freely. This latter group included so-called 'big tech' companies purveying information and knowledge, music and the like gleaned from others to third parties.

The Bill is the battle ground for this conflict of interests, but it is most certainly not simply a contest between the rights of the advantaged and the disadvantaged, because creatives come from all walks of life and levels of society. Solomon Linda is a classic case in point – the epitome of a creative whom copyright should protect in order to be enabled to make a living out of the commercial exploitation of his works.

The Bill was unashamedly biased in favour of the copyists and served their cause. It upsets the delicate balance between private proprietary rights and the public interest, which is crucial to the proper operation of copyright legislation. Its partisan nature and approach were good reason alone for there to be just cause for criticism of it. But there were also a multitude of other reasons to be critical of the Bill. It was badly drafted and is fundamentally flawed. The technical deficiencies were manifest. It used confused and inappropriate terminology and contained some bizarre notions. It violated some of the cardinal principles of copyright law. By changing longstanding and established definitions it (possibly inadvertently) seemed to establish some new categories of copyright works, but which bordered on encroaching on existing categories, thus creating uncertainty and confusion.

Amongst other things it contained a commercially naïve provision which was singularly disadvantageous to creatives. This provision was based on a palpable misunderstanding of *The Lion Sleeps Tonight* case. Let me explain

The term of copyright in South Africa in literary, artistic and musical works, like in the majority of countries in the world, is the lifetime of the author plus a further 50 years after their death. If an author were to write a work when they were aged 30 and die at age 80 (50 years later), the full term of the copyright in the work would be 100 years. Should they wish to assign the copyright in their work to a third party, say a publisher, the latter would be acquiring a property with a lifespan of one hundred years. The value of the transaction, the price for the purchase of the copyright, would be based on this longevity of the property being purchased. Consider the value of the copyright in, say, the songs written by the Beatles which are already 60 years old.

Of course, it lies within the provenance of composers to determine the duration of the assignments in respect of their works, and if they feel that their interests are best served by limiting the effect of the assignment to, say, 30 years, the Copyright Act and the common-law principle of freedom of contract make this possible. The composer could tailor the length of the effect of the assignment according to their wishes and have the rights revert to them after the period has run its course. In general, the longer the term of the assignment, the greater would be the price for the assignment.

The Dickens Clause, which was the crux of *The Lion Sleeps Tonight* case, provided in effect that for the last 25 years of the copyright in a work, the ownership of the copyright in a work that had been assigned by the author would revert to the estate of the author. This had the effect that, in the case of any existing or future assigned copyright, the efficacy of the assignment would be cancelled out and the *status ante* quo would be restored with the variation that the author's descendants would be vested with the copyright.

In our example, even though a composer might have assigned his copyright to another party for the full term of the copyright (100 years), after the elapse of 75 years the copyright would revert to the heirs of the composer in abrogation of the assignment. This is what happened in the case of *Mbube*. In other words, the composer had only around 75 years to play with when it came to assigning their copyright and placing a commercial value on the property.

The Dickens Clause was enacted to cater for particular special circumstances (i.e., the plight of Charles Dickens' family – and others in a similar situation – who had been left destitute by the author's copyright assignments) at a time when it became necessary for Britain to lengthen the lifespan of copyright. It was a short-lived measure. It was removed from British copyright legislation in 1956 and from South African copyright law in 1965, never to return.

The drafters of the CAB in their wisdom seized upon the magical figure of 25 years in connection with assignments of copyright. They provided that any assignment of copyright cannot be for a longer period than 25 years. This means that unlike under the Dickens Clause which, to use our example, gave the copyright owner 75 years to play with in executing an assignment, in this situation the copyright owner's property only has a preliminary life span of 25 years, even during the author's lifetime.

In simplistic terms this could mean that the value of the property on offer for an assignment can only be 25 percent of its normal value. This makes absolutely no commercial sense and is a gross violation of the composer's right of freedom of contract. If it suits a copyright owner to assign his copyright for 100 years, why should he be obliged by the state to limit the term of the copyright, and thus its commercial value, to 25 years? On the other hand, the present law enables the copyright owner to voluntarily limit the term of their copyright assignment to 25 years, or any other specified period, if they wish to do so.

But the drafters of the Bill proclaim that they are actually doing copyright owners a good turn by availing them with the facility of the Dickens Clause enjoyed by the Solomon Linda Estate. This is delusional! It would seem that the drafters have misunderstood the crux of *The Lion Sleeps Tonight* case.

The international implications of this provision have clearly not been taken into account. Take the example of Cullman's film *The Lion's Share*.

On the assumption that the 25 year principle comes into force, if Cullman assigns his copyright (as the maker of the film) in the film (or more particularly, the holder of the copyright in the component works, such as the music and script) to Netflix throughout the world for the full term of copyright, that assignment will be invalid for South Africa as far as the South African copyright is concerned. At best the South African copyright in the works will only be owned by Netflix for 25 years, whereas the copyright in all other countries will be owned by them for the full term of copyright.

Conversely, if a South African filmmaker makes a movie of my book, *The Summit Syndrome*, and assigns the copyright in the film and component works throughout the world for the full term to Showmax, Showmax will only own the South African copyright for 25 years, but will own the copyright for the rest of the world for the full term, perhaps 50 years or more. It is beyond the scope of this work to explain all the complications and difficulties that can result from this situation, but suffice it to say that the commercial exploitation of the films in question will be seriously complicated and compromised. South Africa could become a no-go country for the making and exploitation of films.

The most controversial, and damaging, innovation to creatives in the Copyright Amendment Bill is the introduction of the peculiarly American principle of so called 'fair use' of works. Over the ages, in balancing the private proprietary rights of creatives with the public interest, copyright legislation throughout the world has provided for exceptions or exemptions from the normal principles of copyright infringement. So, for example, users of works are permitted to make unauthorised copies of reasonable portions of copyright works for their personal or private use, or to quote reasonable extracts from them.

In 'British law' countries specified and circumscribed instances of so-called 'fair dealing' are made the subject of exemptions. These exemptions are clearly set forth in the legislation. A measure of certainty as to what exceptions are permitted is provided by these fair dealing clauses. Users of works can be forewarned as to what they are allowed to do with works with impunity. Copyright owners are informed in which instances certain uses of their works can be made without their permission. The Berne Convention governing international copyright law countenances and allows exemptions to be made in national legislation in these circumstances.

Under the American doctrine of 'fair use' exemptions are not specified in the legislation. Instead, the court is given a wide discretion in instances of alleged copyright infringement to decide whether the contentious copying or other dealing with a work that is potentially unlawful should be made the subject of an exemption and thus be rendered perfectly lawful. The law lays down certain guidelines which should be followed in making such a determination, but by and large the court is sufficiently empowered to use its own discretion on an *ad hoc* basis. American law and procedure provide various measures which to some extent mitigate the operation of this far reaching and disastrous principle when viewed from the perspective of creatives.

The main thrust of the American doctrine is to some extent to provide open season for unauthorised copying of works. This is obviously seriously deleterious in principle to copyright owners and their ability to derive commercial rewards for the use of their works.

No doubt for the major part American judges use their discretion judiciously and carefully weigh up the copyright owners proprietary rights with the public interest relied upon by the relevant users. But the potential for widespread violation of the rights of copyright owners is ever present. Moreover, the uncertainty created by this doctrine is unfortunate and highly undesirable. No-one, not the copyright owner nor the potential infringer, knows until the final appeal has been decided in a copyright infringement case several years hence whether the particular contentious dealing with a copyright work is going to be held to be an infringement giving rise to a liability for damages, or will be determined to be an instance of fair use. This situation cannot fail to have strong potential for copyright infringement litigation to flourish, which is in no-one's interest, save perhaps for the lawyers who handle the cases.

American legal practice is characterised by a high incidence of contingency litigation and this situation lends itself to coming to the assistance of copyright owners whose works are abused. An impecunious copyright owner whose rights are being infringed can have recourse to the services to a lawyer acting on a contingency basis. By contrast contingency litigation is relatively rare in South Africa and almost unheard of in copyright infringement cases (save for *The Lion Sleeps Tonight* case where it has been severely criticised by Cullman, ironically an American). Creatives are rarely in a position to fund long and expensive copyright litigation with an uncertain outcome, particularly where an unsuccessful litigant is invariably ordered to pay the costs of the successful party, which does not happen in the United States.

Let us imagine that Disney was able to argue under our law as it currently stands that making an adaptation of *Mbube* in the process of composing *The Lion Sleeps Tonight* amounted to making 'fair use' of *Mbube*, as would be the case if our law had already been amended by the CAB, and that there was consequently no case of copyright infringement! The uncertainty that would have been introduced into the case would have been immense. The validity of this proposition might only have been determined after the case had been pronounced on by the Pretoria court in the exercise of its discretion, followed by an appeal to the Pretoria appeal court (three judges), then to the Supreme Court of Appeal in Bloemfontein (five judges), and finally by the Constitutional Court (possibly eleven judges). Each of these courts (i.e., a total of twenty judges) would in turn exercise their own independent discretions afresh. Predicting the outcome of that process would be a lottery.

Each and all of these judges could decide that, although on a proper interpretation of the law and facts copyright infringement had in principle taken place, they felt that it was in order for the composer of *The Lion Sleeps Tonight* to have reproduced substantial parts of *Mbube*, without the copyright owner's permission or licence, in going about his business. Perhaps they would feel that the two songs appealed to different markets, and they therefore did not compete with one another, or there was some other reason why Solomon Linda or his successor didn't warrant deriving any benefit from his song being incorporated into *The Lion Sleeps Tonight*. Who knows?'

To cap it all, the ultimate loser of the case, possibly the Executor, would have to bear all their own legal costs as well as the legal costs of the victor, in each and all of the courts through which the case progressed. This would have amounted to many millions of Rands! Disney has sufficiently deep pockets to finance all this expensive litigation, but where would the Executor of the Estate of Solomon Linda have stood? You, the reader, in the exercise of your personal discretion, can judge for your self what would be the prospects of any individual copyright owner embarking on a copyright infringement claim in these circumstances. I can, however, say with absolute certainty, that I, despite all the qualities and characteristics that I have described, would never in a million years, off my own bat, have in these circumstances launched the Disney case after Gallo jumped ship. The Disney case would simply never have happened, and the Linda daughters would still be living in poverty. Rian Malan would still be bemoaning and bewailing the inequity of the ways of the music industry. Cullman would have to look elsewhere for a story that he could concoct to further his filmmaking career.

The introduction of the doctrine of fair use into our copyright law cannot fail to have a disastrous effect on the ability of creatives to control the unlawful use of their works and thus earn a living.

I was but one of a legion of proponents of proper copyright law to object vehemently and vociferously against the CAB. I appeared before the parliamentary committees on several occasions mainly under the banner of the Stellenbosch Intellectual Property Chair, the only such chair at the time. We submitted written representations in which we went to great lengths and detail to describe the shortcomings and ills of the Bill. I published numerous articles in the media and spoke from public platforms. I published a booklet entitled *The Gift of Multiplication* through Juta, containing a collection of several of my articles, together with a comprehensive and persuasive academic article analysing the fair use doctrine by Prof Sadulla Karjiker. Even my being billed as 'the lawyer who won *The Lion Sleeps Tonight* case', which had gained me considerable kudos, made no headway in terms of my opposition to the Bill being heard and acted upon.

I might mention that all my work in opposing this misguided legislation was done *pro bono*, save that while I was the Chair of IP at Stellenbosch University, I regarded it as part of my self-determined job description, the execution of which earned my salary. Subject to this, I acted entirely off my own bat and was not remunerated by any client, or at all. I was motivated entirely by my concern for the wellbeing of South African copyright law in the interests of all South Africans and the desire for it to regain its erstwhile status of being of world class for which I had worked tirelessly for many years.

A few minor changes were made to the Bill but for the major part all our protests fell on deaf ears. I was driven to wonder whether the evil of state capture had also pervaded the field of intellectual property, such was the indifference shown by the powers that be to all the protests and the determination to proceed with the Bill at all costs. This approach was cheered on enthusiastically by the copyist camp, which came as no surprise given the Bill's partisan character.

COPYRIGHT WARFARE

A copyright war waged in South Africa like a scene from Shakespeare's *Romeo and Juliet*, with the Montagues (the creatives) ranged up against the Capulets (the copyists). Similar skirmishes had already taken place in countries like France, the UK and Australia, where the copyists had been sent packing with bloody noses. It seemed as though South Africa had been chosen by the copyists as the terrain where the decisive battle would be fought. International forces joined in the fray. International big tech giants, who had a lot to gain from copyright being mortally wounded, brought their heavy artillery into play, either directly or through surrogates. International heavy hitters were deployed to lead the charge. Major forces, including the American Government, the European Union, the film industry, international publishing organisations, the international record industry, to name but a few entities whose lifeblood depended on effective copyright protection being available, came to the party in support of the creatives. The big tech forces driving the copyists were counteracted to some extent by influential international players, like Netflix (who devotes considerable resources and energies into producing material in South Africa), coming into bat for the creatives.

It was particularly ironical and relevant that the American Government entreated our government not to adopt the fair use doctrine. After all the United States (more particularly the American courts) had given birth to the heresy of fair use and are practising it but yet they were doing its best to prevent it spreading worldwide like an international epidemic. Perhaps they were trying to spare the rest of the world the copyright trauma that had seized them! Alternatively, as the world's policeman, they were simply trying to prevent the international copyright system from falling down and having the law of the jungle prevail. It must be said that there has been considerable domestic criticism of the fair use doctrine in the USA.

In South Africa parliament and the media were the principal battle grounds. The Democratic Alliance and other opposition parties strenuously opposed the Bill and a myriad of informed commentators fought it tooth and nail during the parliamentary process. The copyists launched a media blitz which spewed propaganda, making claims about the Bill which simply could not withstand scrutiny. Self-styled copyright 'experts' waxed eloquent about the virtues of the Bill. It was portrayed as being God's gift to the populace to bring about free availability of information and resources, *inter alia* causing a reduction of the costs of education and similar bountiful blessings benefitting mankind. It would be a panacea for all the injustices in the world. It stopped short of saying that it would provide a cure for the common cold!

However, in effect the state would be making a gift of other people's private property to the masses for their alleged wellbeing. In essence it would be an expropriation of the property rights of creatives without compensation. The simple truth that the Bill, if enacted, would probably bring about the demise of the publishing industry, would prove to be a disincentive to the ongoing production of original works, would threaten the livelihood of creatives, and arguably bring South Africa into breach of its international treaty obligations was swept under the carpet.

Branches of the media that one would expect to exercise objectivity, in some instances chose sides in the conflict. The *Daily Maverick* was an example. It was felt in creative circles that it was giving vastly disproportionate airtime and moral support to the copyist cause.

I submitted an article that was critical of the copyist cause to the *Daily Maverick*. I was pleasantly surprised that it immediately published the article electronically. A day later the article disappeared without a trace (it remained in the index for a couple of more days, but then melted away). It was a case of here today and gone tomorrow. When I queried the fact that the article had mysteriously vanished, I was given the explanation that their database had been hacked into and that some of its content, including my article, had been obliterated. My offer to repair the situation by resubmitting my article proverbially flew like a lead balloon and the article went into oblivion, at least in the *Daily Maverick*, but it was published elsewhere by another outlet. As a paid-up and card-carrying so-called 'Maverick Insider' (because I thought that their news service could be a positive force for good), I was dismayed and severely disillusioned by this experience.

In actual fact it is common cause throughout the copyright community that the Copyright Act, 1978, was drastically in need of being updated and that an amendment to it is a dire necessity. Technology is advancing at breakneck speed, and the law has fallen far behind. In the 20-year period immediately following 1978, the Act had been amended eight times. By contrast there have not been any amendments during the next following 20 years, as discussed above.

To its credit the CAB addressed many of the salient issues requiring amendment, and the relevant changes were of a positive nature in principle and were generally welcomed. In particular, it was obvious that further exemptions from copyright infringement were required.

However, this should be accomplished by means of expansion of the existing fair dealing provisions of the Act.

The principle of amendments to the Act was not up for debate, but it was the manner in which the changes were addressed and the quality of the draftsmanship that could not pass muster. The Bill was fundamentally flawed and could not be panel-beaten into good shape. On top of that there were the aberrations like fair use and others that needed to be eradicated.

My stance, which enjoys widespread support, is that what is required is for the Bill to be returned to the drawing board and to be redrafted by a committee of true experts preferably under the chairmanship of a judge with appropriate expertise.

A further problem with the CAB is that it was drafted on the premise that the IPLAA is in force and effect, which it is not. The CAB proposed to insert many new sections into the existing Copyright Act which necessitate significant changes to the numbering and structure of that Act. The CAB presupposes that these substantive and structural changes have already taken place in the Copyright Act, which is of course a fallacy. The changes are non-existent in the light of the status of the IPLAA, which is likely either to be repealed or to remain indefinitely in its current state of suspended animation.

Accordingly, if the CAB becomes law in its present iteration, its structure and numbering will be seriously awry, and it will refer to traditional knowledge for which it does not cater and to sections which do not exist in the Act. This drastic anomaly cannot fail to give rise to confusion and uncertainty and will simply be bad governance. To quote from Sean O'Casey's play *Juno and the Paycock*, 'The world is in a state chassis' (meaning 'chaos'). This will aptly describe the state of our copyright law if the CAB in its present state becomes law.

In March 2019 the Bill was passed by Parliament and sent to the President for signature. Then followed a period of legislative ping pong. Some 15 months later the President referred it back to Parliament mainly on constitutional grounds. Parliament made some changes to it to deal with the President's problems. It is debatable whether these changes indeed disposed of those difficulties. After some four years the revised Bill was passed again and resubmitted to the President for signature.

In the meanwhile, the copyright war raged on and further pitched battles were fought over it primarily in the theatre of parliament. When the Bill arrived back again on the President's desk, he became the epicentre of hostilities. He was bombarded from all sides with missiles launched by both warring factions. It was expected of him to emulate King Solomon. Predictably and sensibly, he referred it to the Constitutional Court for assessment. At the time of writing the referral is pending before the court.

COPYRIGHT IN THE BLOOD

When I first became interested in copyright as an area of practice in the early 1970s, it was a little-known subject. Professor Alan Copeling of the University of South Africa produced a very elementary text book to mark the passing of the Copyright Act, 1965. It did little more than recount the provisions of the Act in a more concise and consequential manner than the Act itself, and it was thus of assistance by providing a readable narrative of the legislation. It was of limited value and usefulness to a practitioner who became seized with practical issues regarding the interpretation, implementation and enforcement of the law. The result was that there was considerable ignorance regarding what the law had to offer to those upon which it conferred rights. Conversely, users of works did not know to what conditions their use was subject.

After I began delving into the law and publishing articles dealing with the subject in the late 1970s, and particularly after publication of my *Handbook* in 1987, something of an awakening and a revolution in copyright began to take place. A resource enabling a better understanding of the subject and facilitating enforcement of the rights available under it became available. A band wagon began rolling in legal practice.

The situation is illustrated by the increment of the incidence of copyright litigation in South Africa. In the preparation of my doctoral thesis and the *Handbook* I conducted extensive and exhaustive historical research on the availability of reports of copyright cases in the past going back to pre-Union and colonial times. The earliest case I could find dated back to 1861 and, interestingly, involved Charles Dickens. The case was *Dickens v Eastern Province Herald*, and it dealt with the unauthorised reproduction of part of one of his works in the newspaper of that name. It was decided under the colonial legislation of the Cape Colony. The Colony had adopted legislation dealing with copyright in Act 4 of 1854.

My research brought to light that during the century that followed the Dickens case, i.e., 1861 to 1961, when the Republic of South Africa came into existence, there were 22 known copyright court cases throughout the country. In the next ensuing 50 years, i.e., 1962 to 2012, there were 168 known copyright cases that gave rise to judgements. Of course, there were very many more cases that were launched but did not go all the way culminating in judgments being handed down. Based on my own experience I would say that only around ten percent of copyright cases initiated made it through to the judgment stage. The vast majority of cases were settled, as happened in the Disney case.

My involvement in copyright and my expertise in copyright grew in tandem with the development and awareness of the law. All but four of the 168 post-1961 cases, took place subsequently to my entry on the scene in 1972. One hundred and twenty-one of those cases occurred after the publication of my *Handbook* in 1987. I estimate that I personally handled in excess of 60 percent of the post 1972 cases. Such was the extent of my involvement in copyright law and its evolution in South Africa.

My account of my personal history in respect of copyright goes to show that, like it or not, I have copyright in my blood. It is like a fever in the blood. It is an integral part of my essential make up as a person. In the same way as a minister of religion or a missionary is imbued with the doctrine that he propagates; I am committed to the doctrine and effect of copyright. Try as I might to live a quiet and professionally uneventful life in retirement, I cannot get away from involvement with it.

As a result, when aspersions are cast on my integrity in connection with my living and implementing copyright, as was about to happen, it cuts to the quick and I cannot take it lying down. I must inevitably counteract the assault not only on my person and character, but also on the principles that served as the foundation of my career. This was about to unfold.

XV

Enter Netflix

THE PROPOSITION

In or around early 2018, while the South African copyright war was being waged in all its fury, and against the background of my involvement in it, late one night out of the blue I received a telephone call from Netflix in the USA. At this point I had already long since retired from the Chair of Intellectual Property and was aspiring to live a life in full retirement although I was being drawn on a rapidly increasing scale into the copyright war. The caller advised me that Netflix had decided to make and disseminate a documentary film on *The Lion Sleeps Tonight* case. He enquired of me whether I would be willing to assist and co-operate in the making of the film in South Africa. The film would be part of a series called 'Remastered' and its episodes would relate to important and noteworthy aspects of events that took place in the music industry, of which *Lion* would be one.

It did not take me long to make up my mind that I should answer in the affirmative. I thought that it would be opportune to highlight the nature and outcome of the case at this particular juncture of the copyright war, when copyright was under threat. More than ten years had passed since the case had been concluded and the public in South Africa should be reminded at this critical time regarding copyright in South Africa of what the benefits of this area of the law held for creative persons and indeed for society as a whole. A success story where a poverty stricken family rose from the depths of despair to be given the opportunity of a new and rosy way of life, and their ancestor could be seen to have achieved undreamed success on account of his creative talents, all on account of copyright, was just what was needed to bring some perspective into the underlying causes of the copyright war. It seemed to me that fate was playing its hand once again.

I expressed my willingness to the caller to be of whatever service I could for the making of the film. I referred him to my short e-book, *Awakening the Lion*, that was available on Amazon and to the various articles that I had written on the case that could be accessed on the IP Chair's blog by way of background material that he might find useful. He thanked me for this and in anticipation for my co-operation and advised me that I would be contacted in due course by the director/film maker who would be appointed to make the film, and that I should henceforth deal with him.

Some months later I received a call from Sam Cullman, who advised me that he would be making the film and would shortly be arriving in South Africa to commence work. He is an independent documentary film maker, and I welcomed the prospect of working with him. He told me that he had taken steps to inform himself about the case and had referred to my written materials. I advised him that I saw the story of the case as being a feel-good, rags-to-riches fairy tale – a David vs Goliath success story, but that there had been a sting in the tale in that the family had recently been badmouthing the outcome. I suggested to him that stopping short in his story at the conclusion of the case and not venturing into the aftermath may perhaps be his best approach. I also suggested to him that he should make contact with Rian Malan and Hanro Friederich as they could give him important insights into the case.

GETTING THE SHOW ON THE ROAD

Sam Cullman is a cinematographer, director and editor of documentaries, and the founder of Yellow Cake Films, a film production company. He has been nominated for and/or won several awards for film making. He is married to the activist Purva Panday Cullman. On the strength of what was later to unfold it is possible that activism runs in the family.

When he arrived in South Africa he was accompanied by a full-time researcher who would help him compiling the facts of the case and putting together the story. I arranged for them to visit Spoor & Fisher's offices in Pretoria and for them to be given full access to all the documentation pertaining to the case in the firm's possession that was not subject to privilege, and I secured the firm's agreement that they could use the firm's offices for conducting their research and even as a location for filming if they wanted to do so. The documentation, including the full court record, was perused.

Agreement could not be reached on the use of the firm's office facilities because Cullman laid down such onerous conditions with which the firm was required to comply, such as providing warranties, indemnities and the like – uncalled for when the firm was actually granting a favour – that the offer to use the offices was withdrawn.

I was then asked to travel from Cape Town to Johannesburg for the purpose of being interviewed and filmed by Cullman. I did so and underwent a full day of interviewing at premises that had been hired for the purpose. I spent an entire day being questioned by Sam Cullman. Virtually the entire duration of the question and answer sessions were filmed over a period of around five hours. The *modus operandi* was for Cullman to raise issues with me off camera for us to establish what the approach would be in dealing with them, whereafter we would deal with them in a focused manner on camera.

OPENING GAMBIT

The session commenced with the approach made to me by Gallo for an opinion. From there it progressed to the substance of the opinion, and the meetings held with the Gallo team. We traversed the decision to conduct a test case against Disney and the preparations made by me for commencing the case in the United Kingdom. The meetings that I described were all attended by Paul Jenkins, Hanro Friederich and Rian Malan. All the information that I gave him had been foreshadowed in my e-book, *Awakening the Sleeping Lion*, and the journal articles to which I had referred him, so he was forearmed. Consequently, I emphasised, and we dwelled on, particular issues.

We commenced with the early discussions regarding the proposed case. I paraphrase and summarise below what I had to say to him. The substance of what I communicated to him is presented in italics. I was at pains to inform him fully on what we did, why we did it and what the implications were. I wanted him to understand thoroughly what our thought processes and objectives were.

TELLING IT AS IT IS

The object of the exercise had been to conduct a test case in order to establish for future use and further action the principle that the Dickens Clause was applicable and that as a result the ownership of the copyright in Mbube *had vested in Solomon Linda's estate in 1987. We addressed the finding to this effect by the court in the attachment application and that the unauthorised use of the derivative work,* The Lion Sleeps Tonight, *by Disney in* The Lion King *constituted infringement of that copyright; this would provide a platform for a damages claim in theory, as well as for subsequent damages claims against other parties.*

I was following the examples of the several test cases that I had conducted in the past and most noticeably the Adidas and the Paramount Pictures cases.

While we may, depending on the advice we received from the London solicitors we had lined up, and the barristers whom they would brief, throw in a perfunctory damages claim, procedurally it would not be feasible to earnestly pursue a damages claim at that stage. That could follow later if necessary. Although I had held discussions with London solicitors, I had not as yet instructed them to take any action.

The decision to target Disney in the test case was a joint one by consensus amongst all the participants in the meeting, including Paul Jenkins. I had wanted a high profile target because I wanted to get maximum publicity and effect from a successful case. Ideally, I would have preferred to take on someone like the theatre company staging the show rather than what was probably the most powerful entertainment company in the world who would be equipped with a legion of high powered entertainment lawyers, but the lot fell on Disney.

Gallo were obviously aware at the outset that Disney was the licensing principal of some of the companies in their group, but this did not deter Paul Jenkins from agreeing to the case being conducted against them. Prior to joining Gallo, Jenkins had been a prominent Johannesburg attorney practising in the entertainment law field, and he was consequently familiar with what would be involved in conducting the proposed litigation. Rian Malan, who was a party to the discussions, had virtually no experience with litigation, was rather tickled at the prospect of taking on an entertainment giant like Disney.

I moved on to what followed after that watershed meeting.

In the course of doing the preparatory work on the case I had met with the daughters at their house in Soweto on two occasions in order to make their acquaintance and to assess what kind of witnesses they would make if it became necessary for them to give evidence. I also wanted to explain to them what I proposed to do and to advise them that, while I believed we had a good case and would conduct it to the best of my ability, there were no guarantees of success, and they must not get their hopes up unduly.

On the first of these occasions, I was accompanied by Hanro Friederich, but he was unable to attend on the second occasion. I was taken on that visit by Hanro's driver who competently acted as my driver and go-between. In fact, Hanro's driver, who could speak the same language as the daughters (whose English was not good), played an invaluable role as an interpreter and a conduit of information.

The information that I was conveying to the daughters was complicated and I tried to simplify it as best I could. I fondly believed that they had some notion of what we were about.

At that stage, having been instructed by Gallo to bring the case, I was billing them for my services in the normal way in an attorney and client relationship. The daughters were not my clients – they were the beneficiaries of the action my client proposed to take.

My discussions with Cullman then turned to the dramatic turn of events that occurred when Gallo abandoned the case and left us high and dry.

What follows is the gist of what I told him.

It appeared that we had reached the end of the line and that the project had ground to a halt. Jenkins simply walked away from it and Rian Malan later followed suit soon afterwards. It was an absolute moment of truth in the case. Hanro and I were devastated.

I described how Hanro and I had agonised over the matter but decided to go ahead with the litigation.

We were very reluctant to leave the daughters in the lurch, having raised their hopes to some extent. Also, we had spent so much time and effort on the case and had invested in it both emotionally and intellectually. We decided we would go ahead with it off our own bat.

In retrospect the decision we took to carry on with the case, acting pro bono with no source of funding and no assurance that any would be forthcoming, bordered on being insane. The risk for me, or more correctly for my firm, Spoor & Fisher, was enormous. Commencing litigation had serious costs consequences. If the case was unsuccessful costs would be awarded against the Estate, which was to be the plaintiff. There would be absolutely no funds in the Estate, so it could not pay them. This could mean Disney would turn to Spoor & Fisher, the Estate's attorneys of record in the litigation and seek to hold us liable for all their costs of litigation, which would be substantial. This was not idle conjecture on my part because when Disney subsequently brought their application to set aside the attachment of their trade marks, they indeed sought an order that the firm should pay their costs out of our own resources, which demand was fortunately rejected by the court.

Although I had informed the firm what I was doing I did not consult them on the decision, so the responsibility fell entirely on me. My standing in the firm (I was chairman at the time) would have been seriously jeopardised and the misfortune would have been a serious blot on my career. When the trial action continued after the application to set aside the attachment of the trade marks, I continued to run the risk that, if the action was ultimately unsuccessful, the court would order our firm to pay all Disney's costs, which probably would have been in excess of a million Rand at that stage.

These risks were incurred without any assurance at that stage that we would achieve anything positive with the litigation. Hanro did not run any of these risks because he had no official status in the litigation. His role was largely that of an interested bystander (but was the representative of the daughters, the intended beneficiaries of the litigation), although he played a valuable role as an adviser and a confidant.

When we launched the litigation with no funding available both Hanro and I had to reconcile ourselves with the possibility that we would devote a lot of energy and time in pursuing the litigation without earning a cent for our trouble and efforts. We were willing to do this because we felt that we were pursuing social justice, a worthwhile and righteous cause. We felt great empathy for the daughters, and we thought that as Solomon Linda's daughters, they deserved to reap some of the rewards that ought in all fairness to have come his way for creating a worthwhile musical work. That was what copyright was all about. I personally felt that I had unfinished business to accomplish on their behalf and that I had to take the matter through to its conclusion. It was a case of personal pride. I was not at all influenced by any political factors and had no feelings of guilt to assuage.

I justified to Cullman why it was out of the question to give effect to the original intention of suing Disney in London. Because of the vastly changed circumstances our only option was to conduct the case in South Africa. I explained the jurisdictional problems that had to be overcome in order to found jurisdiction over Disney, a foreign-based company in South Africa, and how we had gone about in overcoming this hurdle, by means of a unique and as yet untried process which proved to be successful.

The change in the theatre of action involved a variation in the ostensible purpose of the litigation because it was necessary to cast the case in the form of a claim for damages, whereas in London the ostensible and real purpose of the litigation had been to obtain an injunction against Disney continuing to use the song in The Lion King. *To all outward appearances an injunction or interdict theoretically and formally only assumed the role of a secondary objective in the South African case. However, in fact it remained the real actual goal. The case remained a test case despite having the façade of a case for damages.*

I continued my exposition of our thinking and actions.

For effect we had trumped up a ridiculously large sum, R15 million, as the Estate's avowed damages suffered, whereas we knew full well that the actual damages suffered were confined to what had taken place in South Africa and were purely for lost royalties for the song being played in cinemas as part of the sound track of the animated movie version of The Lion King *or through the sound track version of that film or of the stage show being played over the radio and elsewhere in public. Those damages were minimal, assuming that we could ever properly quantify them and prove them. They would probably barely have amounted to around R5 000 at the most.*

The vastly inflated amount was stipulated to cause Disney to sit up and take serious notice of the case and to defend it. This was an essential factor as the case was after all a test case to prove the availability of a legal cause of action and remedy and this goal would have been frustrated had Disney simply agreed to pay a trifling sum like R5 000 to get rid of the case. It would probably not have been worth their while to engage in litigation in faraway South Africa over an amount of in the region of US$300.

We also wanted to make the public and media take interest in the case and side with the Estate, because this was an essential ingredient to our being able to bring moral pressure to bear on Disney.

The downside of this approach was that a trial action for damages would potentially run up far greater costs and be more complicated and time consuming than an application to court for an interdict where all the evidence would have been given by means of affidavits instead of by live evidence in a fully-fledged trial. The prospects of possibly having to expose one or more of the daughters to giving live evidence in the witness box and enduring hostile cross-examination by a seasoned advocate was daunting but we had no other choice.

It was necessary for me to appoint advocates to act on our behalf in the action as it was not competent for me as an attorney to appear in the Supreme Court, and in any event, I had no real experience in that regard. Arguing a completely novel and untried theory, which, if successful, would make new law, required the services of a formidable and tried and trusted senior advocate. This would mean that a junior advocate would have to be appointed to assist him as was required by convention. As we in any event had no money to pay any advocates, and were going to have to rely on their goodwill and sense of altruism to get them to act, the theoretical costs involved were unimportant.

I approached the best senior advocate in the business, Cedric Puckrin, whom I had used very frequently in the past, and with whom I had a good relationship, to act, and chose as his junior, Reinard Michau, who had previously been an assistant of mine at Spoor & Fisher before he moved to practising at the bar as an advocate. To my relief they agreed to act in the case, but subject to entering into a contingency remuneration agreement as required by the Bar Council in this situation. This entailed acting pro bono at the outset, but subject to their being entitled to charge double their normal fees if they were successful to the point that the outcome of the case made payment of such fees possible. I was not too bothered by this condition as I could not foresee us obtaining payment of more than around R5 000, even if the outcome of the case was entirely favourable, and a payment in this ball park would have been insufficient to call the contingency agreement into play.

I told Cullman that the counter claim for setting aside the attachment of the Disney trade marks caught us off guard and by surprise.

The advent of this additional court case to our program made obtaining funding for our venture, if possible, a high priority. The complexity of the matter and the legal costs issue had escalated to a significant extent.

Hanro and I had kicked the funding issue around from time to time, but had so far had done nothing concrete about addressing it. We racked our brains and came up with suggestions of some major corporations which we felt might be sufficiently public spirited and altruistic to come to our assistance. Before we took any steps in this regard, Hanro had the good fortune to coincidentally run into the Minister of Arts and Culture and had raised the case and the costs issue with him. He appeared to be possibly amenable to assisting us and we decided to take the bull by the horns and seek a meeting with the Director General of Arts and Culture.

The application to set aside the attachment of the trade marks was already well under way and we used this to underline the urgency of the costs matter. To our great relief and delight, we managed to persuade the Department to provide us with funding up to a certain amount which we thought ought to be sufficient to carry us through to the end. We had to be cautious not to overreach ourselves.

Thereafter, Spoor & Fisher billed the Department for fees and disbursement on a standard and regular basis and the matter proceeded as normal. These bills were accompanied by detailed explanations of the services they covered, and the time spent on providing them. I proceeded in this respect as though the Department was my client and were entitled to be fully informed as to what they were paying for. In a limited sense they were of course my client since they were bearing the cost of the litigation.

While the financial backing of the Department came as a considerable comfort to me, it did not relieve Spoor & Fisher, and me, from the risk of an adverse costs order for Disney's legal costs if it came to that. In the circumstances that were obtained the Department could not be expected to fund any adverse costs order that may be made against the Executor. Such costs would have to be borne by Spoor & Fisher. Nevertheless, the hopeless and drastic imbalance that existed between risk and reward was alleviated to some extent.

Apart from the enormous risks that I took, I also suffered serious immediate harm in other respects in launching the litigation. My position as the attorney of the MPAA on retainer, which probably accounted for around 20% of my fee earnings at the time, was immediately terminated by them at the behest of Disney, a leading member of that organisation. This also impacted on my position as the attorney of several of the individual members of that organisation, like Universal Studios, Paramount Pictures and MGM. My position as a director and the attorney of SAFACT, the local anti-piracy agency operating under the auspices of the MPAA, was

also terminated and I became persona non grata with members of SAFACT
(except for the operations head of the organisation, Ted Askew, with
whom I had a working relationship going back over several decades). The
members who severed relations with me included Nu Metro, the movie arm
of the Gallo group. Even Gallo shunned me in view of their relationship
with Disney.

As an aside, although I never said this to Cullman, my sentiment towards
this betrayal was 'this was the most unkindest cut of all', to quote from
Shakespeare's *Julius Caesar*.

I was treated like a leper in the movie industry, an industry that I had
loyally served for 30 years. My argument that acting against Disney (who
was not a client) in regard to the copyright in a song did not in any way
place me in a position of conflict with all these entities in the work that
I was doing for them in matters relating to piracy in the movie industry cut
no ice with them. Such was the power and influence of Disney and the depth
of their desire to take revenge and retribution against me for suing them
and to bring pressure to bear on me personally.

I outlined the course that the trial action had taken.

After Disney's counter-application had been dismissed, the procedure for
the trial action went its normal course. Pleadings were exchanged and the
issues in dispute were defined. It was apparent that Disney were relying for
their defence on a few issues. They did not admit that a valid assignment of
the copyright from Solomon Linda to Gallo had taken place, but were not
challenging the principle of the applicability of the Dickens Clause and our
reliance on it. They appeared to accept that the argument per se was valid.
Indeed, they had not challenged it in their counterapplication regarding
the attachment of the trade marks either. They placed their eggs primarily
in the basket of contending that Mbube was a traditional song and not an
original copyright work, and that they therefore had no case to meet.
   This argument had been advanced in the American litigation involving
The Lion Sleeps Tonight *and had not been definitively resolved. It was*

an argument that had worried me all along and I regarded it as being in principle our Achilles heel. I had gone into the situation before launching the case and had consulted with an expert witness with good credentials who had assured me that there was no substance in it, because the genre of music in South Africa known as mbube was spawned by Solomon Linda's song subsequent to its success and only in that sense had the music become generic. However, it seemed to me that there was some possibility of a chicken-and-egg situation becoming a crucial issue. I had been around IP litigation for long enough to know that for every expert that could be found to propagate a particular view another could be found to propagate the opposite view. I had no doubt that with the resources available to them, Disney would be able to present an expert who would say that Mbube *had simply been a longstanding tribal song that Solomon Linda had adopted for use in his performances.*

At the end of the day, it would be a case of the court having to decide which expert view to favour. Having no basis to evaluate such conflicting evidence in advance, there was no way of knowing which way the matter would go. We did, however, have a card up our sleeves in that the Copyright Act provided for a rebuttable presumption that where an author of a work was deceased, it would be presumed that in the absence of persuasive evidence to the contrary that his work was original. This meant that Disney bore the onus of proving that the work was not original, and we would thus enter the debate in pole position. It was nevertheless a worrying factor.

I explained that the case moved on to the discovery phase where the parties were required to disclose under oath all documents in their possession that were in any way relevant to the dispute. We had to discover, *inter alia*, the assignment agreement that Solomon Linda had entered into with Gallo in 1952, the validity of which they had not admitted. I addressed the question of that assignment.

This was possibly another Achilles heel in our case. Rian Malan and Hanro had right in the beginning of their quest for a leg to stand on wanted to use the angle that the assignment was invalid as a means to claim monies for the family. Their argument was that Solomon was duped into executing the assignment and/or undue influence had been brought to bear on him to execute it. In other words, although he had signed the agreement there had not been an informed and voluntary act on his part in entering into the assignment. The agreement could thus be set aside on the basis that it was invalid.

I was not too worried on this account as, although the theoretical argument was valid in law (if the facts supported the proposition), I did not feel that there was any evidence available to support it and without any evidence it would be stillborn. None of the people who were involved in the transaction 50 years previously were alive to tell the tale, However, it was an argument that, if sustained, could be fatal to our case because the availability of the Dickens Clause, the cornerstone of our case, was entirely dependent on this assignment being valid. Unlike Rian who wanted to argue that the assignment was invalid, it behoved us to adopt the stance that it was indeed valid. It was thus necessary for us to shy away from any suggestion to the contrary.

We then addressed the topic of the settlement that was reached. Cullman queried the wisdom of entering into the settlement. I dealt with these issues at some length and what follows is a resume of what I told him.

The final preparatory phase of the trial action process was the holding of a compulsory pre-trial conference between the parties. Such a conference is designed to provide the parties with an opportunity to try and devise ways and means to simplify or shorten the trial, and maybe even reach a settlement which would avoid the trial altogether. We prepared ourselves for the holding of this conference and in discussions with our counsel, who would be the principal actors for our side at the conference, it emerged that it was common cause amongst us that Disney might advance a settlement proposal.

At that stage Disney had for a while been taking a pounding in the local and international media which was seriously affecting their wholesome family orientated reputation. We had been fuelling the fires of this adverse publicity precisely to put pressure on them to be amenable to a settlement. They had already incurred substantial legal costs, and these would increase exponentially as the trial progressed, augmented by any damages that they might ultimately be ordered to pay if the matter was taken through to its conclusion. Disney were also very uncomfortable about their priceless trade marks being under attachment. We hoped that they would make an offer of a money payment that would be acceptable to our side.

There was another important factor playing a major role with Disney that we were unaware of, and which was only revealed to us later at the conference. They had obtained what they believed to be a valid licence from Abilene to incorporate The Lion Sleeps Tonight *in* The Lion King. *This licence had been accompanied by a guarantee and an indemnity from Abilene that their licence was good. Since this litigation had shown this not to be the case, they were entitled to recover all their losses from Abilene. Any money that they agreed to pay to us would in fact be coming out of Abilene's pocket. In the light of this Disney would involve Abilene themselves in any settlement, and make them a party to any agreement that was entered into. In effect, Disney had nothing to lose and everything to gain from a settlement that would result in curtailing the haemorrhaging that their reputation was undergoing.*

From our side, we had reached the limit of the financial support that the Department of Arts and Culture had provided. Our enquiries as to whether further support to take the case through to finality would be forthcoming had not been answered, and we had no certainty in this respect. There was a possibility that we would be able to obtain further funding from some other philanthropic source but that was mere conjecture at this stage.

The costs of undertaking the actual trial were daunting. We had concerns about the merits of our case on the originality of the song issue. We had already achieved the aim of the litigation in the first place, namely establishing that the Estate had a valid legal basis to claim ownership of the copyright in Mbube; *by means of the favourable outcome of the attachment litigation our test case had proven to be successful. This was achieved. What was to be accomplished by taking the case through the expensive trial phase? Very little, if anything at all.*

Even if the trial gave rise to a judgment in our favour, in order to recover damages, we would have to proceed with the second phase of the litigation, namely conducting the enquiry into what the estate's damages were and proving them. This was not likely at best to yield more than a few thousand Rand and would be offset by many multiples of that amount in costs in the process. Then there was also the prospect of possibly losing the case and coming up with nothing to show for it and incurring an order that the Estate should pay Disney's substantial legal costs, which the Estate could not meet and there would be dire consequences that would flow from that. It was plain for all to see that it would be a no-brainer for us but to accept any reasonable settlement offer that Disney might come up with.

The pre-trial conference took place almost two years after the trial action had commenced. This is not unusual for a trial action. At the commencement of the conference the parties indulged in the usual verbal jousting that is calculated to promote themselves into the best possible negotiating position. It was apparent to us that the Disney team was under the impression that we had sufficient independent financing for our case. This was important to us as we did not want it to appear to them that we were negotiating from a position of weakness. We told them that they should not think that this particular case was all there was to our campaign to do justice to the Linda family. We pointed out to them that our rights to Mbube, *that had now been established, existed throughout the countries of the former British Empire and Commonwealth and that they could expect similar actions to be instituted against them in other jurisdictions. This was unbridled puffery on our part for effect.*

Pursuing my discussions with Cullman, we moved on to the subject of reaching agreement with Disney on the settlement and its terms. I summarise these discussions below.

The Disney team wasted no time in getting to the point. They introduced us to the role of Abilene and said that the settlement proposal they were about to put forward came from both Disney and Abilene and that if a settlement agreement was reached Abilene would also be a party to it. The essential elements of their proposal were the following:

- *They would make a lump sum payment of a substantial amount to atone for past infringements. No attempt would be made to quantify damages;*

it would be an ex gratia payment i.e. a payment without recognition of any legal obligation.

- *In addition, Abilene would pay a royalty on all their receipts for uses of* The Lion Sleeps Tonight *throughout the entire world for the next ten years.*

- *The Estate must grant a licence to Abilene, with the right to sub-licence others throughout the world, to use derivatives of unital, including* The Lion Sleeps Tonight *for the duration of the copyright in* Mbube, *which was due to expire in 2012, some six years hence. The payments to be made to the Estate in terms of the settlements should be administered by a responsible trust.*

- *The details of the amounts of the payments to be made under the settlement were to be kept strictly confidential on pain of immediate cancellation of the agreement and all its benefits if this confidentiality stipulation was breached.*

- *The terms of the settlement were to be reduced to writing and the agreement should be signed by and binding on the Estate and each of the individual daughters.*

- *The obligations under the agreement were to be made binding on the successors in title of all the parties.*

- *This was a once-off offer, and it would be withdrawn never to be repeated unless accepted forthwith. It was a question of take it or leave it.*

We said that we would consider the offer and revert to them shortly subject to two further items being included, namely the following:

- *They should concede that* The Lion Sleeps Tonight *was derived from* Mbube *and was a reproduction of a substantial part of it.*

- *Solomon Linda should henceforth be acknowledged in all future statements in respect of the origins of* The Lion Sleeps Tonight *as a co-author of it.*

It was clear that Disney had had enough and wanted out expeditiously and were prepared to pay to achieve this objective. They had made an offer that any experienced lawyer in their right mind could not refuse.

The Disney team agreed to the inclusion of these two additional stipulations. They offered as an explanation for the confidentiality stipulation that they were perpetually bombarded with all sorts of spurious claims from a variety of sources, most of which had no merit or substance, and they felt that if it became public knowledge that they had agreed to make as substantial payment in this instance, this would act as an open invitation and incentive for the submission of future frivolous claims.

The conference was speedily concluded without even broaching the normal subjects discussed at such meetings. We retired to consider the offer.

We were gob-smacked and incredulous at the amazingly favourable terms offered. They by far exceeded our wildest dreams of what we could expect from a settlement. We had absolutely no hesitation in deciding that the offer should be accepted. Against the background of the limited territorial rights that the Estate enjoyed in respect of Mbube, *and the fact that not only Disney's uses of the song would be swept up in the settlement net, but also all uses by all parties licensed by Abilene throughout the world would fall within the settlement, was absolutely incredible. Importantly the settlement would encompass the United States of America, the European Union and many other countries in which the Estate held no rights. Moreover, the financial benefits would continue to be enjoyed for five years beyond the expiry of the copyright in South Africa when the Estate would no longer enjoy any rights whatsoever in unital. To weigh this up against the possible recovery of a few thousand Rands damages after maybe a further year or two of expensive litigation was a joke.*

We saw little point in discussing the settlement proposals with the daughters because they would not begin to understand what it was all about. They were in blissful ignorance of anything to do with the litigation. Their only interest was to get their hands on money, and we would be getting them plenty of that in a measure of thousands of times more than they would get by our persevering with the litigation. Hanro, as their attorney and representative, was prepared to agree to the settlement on their behalf. He was charged with securing their signature of the settlement agreement, which he duly accomplished after the settlement was explained to them as best possible with the help of Rian Malan.

The settlement was speedily consummated, and the action was withdrawn with no costs order being entered. A press conference was held to mark the outcome of the case which was widely hailed as an outstanding success.

This last discussion marked the end of the interview, and I returned to Cape Town. Cullman advised me that he would probably be contacting me again from time to time for further information and discussions. The interview had been conducted in a friendly and open manner. His researcher was present most of the time during the discussions. I gained the impression that Cullman's objective had been to get to the bottom of the case and to solicit useful information from me on a neutral and unbiased basis. I was willing to continue working with him on that level. I was later to have good cause to reassess and revise this impression, which later proved to be fallacious.

XVI

Second Take

THE GARDEN PATH

During the weeks that followed the interview I received telephone calls from time to time from Cullman. These generally dealt with requests for further information or comments on particular points. He asked me whether I could provide him with photographs or other visual materials pertaining to my earlier career. I searched my own and Spoor & Fisher's records for suitable materials and came up with a few photographs which were not particularly suitable. In a subsequent call he advised me that his researcher had discovered film material at the SABC portraying a previous interview that I had done. He enquired about the nature of the interview. I racked my brain but couldn't immediately recall such an interview. I had from time to time been featured in television news programmes, but I had no specific recollection of them. When he told me that it had apparently been part of an actuality programme called *Carte Blanche* I remembered what it was.

When I had brought and won the Paramount Pictures test case in the 1980s, quite a media splash had been made of it. It had achieved recognition that dealing in parallel imports of video versions of films could be prevented by means of utilising a copyright infringement cause of action. This in turn had opened the door for the legitimate international video industry to come flooding into South Africa. I had done an interview with *Carte Blanche* on the subject of that case. Footage from this interview was subsequently brought into Cullman's film without any mention of what it was.

It struck me as being ironic that my two most noteworthy test cases had been joined together in this way, particularly since the Paramount case had marked my entry into doing legal work for the film industry, while the present case had brought about my exit from it. Moreover, the South African distributor of video versions of Paramount films was a company in the Gallo group. The two cases were thus at the opposite ends of my relationship with Gallo!

I learned during this time that Cullman and his researcher had parted company and that he had taken over doing his own research. I was not told what had prompted this, but once his film had been released and I saw the line it took I wondered whether perhaps they had not seen eye to eye on the direction that the film was to take.

About a month after the Johannesburg interview had taken place, Cullman contacted me and said that he wanted to film a second interview with me and would travel to Cape Town to this end. This was in March 2018. He had in the meantime interviewed all the role players in the case, including the trustees, the daughters and the Gallo people. We arranged that he would do the interview at my home in the De Zalze Winelands Golf Estate in Stellenbosch. He did not give me any details about what he wanted to discuss.

The appointed day dawned, and he arrived at my home with a posse of people. It included a camera man, a sound technician, a producer together with all their paraphernalia and equipment. They proceeded to take over my house, removing and rearranging most of the furniture to convert it into a film studio, and effectively banishing my wife from it, for virtually the whole day. This impromptu film studio was obtained at no cost to them, not even of a bunch of flowers for my wife to compensate her for the inconvenience!

The most remarkable aspect of this invasion was that the occupiers included Rian Malan, whose participation was completely unannounced. Not a word of this was mentioned to me either by Cullman or Malan, despite the long association I had with the latter. I was advised that the interview was to take the form of a filmed discussion between him and me on topics which were not foreshadowed. I was caught completely unawares.

As the discussion advanced it became obvious to me from the direction it was taking that this interview was all about the settlement, the performance of the Trust and above all the money that had been forthcoming from the settlement. I realised that this was going to be the focal point of the forthcoming film. The niceties of the actual court case would serve to provide a curtain raiser for the main event. It was not going to tell a good fairy tale. All along Cullman had been looking for something that could fuel a controversy coming out of the case that he could sensationalise. My earlier interview with him had largely been a fishing expedition to find a suitable catch. Something that could facilitate putting together a tasty controversy that would provide spice for the story of his film. It dawned on me that I was being led up the garden path.

THE BOUT

Rian's presence and role here was to be that of a foil. It was apparent that Rian had become an ally of Cullman's, or at least identified with some of the views that he wanted to propagate in the film. I didn't know whom I should regard with the greater circumspection – Rian, who had been in on the matter at the beginning and had heard all the issues canvassed and therefore ought to know better, or Cullman, who had a private agenda which may not be in unison with the facts of the matter.

The merits of the settlement were canvassed. The daughters had apparently expressed unhappiness to them about settling the case. I couldn't believe that anyone in their right mind who was prepared to be objective could doubt that it was an amazingly beneficial outcome for the family in all the circumstances of the matter. I briefly reiterated what I had already explained at length to Cullman at the previous meeting. Rian too had been fully apprised of the situation when he had been recruited to explain it to the daughters in order to secure their signatures to the settlement agreement. On that occasion he had been accompanied by Hanro who was fully steeped in all the issues and was a true believer in the exceptional merits of the settlement and doubtless amplified the arguments.

The simple facts of the matter were that we had brought a highly risky test case with no prospect of securing any meaningful damages and had come away with an incredibly favourable outcome. This was achieved by a notable settlement involving payment of substantial amounts of money to the daughters, which had far exceeded our wildest dreams. The outcome had received widespread popular acclaim even though the precise details of the financial arrangements were not known.

Rian incidentally would have known these details because they were set out in the agreement which the daughters had to sign and which he had to explain and motivate to them, which he successfully accomplished. Presumably these details as well as the reasons and circumstances of the settlement would have been spelled out to them in the process. It is inconceivable that he would not have dealt with the content of the settlement while going about his mission. He or Hanro would presumably have explained to them that the original damages claim, R15 million, had been a strategy to achieve a favourable judgment and the best possible deal for them, not the pot of gold at the end of the rainbow.

The discussion then turned to the money realised by the settlement and the management of it by the trustees of the Trust. Both Cullman and Rian Malan proceeded from the premise that some form of maladministration had taken place, and their questioning in my own home (lulling me into a false sense of security) and without any advance warning was aimed at exploring this and establishing blameworthiness.

They linked Spoor & Fisher with the operation of the Trust and intimated that the firm had some responsibility for the trustees' conduct. I in turn had vicarious accountability in that regard. I disabused them of this notion, saying that Spoor & Fisher, and I personally, were specialist intellectual property practitioners and had no involvement whatsoever in managing the finances of third parties and the setting up and administration of trusts. Our involvement in the matter had been strictly confined to conducting copyright litigation, which fell within our field of practise and expertise. Our involvement ended with the finalisation of the litigation, which included arranging for the Trust to be set up by practitioners in that field and attending to the assignment of the copyright in the song from the Executor to the Trust. We had then bowed out of the matter completely.

The fact that Glen Dean, who was employed by the firm as its Financial Manager, was appointed and acted in his personal capacity as a trustee was entirely due to circumstances.

I made it clear that despite sharing the same surname we are not related and that I had no knowledge of him before he joined Spoor & Fisher. His role in the Trust and the fact that it had no connection to Spoor & Fisher was made abundantly clear at the time. As mentioned earlier this came about purely on account of my being of the view that the trustees should include someone with financial acumen, and I had not been able to find any other volunteers despite strenuous efforts in that regard. Throughout the case I had to call in favours and persuade people to assist in the interests of the Linda daughters. Glen taking on this role had been as a last resort, and with the benefit of hindsight had probably been unwise.

Cullman and Malan then cast aspersions on the integrity of the trustees and their honesty in carrying out their duties. They insinuated that there appeared to have been some sort of embezzlement of monies on their part. I responded that I considered this to be highly unlikely as I had chosen each one of them on the basis that I believed them to be persons of the highest moral character and integrity. Moreover, I reminded them that Malan had a few years earlier investigated the financial affairs of the Trust and found absolutely no trace of any irregularities or untoward conduct.

I pointed out that the daughters had ridiculously high and totally unrealistic expectations as to the amount of money that they would receive, and their claims of money having gone missing were probably due to the misapprehensions under which they laboured. I also averred to the fact that the estate duty, the Executor's standard fees for winding up the Estate and counsels' fees had been deducted from the lump sum payment made in terms of the settlement. Income tax would also have been paid on an annual basis on the payments made to them by the trustees. They clearly paid no regard to these inconvenient details.

The truth of the matter was that they had no facts whatsoever on which their suspicions could be based and were relying purely on their misguided impressions and prejudices.

The duo claimed that I had a personal responsibility to explain and justify how the trustees had managed the Trust and in particular the finances. They expected me to now undertake a thorough investigation of the administration and management of the Trust by the trustees and in particular their dealings in the monies paid into the Trust.

More than a decade had passed since the end of the case and my path over this period had taken me to destinations far away and removed from anything to do with the case. I felt no obligation, inclination or even competence to undertake such a task, particularly because I thought it was a fool's errand. I suggested that if they or the daughters really believed that the trustees had been dishonest, and malfeasance had taken place they should appoint forensic auditors to go into the matter and get clarity for once and for all.

I mentioned that it had been suggested to me on occasion when encountering Glen Dean that the daughters had adopted a spendthrift attitude to the monies that had been paid out to them and had squandered large amounts. One of the daughters had wantonly indulged herself with a substantial payment made to her.

I confessed to being thoroughly disenchanted and disillusioned with the daughters' attitude to those who had gone out on a limb for them and gained a substantial amount of money for them at no cost to themselves. Indeed, they had at no stage even thanked me for my efforts on their behalf. I ventured the view that they had abused Rian Malan in getting him to fight spurious battles for them, in particular with regard to the alleged misuse of the Trust's funds.

It was apparent that Cullman, abetted by Rian, were pushing a particular agenda and were working on a narrative to support it. The gist was to be that the settlement was something of a cop-out and that we had conceded too much. Their point was that we had claimed R15 million and achieved less in the settlement. I will revert below to the amount of the damages that had been claimed and what had been said about it. Even then only a portion of what had been obtained had ever reached the daughters. What had happened to the rest of it? Enquiries made in that regard had been met with evasive replies.

Scant attention was being paid to what had been told to them time and time again, and in the case of Rian Malan what he had witnessed and experienced in being part of the team during the conception of the whole project and through its initial stages. The purpose and objectives of the case, the procedure to be followed for computing damages in a South African court, the sleight of hand in stating the damages claimed in the court papers, and in particular, the severe limitations on what could actually be claimed from specifically Disney, the defendant (no one else besides them were in the firing line in the litigation), in the South African court were being swept aside. Above all the fact that the Estate in reality had no more than a trifling claim, relatively speaking, to a share of the fortunes made by the song, and not the tens of millions that the daughters dreamed and fantasised about, appeared to be of little or no interest or consequence. I felt very disappointed and perplexed at the end of the interview.

They clearly paid no regard to the dynamics of a settlement of a dispute. It is inherent in the nature of a settlement that both parties should make concessions in order to find middle ground. Somebody once said that 'a good settlement is one that made both parties equally unhappy!' In my experience this is a truism. In anticipation of a conflict of interest arising in any situation one invariably initially asks for more than can realistically be expected in order to provide latitude for making concessions and enabling an acceptable conclusion being arrived at. This applies to selling a house or a car as much as it applies to a damages claim. Both Cullman and Malan could have benefited from a healthy dose of realism in the ways of the world.

Cullman sought no further comments or information from, or contact with, me during the remainder of his stay in South Africa. He returned to the USA to process and produce the film which was to be aired by Netflix. It was by now 18 years since the beginning of this saga and 12 years after the conclusion of the court case.

XVII

The Lion's Share

REMASTERED STORIES

Wikipedia explains the meaning of the term 'remaster' thus:

> A 'remaster' is a change in the sound or image quality of previously created forms of media ... In a wider sense, remastering a product may involve other, typically smaller, inclusions or changes to the content itself. They tend to be distinguished from remakes based on the original.

The term 'remastered' is the past participle of the verb 'remaster'. This would entail, in the case of a story, an altered version of it involving changes to the content.

Sam Cullman's documentary film of the case is entitled *The Lion's Share*. It is the final episode of an eight-episode television series made and flighted by Netflix under the rubric 'Remastered'. Each episode had an extended title incorporating somewhat descriptive wording as in *Remastered: The Lion's Share*. For instance, another episode dealing with the life and career of the famous singer, Bob Marley, is entitled *Remastered: Who Shot the Sheriff*, an allusion to one of his best-known songs, *I Shot the Sheriff*. An episode featuring the singer Johnny Cash is entitled *Tricky Dick and the Man in Black*, the latter description referring to the fact that the singer generally wore black clothing when he performed. In each instance the extended title of the film has some relevance to, and hints at, the content or message of the film.

I viewed each of the seven episodes as they were progressively aired on the Netflix channel on a weekly basis. By the time I had viewed the first seven episodes a clear pattern had emerged. Each film told the story of a famous person, for instance Bob Marley, or Johnny Cash, or a noteworthy episode, in the music industry, and highlighted or championed a perhaps little known, or even unknown, aspect of the subject matter, making it into a controversy and sensationalising it. At the end of the trailers of each of these films, and specifically Cullman's one, the bold statement 'the stories you don't know' is made.

In effect each episode, made by a different film maker, 'remastered' a particular piece of musical industry history by including new material, a new angle and/or changing the story of it. Hence the description *Remastered* for the series. The novel slant given to each of the stories made for compelling and entertaining viewing, while perhaps adopting some poetic licence – being at the expense of accuracy. Netflix had ordained this approach when it conceived the idea and theme of the series and named it *Remastered* consistently with its intended thrust. The individual filmmakers' hands were seemingly tied. They were discharging a specific mandate. I have no doubt, however, that Netflix's mandate to the filmmakers did not encompass fabricating situations which had little or no substance in fact.

By the time I had viewed the first seven episodes of the series I already had a shrewd idea of what was coming in the eighth episode. The name, *The Lion's Share*, gave it away. That name alluded to the message Cullman intended the film to convey. It was going to address the question of what became of the vast 'fortune' that, according to his narrative, ought rightfully to have accrued to the Linda daughters from all the millions that the song made throughout its lifetime. There would be innuendo to the effect that most – *the lion's share* – of the proceeds of the litigation had gone elsewhere and the daughters had been cheated out of their full inheritance.

Having been commissioned by Netflix to make a film that 'remastered' the story of the court case, and which told a story the viewer did not know, the spiriting away of most of the money was no doubt his pre-conceived theme from the moment he first set foot in South Africa. He was on the lookout for dirt and ammunition for his quest. I had unwittingly put him on the scent of this angle in my very first telephone conversation with him. After all, there is nothing controversial and sensational about a feel-good fairy story that was already old hat, having been widely emblazoned across the media. Moreover, as the former British Prime Minister, Margaret Thatcher, once said, 'Good news is no news'.

THE WORLD ACCORDING TO MALAN

Netflix's documentary film, *The Lion's Share*, made and directed by Sam Cullman, was flighted during 2019. It purported to tell the story of the court case in which the Executor of the Estate of Solomon Linda sued Walt Disney and Others for copyright infringement on account of the reproduction and public performance of a substantial part of the song *Mbube* without the permission of the copyright owner. The infringing acts consisted of the commercialisation of the song *The Lion Sleeps Tonight*, which is a derivative of *Mbube*. The commercialisation of the song took the form of its incorporation in the stage show and subsequent animated movie, *The Lion King*. As such, the song formed a part of the sound track of both the show and the movie, and of records of the soundtrack which were released in the record industry. The film also dealt in particular with the aftermath of the court case and the benefits which a negotiated settlement of the case bestowed on the heirs of Solomon Linda, his three surviving daughters.

Cullman's film should perhaps have been subtitled 'The Life and Times of Rian Malan' as 'the lion's share' of what it catalogued was in fact his biography. In doing so it made reference to the commercialisation of *The Lion Sleeps Tonight* as a component of the soundtrack of *The Lion King* and the role that it played in his existence. Malan was essentially the narrator of the movie, and it told the story of Disney's use of the song and what transpired in and after the court case as seen through his eyes, as focused by Cullman. In the process Malan dominated the film.

Never himself appearing on camera (but being the ventriloquist or puppet master for the content of the film), Cullman effectively presented his story of the film through the medium of the words and gestures of Rian Malan. A supporting act was performed by the daughters. These *dramatis personae* were his dominant mouthpieces.

The film related that Rian Malan was born into and grew up in a prominent traditional Afrikaner family and was related to

Dr DF Malan, a former Prime Minister of post Second World War South Africa. Dr Malan became the first National Party Prime Minister in 1948 when the party won the national election of that year and came into power. It introduced the Apartheid doctrine as the official philosophy and policy of the country and brought about formal strict racial segregation. DF Malan is generally regarded as the initiator of Apartheid in government policy.

The documentary went on to recount that a young Rian Malan was opposed to the Apartheid policy and became an activist. His approach and conduct were completely at odds with his illustrious, or notorious, relative, and he became estranged from his family. He was ashamed of their political views and conduct and his rebellious attitude caused him to clash with the authorities. When he became liable to be called up for military service, which was the lot of all young white male South Africans at the time, rather than becoming a collaborator in the execution of the government policies that he abhorred, he fled the country and took up residence in the United States where he became a journalist and an author. He wrote a book entitled *My Traitor's Heart* in which he related his opposition to the South African government and its Apartheid policy. He felt guilty on account of his relative's role in the establishment of Apartheid South Africa. It was something of a chip on his shoulder.

When the first democratic government came into power in South Africa and Apartheid was abolished in 1994, he returned to the country and resumed residence in it. He continued his career as a writer and a journalist. He had high hopes for the future social and political development of the country. It should become a normal society.

In the late 1990s he became aware of the story of Solomon Linda and how his song had evolved into a famous international hit song, *The Lion Sleeps Tonight*, and the fact that none of the financial fruits of it had been bestowed on him, while he and his family lived in poverty. He wrote his article 'In the Jungle' which was published in the magazine *Rolling Stone*, whereafter the whole saga leading to the court case got underway.

Rian Malan's life story, recited in detail at some length, set the tone and the mood of the film. Malan explained that the high hopes he had that White South Africans would become transformed with regard to their attitudes to Non-whites in the new political dispensation that had come about had not come to fruition, and in effect the more things changed the more they had stayed the same. Whites were still guilty of holding and exercising racialist attitudes towards, and supremacy over, Non-whites. White guilt prevailed both in South African society and in Malan's conscience.

Through Malan's narration and the expression of his views on White guilt, Cullman transposed Malan's cynical attitude onto the unfolding story of the aftermath of the court case. What transpired was simply a manifestation of the scenario that had been sketched by Malan. He used Malan to portray a situation where the Linda daughters were allegedly abused by bigoted Whites being true to form (the leopard had not changed its spots), and money that should have come to them had been purloined away by greedy individuals. Cullman had created his desired controversy.

Malan had, of course, stood on the sidelines and stayed aloof from all the multiple risks and perils that had been part and parcel of the fruitful legal result for the Linda daughters.

THICKENING PLOT

The premise on which Cullman's plot was predicated was that huge sums of money were rightfully due to the daughters and that this had not materialised. Then too, only a small portion of the money that had come their way actually made it into their pockets. The lion's share of their due rewards had gone elsewhere.

In putting together his story in the film Cullman worked backwards from the conclusion that he wanted to reach. In so doing he made selective use of the facts and the interview material that he had assembled. He also steered some of the interviews and content of the film in a way to suit his thesis. He had Rian Malan making some surprisingly erroneous statements about the course of proceedings given his earlier direct involvement in the case and his personal knowledge of what had transpired. Either that or Rian had some memory lapses and changes of heart over the six-year period during which the case ran its course. The result was that Rian came over giving a less than accurate account of the proceedings. The most extreme of these was the astonishing averment on screen that in the South African court case we had claimed damages in the amount of R60 million, whereas in fact we had claimed R15 million, already a grossly trumped up amount. This can be seen in paragraphs 24 and 25 of the Particulars of Claim to be found Appendix III at page A19. This set the stage for the melodramatic accusation that the lion's share of the booty had been spirited away by the lawyers and/or the trustees.

The very premise of Cullman's story as related in the film was totally wrong. The plot ran as follows.

The American players who had 'stolen' *Mbube* cheated Solomon Linda and his family of their dues, namely all the proceeds of the commercialisation of all the multiplicity of derivative versions of the song, no matter by whom and when or where they were commercialised. All those proceeds, over a period of more than five decades, which were many millions of dollars, should by rights have gone to the family. The family had a 'right' to receive that money but prior to me, Owen Dean, coming along nobody had formulated and pressed for that 'right'.

Disney, by virtue of *The Lion King*, had appropriated a large portion of that bounty. *The Lion King* has been very successful and has made an enormous amount of money. Somehow the family had an entitlement to this money or a substantial portion of it. By some twist of logic, I, in suing Disney, was now going to recover the totality of the 'missing fortunes' generated by the song over all the years for the family, in a court case in South Africa. However, I had only succeeded, by means of a dubious settlement, in gaining a very small portion of the family's just desserts. And even then, I and the other lawyers, as well as the trustees of the Trust, had misappropriated or spirited away a substantial part of these monies and had thus deprived the daughters of a lot of the meagre pickings that had come their way by virtue of the court case.

A DOSE OF TRUTH

The daughters believed implicitly in the veracity of this plot and felt very hard done by through the whole exercise. Nothing was done to disabuse them of their false notions; indeed they were pandered to and encouraged to think along these lines and express their views accordingly.

Of course, the truth of the matter was that due to the 1952 assignment executed by Solomon, the family had no such historic entitlement to receive any monies and the American players had acted perfectly correctly (at least on a legal basis) in not remitting any of the proceeds of the song to them. The family's right to receive royalties in principle only commenced in 1987, a fact of which no-one was aware until the advent of the court case in 2002.

RAINDROPS OF ROYALTIES

Our litigation, an archetypal test case to prove a legal principle, only indirectly concerned damages. These were the lost royalties payable by Disney for the use that was made of the song as a component of the sound track of *The Lion King*, solely in South Africa, and nothing more. Other uses of the song made in other countries and by parties other than Disney did not enter the frame.

The Lion Sleeps Tonight was but one of around twenty songs included in the show. The remainder of the songs in the show were composed by Elton John and many of them became international hits in their own right. The amount of money made by *The Lion King* as a stage show and movie was irrelevant in the overall scheme of things. What was relevant was the royalties payable by Disney to the copyright owner for the use of that particular song. This amount would not have been calculated on the basis of the funds generated by the show/movie. In any event the contribution of that particular song in itself to the overall value of the show/movie was minor.

The amount of money generated by the royalties payable by Disney for the use that was made of the song in the commercialisation that took place of *The Lion King* and its sound track in South Africa would have been a decimal point fraction of the total royalties payable for the use of the song in this context worldwide. I estimate them at being around R5 000. Such royalties were a trifling pittance and as damages were certainly not worth litigating about. Such damages emanating from unpaid royalties were not a torrent in a cloudburst of rain as envisaged by Malan and the daughters, but rather sparse intermittent rain drops. Claiming them was simply a pretext in order to found jurisdiction in the South African court against Disney, a foreign company, which was a prerequisite for litigating against them in South Africa.

The film made a monstrous mountain of what was in fact a tiny molehill in regard to the question of damages. The damages claim was but a means to an end. They were a mere side-show. On the other hand, the main event was the legal significance of the successful outcome of the case and the implications that these held for the future. This was an entirely different matter. This major issue was entirely glossed over or overlooked in the film. The film actually missed the entire point of the case.

The amazing feature of the court case was that, despite its limited objectives and scope, it actually ended up making an unexpectedly substantial amount of money for the family. This was manna falling from heaven, not sparse raindrops. This factor achieved no recognition in the film. A case that was intended to essentially establish a platform for future collection of damages turned out to be doing a pretty reasonable job of obtaining monetary reward itself!

COMMISSION BY OMISSION

The most palpable inaccuracy in Cullman's version of the facts concerned the launching and early conduct of the case before the South African court. Gallo had walked away when we were due to launch the case in the United Kingdom. Hanro Friederich and I took the decision to launch the case in South Africa without any funding and no tangible prospect of obtaining any. At best we had the supremely optimistic hope that we would be able to obtain some funding down the line. Rian was part of the discussions at that time.

In this parlous state we prepared the case, secured the services of Puckrin and Michau on a contingency basis, instituted the trial action in the Pretoria court, served the court papers in Los Angeles through attorneys based in that city (it was difficult to find attorneys in that city who were prepared to be seen to be acting against Walt Disney), and received the court papers filed by Disney in the counterclaim and assumed and undertook the defence of the counterclaim. The latter involved preparing court papers and once again enlisting the services of Puckrin and Michau. All these activities caused expenses to be incurred, which were borne by Spoor & Fisher, and done without receiving any income or even having a tangible prospect of receiving any in the future.

All the while there was no funding in the offing. For all we knew this situation would endure indefinitely and we would be entirely on our own in continuing with the litigation. Puckrin and Michau joined us in being willing to act on an essentially *pro bono* basis with the extremely faint hope of someday getting some remuneration for our services. The prospects of this happening were very slim because we all knew that we were conducting a test case where, even if we were entirely successful, no more than a few thousand Rands damages would be forthcoming which would not be enough for securing contingency remuneration. All of us were willing to act and give of our best in these circumstances because we believed in the righteousness of our cause, and this made it worthwhile.

This state of affairs endured for the best part of six months. During this entire difficult period and afterwards Rian Malan had exited from active participation in the drama. He was nevertheless aware of what was happening, and it may have been the cause of his fading out of the picture. Happily, during the course of the counterclaim proceedings we were able to secure funding from the Department of Arts and Culture and this came as a great relief to me and lessened the extreme stress and pressure under which we had been operating.

I explained this whole situation at great length to Cullman in the interviews that I had with him. It was also described and explained in the e-book and articles that I had written and to which I had referred to him. I considered this entire episode to have been of great significance to the whole matter because I felt proud that we had been very altruistic and public spirited in our actions, something that could be an inspiration to other lawyers, and I felt that we deserved some credit for having taken the risks we did.

This entire period of striving and acting without recompense was completely overlooked and not a mention was made of it in the film. Indeed, the film version of the facts was that when, and only once, we had obtained funding from Arts and Culture did we decide to launch the proceedings in the South African court. Rian Malan is on record describing me as some sort of out-and-out mercenary with the attitude of 'pay my fees and then I will act' – like a juke box or a wind-up toy that only springs into action once it has been fully armed. His verbatim comment on screen, referring to me, was: 'But it was always the case; if you want my services pay my fees, okay'.

This is a gross misrepresentation of both my attitude and what had actually happened to Malan's own personal knowledge in this matter. But it suited Cullman's thesis to have me portrayed in this light. Malan's comment was very wide of the mark as I will explain.

My wife Dana was very active in doing charity work. In particular she did voluntary work as a counsellor at the Citizens Advice Bureau (CAB) in Pretoria for 21 years, during the period from 1986 until 2007, when we re-located to Stellenbosch. The offices of the CAB were located at St Albans Cathedral, the Anglican cathedral in the centre of Pretoria. We were both members of the Anglican Church. The CAB provided advice and support to persons in need, mostly indigent individuals. As it happened most of their 'clients' were poorly educated Black people. The policy of the CAB was to help people to help themselves, although in many, if not most cases, this entailed acting on their behalves. However, the counsellors were strictly forbidden to furnish legal advice, for which they were not qualified.

It transpired in many of the hundreds of cases that Dana handled during her tour of duty that some measure of legal advice or assistance was necessary. Dana's approach in these cases was to call on me to provide the necessary assistance, which I did on a private basis unconnected with the CAB or my firm. I did this on a *pro bono* basis. I virtually operated an informal legal clinic. In this capacity I aided countless needy people.

I have continued to do this up to the present day. Indeed, as I write I am involved in assisting a gardener with an insurance claim for damages to his vehicle, a domestic worker with her divorce and an Asian gentleman who is involved in a property dispute. Over the years I have provided legal assistance for free to a value of many thousands of Rands if calculated in terms of my standard fees.

Indeed, this mindset and practice on my part played a significant role in my deciding to continue aiding the Linda daughters when they were abandoned by Gallo, even if it required me to act on a *pro bono* basis. Apart from any other considerations I considered that as a privileged lawyer I had a general duty to render assistance without charge to underprivileged needy people when circumstances made it possible to do so.

By glossing over this whole episode, Cullman deliberately concealed pertinent facts which were inconsistent with the scenario which he was presenting in order to achieve his purpose. He consciously made a misrepresentation by omission which in law is as reprehensible as wilfully telling an untruth.

CONSTRUCTING THE TRUTH

The way in which the story is told in the film is incorrect, but fits perfectly into Cullman's scenario which entails portraying the lawyers who acted for the family as being money-grabbing and greedy mercenaries. What else could one expect from White South Africans steeped in Apartheid? Moreover, these dastardly characters had the temerity and cheek to actually expect to be paid for the services that they rendered to the family in making them multi-millionaires! Shame on them!

It must be said that neither I nor any of the lawyers who acted for the family can remotely be said to be the kind of neo-Apartheid adherents that Rian Malan sweepingly and inaccurately described as prevailing in modern day South Africa.

What had happened was that Cullman had concocted his own version of the facts – his 'truth' of convenience – to enable him to arrive at his preconceived conclusion. In this regard I quote below from an article written by Randy Lewis and published in the *Los Angeles Times* on 14 May 2019 under the title 'Who wrote *The Lion Sleeps Tonight?* A Netflix film seeks answers, and closure':

> '*I definitely experienced a bit of whiplash a number of times during production,*" Cullman said by phone from Brooklyn. "*As we were filming and uncovering the story we had to follow the truth of what we were uncovering...*'

I am not surprised, and give him some credit, for the fact that he 'definitely experienced a bit of whiplash a number of times during production' while following the truth during making his film. He is perforce referring to his own self-constructed 'truth'. Were these 'whiplashes' pangs of conscience at what he was doing?

MONETARY MISINFORMATION

The most striking and damning aberration in the film is the perpetuation of the myth that the family was entitled to expect to receive many millions of dollars as their just reward from the fruits of the exploitation of 'our father's song'. As previously explained, this perception was fanciful in the extreme and simply wrong. This is particularly so in regard to the court case which was only concerned at best with lost royalties stemming from the use in South Africa of the soundtrack version of *The Lion Sleeps Tonight* in *The Lion King* production.

Even the worldwide royalties accruing through Disney's use of the song were a miniscule proportion of the total revenue of all uses by all perpetrators of the song. We were not suing the international entertainment industry at large for all uses of derivatives of *Mbube*. Our defendant was Disney alone. Our case was solely concerned with Disney's actions in regard to the song, and then only in South Africa. However, the case was not about obtaining a significant damages payment. The goal was to establish that the family had acquired the copyright by virtue of the reversionary interest in terms of the Dickens Clause and were thus in a position to take infringement action. I put this point on screen in the film as follows:

Money was never really the object. The object was to establish the rights and to make a big splash. Since we wanted to make the world out there to take notice, the more prominent the target the better.

Both Cullman and Rian Malan were well aware of the position. It had been spelled out to them on numerous occasions in my discussions with them. Rian Malan was party to the original discussions when we formulated the legal claims, and being a media man must have had some insight into royalty rules. Most pertinently, Cullman had actually even included my above statement in the film. Yet the view is propounded in the film by Cullman's cast members that the case was about obtaining a fortune in damages and many millions were not realised by the court case.

This echoed the views expressed by the daughters for several years previously. No attempt was made in any of the scenes featuring the daughters when this issue was discussed to disabuse them of their delusional view as to their 'entitlement', or to remind them that Rian had participated in the process of them agreeing to and signing the agreement. They were simply humoured in these views (perhaps even encouraged!). Small wonder that they considered the 'meagre' sums of money that they received from the case as indicative of the fact that they had been cheated out of their birthright.

Rian Malan did not assist the situation by expressing doubt on screen to the daughters about the wisdom of the settlement that was reached. It defies belief that someone who knew the facts of life regarding the money situation could express such a view.

Let's look at the publicly available facts. According to information given at the conclusion of the film (i.e., provided by Cullman from his own sources and not from me or Spoor & Fisher) each of the three daughters received around US$250 000. This translates into roughly R4 million, thus making a total of R12 million. This amount is calculated after deduction of estate duty of 35% of the original payment and 3.5% in executor's fees (the standard fee). In addition, counsels' fees at double their normal amount had been paid by the Executor. Accordingly, the gross amount of money accruing to the daughters was probably in the region of in excess of R15 million. This can be weighed up against the grossly trumped up and exaggerated amount claimed as damages in our court papers. The settled amount exceeded even that amount.

The net amount of money received by the daughters made each of them millionaires four times over! Given all the circumstances of the case this was an extraordinarily favourable amount to have received in the settlement. And it cost them not a single cent of their own money to achieve this outcome. It was presented to them on a platter.

The only legal fees that were debited against the amount of the settlement were those of senior and junior counsel. My fees (Spoor & Fisher's) were debited to the Department of Arts and Culture, an arrangement Hanro and I had facilitated. A payment was made by the daughters to Hanro Friederich but that was in terms of a personal arrangement between them and him at the time when he was appointed as their general attorney more than two years prior to the litigation being commenced or even conceived and was not a litigation expense charged against the amount paid in terms of the settlement.

It is abundantly clear that the cause of the daughter's disenchant-ment with the outcome of the case was brought about by a total misun-derstanding of the purpose and effect of the court case taken together with a wildly uninformed and unrealistic belief regarding what rewards they could expect to receive from it. Rian Malan somewhat grudgingly largely confirmed this by saying on screen that, 'it is a story of dashed expectations'.

This false and contrived notion that bounteous rewards ought to be forthcoming for the daughters from the case was the basis for Cullman's assertion that the lion's share of the proceeds had gone elsewhere than to the daughters. The daughters in their ignorance can perhaps be forgiven for holding this misconceived view, but the same is not true of the views espoused by Cullman and expressed by Rian Malan. The latter had, of course, personally conducted investigations into the accounting of the application of the proceeds of the case at the request of the daughters and had come up with a clean bill of health.

Indeed, it seems that he conducted such investigations on two separate occasions. The first was in 2014 after he had interceded with me on their behalves and, to judge by what he said on screen, the second was at a late stage in the making of the film. In regard to the latter investigation, he said the following on screen:

> *The family was able to provide us with a few bank accounts and, uh, I plowed through all the statements I was able to lay my hands on and I made certain deductions, and I could not find any illegitimate payments leaving that account. I said I am afraid to disappoint the family that there isn't any evidence of the fraud that they allege.*

A factor that may have played a role in the daughters' disenchantment with the money they received was that the copyright in *Mbube* expired in 2012 in South Africa and the family's rights in the song thus came to an end. Theoretically they were therefore not entitled to receive any monies from it after that date. However, the settlement agreement extended to 2017, but it then also came to an end and the flow of money dried up. Doubtless Cullman and Malan never saw fit to explain this to them when they embarked on the 'documentary' in 2018, and this probably fuelled their belief that their money was being misappropriated.

THE CRITICAL 1952 COPYRIGHT ASSIGNMENT

In his resolute pursuance of his own agenda, Cullman has done inestimable harm to the daughters' cause. The primary purpose and effect of the litigation was to achieve a favourable result in a test case by establishing the family's rights to ownership of the copyright in *Mbube*. As a result, the family has in principle been placed in a position to pursue further claims against other misusers of derivatives of the song, besides Disney and Abilene.

Folkways and their exploitation of *Wimoweh* immediately come to mind, but there is a plethora of others. These claims could be brought in all countries that were formerly part of the British Empire up to 2012 when the copyright expired in most countries. However, in certain countries the copyright endures until seventy years after Solomons death, i.e., until 2032. Theoretically there is the opportunity for further money to be made. Alas, Cullman in his film has nullified these opportunities. I will explain.

An absolute kingpin in our legal argument is that there must have been a valid assignment of copyright in *Mbube* from Solomon Linda to Gallo. Absent such an assignment, the Dickens Clause cannot apply and the case collapses. The whole case turns on the applicability of the Dickens Clause. I have described the validity of this assignment as one of the possible Achilles Heels of our case. A possible challenge to the assignment by Disney (which was foreshadowed in their pleadings) was one of the factors which weighed with me when taking the decision to accept Disney's settlement offer. In the circumstances it is foolhardy for the family and their allies to do anything which can facilitate an argument that the assignment was invalid.

Against this background it was injudicious to say the least for Cullman to devote considerable time and attention in the film, as he did, to making out a case that the assignment was indeed invalid. This was done in his fervour to show how Solomon had been abused by White guilt. He has the daughters, i.e., close relatives of Solomon who knew him intimately, intimating that his purported signature on the document is not genuine because he could not read or write and thus had no signature. They say the following in that regard on screen:

Also, an uneducated person's signature does not lie. Sometimes they make a cross or otherwise a thumb print.

Upon focusing on the purported 'Solomon Linda' signature they stand by their earlier statement. In other words, they assert that their father, an uneducated person, would not have signed his name in full and, if he had indeed executed the document, he would have done so by means of a cross or a thumb print.

This boils down to their saying that the document was forged! Or at least their statement is capable of this interpretation. It is difficult to comprehend that they are saying anything different. It follows from this that the forger must have been Gallo.

The daughters also advanced other arguments on screen which go to the point that the assignment agreement and Solomon's execution of it were irregular. Cullman, the ventriloquist, is thus effectively contending in the film as trenchantly as possible that the assignment agreement had no force or effect.

The presentation of this damning information in a film which has been publicly distributed with acclaim throughout the world will go a long way towards rendering nugatory any future claims of copyright infringement. Such claims would in principle still be possible in those former British Empire countries which have extended the term of copyright to 70 years after the death of the author. However, Cullman has gratuitously delivered information which, if true, serves to destroy the family's ability to mount claims against possible future defendants. He has gifted it to them in a neatly wrapped package. One can imagine a defence counsel rubbing his hands in glee and making a meal of this scene in the film at any future infringement trial. If his very own daughters and heirs, contrary to their own interests, believed that he did not validly execute the assignment why should the court hold to the contrary, particularly in the absence of any refuting evidence? On this basis any future claims will be dead in the water.

By undermining and compromising the validity of the assignment, Cullman has effectively undone all the good achieved by the successful test case, and has probably brought about a situation where the Disney case will prove to be the first and last case in which copyright infringement and damages can be claimed by the Trust. This is most unfortunate. If I had to decide anew whether to launch the Disney case in the knowledge that the daughters would make this statement about the signature of the 1952 assignment, I would definitely not have gone ahead. I believe that most lawyers would in the future reach a similar decision.

But worse still, if the 1952 assignment is indeed fraudulent then the daughters should not have received any money at all because the family had no claim to the copyright and thus of copyright infringement. The Estate's acquisition of the ownership of the copyright in 1987 on which the whole case is based never came about. The copyright never reverted to it in terms of the Dickens Clause. All the money they received would in fact have been wrongfully paid to the Estate and ultimately to them!

The daughters never disclosed this evidence to me on either of the two occasions that I met with them at their house during the course of handling the case, or at any stage, nor to my knowledge to Hanro Friederich, their lawyer. I cannot vouch for Rian Malan. Had this in fact been the case it would have been traversed by them in their earlier valiant but unsuccessful attempts to find some way to assist the daughters to derive income from *The Lion Sleeps Tonight*. Why did the daughters fail to disclose this vital evidence to me or anyone else earlier? Why was it only mentioned for the first time 20 years after the conclusion of the court case? Was it perhaps coaxed out of them by Cullman?

Let us suppose we had not accepted the settlement offer and had continued with the trial, as Cullman intimated that we should have done. It would have led to a hearing. As the plaintiff we bore the onus of proof that the *Mbube* is the subject of copyright. This entailed presenting evidence that it is an original work composed by Solomon Linda. The best available evidence to prove these facts would have been forthcoming from one or more of his daughters. We would have put them in the witness box and required them to present the facts, as best they could, to the effect that he had composed the song and that it was his own original work. Having testified to that effect they would have been subjected to cross-examination by Disney's senior counsel.

Disney had pleaded that they did not accept that the song was original but rather was traditional. They would undoubtedly have lined up an expert who would testify that the song was traditional and merely adopted by Solomon. Furthermore, they had challenged the assignments of copyright which were critical to our case in the earlier application to set aside the attachment of the trade marks. They would once again explore this avenue. They had intimated this in their pleadings.

Imagine what would have happened if during his cross-examination Disney's advocate had questioned the daughters about the validity of the 1952 assignment and they had responded by saying that they believed that the agreement had been forged and that their father had never signed it (which they were bound to say, if this was the truth). This would have been catastrophic and would have blown our case sky high. Our action would have been dismissed, and the costs of the case would have been awarded against the Executor. These costs would have also included the costs of the earlier counter-application by Disney, because that court had reserved the question of who should pay those costs for decision by the trial action court. How would this costs claim, amounting to millions of Rand, have been met by the Executor?

The successful and prized judgment in the attachment application would have been overridden and we would have been left with absolutely nothing to show for more than six years of hard work. The daughters would have gained nothing, not one cent, from the case that had in principle cost millions of Rand to pursue. The taxpayers' money expended by the Department of Arts and Culture in financing the case would have been completely wasted.

Just as well then that we settled the case when we did! If, in our ignorance of this crucial and damning information, we had continued with the trial, we would have been hurtling headlong towards a precipice. On this account we can thank our lucky stars for settling the case before it was too late. So much for the Cullman's suggestion that we ought not to have accepted Disney's offer and settled the case when we did!

Given the daughters' astounding revelation, Folkways can mount a good argument that they are the current copyright owners in respect of *Mbube*. That's because the copyright, never having left Solomon in 1952 on account of the fraudulent assignment, was still owned by him at the time of this death in 1962 and passed to his heirs, i.e., his wife and children, whereafter it passed to them (Folkways) in 1983 and1992 when his wife Regina and his daughters, being his heirs, respectively executed assignments of copyright in their favour. Disney tried to rely on these assignments in their counter claim, but we successfully argued that the copyright had already flown the coop with the 1952 assignment, so the 1983 and 1992 assignments were ineffective and valueless because they dealt with copyright that the purported assignors never owned. On the revised facts, this argument would have been wrong.

The daughters had at least two opportunities to drop their bombshell that the 1952 assignment had been forged on me. These were on the occasions that I met with them when I was assessing the merits of the case and their suitability as witnesses. But in the film the daughters alleged that I never met with them, which they claimed was indicative of my showing no interest in them. This is blatantly untrue. As if I, or any competent lawyer for that matter, would embark on a precarious trial action with exceptionally high risks and stakes, especially for me personally, without first meeting with the beneficiaries of the litigation and key witnesses to hear what they had to say and assess them as potential witnesses in the witness box!

As I have said one or more of them would have been required to give the best evidence available that their father had composed *Mbube,* and that the song was original. These were essential elements of the case and critical issues to be proved.

For goodness' sake! I am not given to riding into battle without first checking whether I have bullets in my gun, or perhaps even whether I have a gun at all! That would be suicidal. I might have been mad to persevere with the project once Gallo had bailed out, but I wasn't crazy in executing it. On the contrary, because of the risks I was taking in doing so I was doubly cautious in going about it. Give me some credit in knowing how to do my job after thirty years' litigation experience!

As it happens, my assessment of them as witnesses was not favourable, at least not for appearing in the British court. This was something that we would have to work around if we had proceeded in the British court and was the subject of discussion amongst the lawyers.

The startling statement that I never met with them emerged during a filmed discussion involving Malan and the daughters and choreographed by Cullman. Questions arise about its spontaneity. It conflicted with information that was contained in my e-book *Awakening the Lion* and moreover that I had previously imparted to Cullman and Malan, but it was not discussed further on camera. It was not put to the daughters that I had positively stated that I had indeed visited them in contradiction to what they were alleging. What possible reason would I have to make such a misrepresentation in a book published in 2013, years before the film project was dreamed up? The improbability of this allegation that I never met with the daughters being true is manifest. The daughters were simply telling an untruth in this regard. This question has further implications which will be discussed below.

A SHOT IN THE FOOT?

My above analysis of the consequences that flow from the invalidity of the 1952 assignment is entirely predicated on the premise that the daughters were being truthful when going on record in the film in saying why their father could not have signed the document. But what if there is no substance in their allegations? In that case the whole problem is avoided, their copyright infringement claim is valid, and the money paid out to them in terms of the settlement was legitimately obtained.

Their revelations about the circumstances in which the 1952 assignment was executed – the process of shooting themselves in the foot – came in an interview in which the whole tenor was how badly the daughters suffered from the ills of White guilt. The influence and of White guilt was an important point for Cullman to make in pursuing the theme that he had chosen for his film. That is why he got Rian Malan to wax on about it in the film. It was a vital component of his plot of the film. My alleged indifference or even disdain towards the daughters in ignoring them and not bothering to meet with them was thrown into the mix. After all, I was nothing but a fat cat White lawyer out to further his own interests at the expense of the daughters!

The crowning glory of this particular scene was the revelation about the signing of the agreement. It is of course possible that the daughters were giving vent to hyperbole for effect and that they were misrepresenting the situation. Their allegation that I never visited and met with them certainly was a misrepresentation. It was simply not true. They thus showed a propensity to be economical with the truth, particularly when, according to their perception, they were advancing their cause. Could it be that their allegations about their father and the signing of the agreement fell into the same category? Why was the point not raised with me when I was gathering information and evidence at the outset of the matter? For someone uninitiated in copyright law, and particularly the niceties of the Dickens Clause, it would have seemed to them to be advantageous to their cause. It was of crucial importance then and if it had come to the fore would probably have changed the course of events completely.

As previously discussed, Rian and Hanro had at the outset, and before we joined forces back in 2002, tried to argue that the assignment was invalid because Solomon had been duped into signing it. Duly instructed by the daughters (armed with their power of attorney according to their statements on camera) they discussed the existence and effect of the 1982 and 1993 assignments executed by family members with the daughters' previous attorneys, whom they replaced. This was at a time before the Dickens Clause had come on the scene and the perils of the invalidity line of argument had become apparent. It was the only string that they had in their bow, but it was to no avail as it was only conjecture, and no evidence was available to support it. Rian argued that the imbalance of power between the parties made it likely that Gallo could have forced Solomon into signing the agreement against his will. Alternatively, Solomon had no idea what he was doing when he signed.

These are all theories unsupported by facts and do not constitute evidence, which is the currency of the court. But they were rehashed on screen in the film. The simple fact of the matter was that some 50 years after the event there was no-one around who could testify as to the circumstances in which the document was executed. The invalidity point based on their arguments at the time was a dead letter. All this would have changed if the forgery point had come to the fore. But it didn't – because it was unknown at the time. The daughters were silent on it.

Surely when ways and means of knocking out the assignment were desperately being sought by Rian and Hanro that was the opportune time for the daughters to come forward with their remarkable evidence, but this never happened. Why not? There is no apparent reason. Unless this was a subsequently dreamed up argument of convenience? If you are intent on knocking out the assignment, this point was a winner. The beauty of the forgery argument is that there are indeed witnesses available to testify to the relevant facts. Having this argument available to them at that time would have been a trump card for them to play. But that card was not brought out of the pack. The box must have been empty.

But after the advent of the Dickens Clause the last thing that you should be doing is to try to knock out the assignment. The availability of reliance on that clause changed the landscape completely. Now knocking out the assignment would destroy the entire case – not a sensible or desirable move. This evidently was not appreciated by Cullman and Malan. They blundered on with a superannuated and counterproductive argument that Solomon never assigned the copyright. Most unfortunate!

The million dollar question (literally and figuratively) is whether the daughters' statements regarding the forging of the signature are true and credible. Let's examine the known facts. The event took place in 1952, i.e., roughly 70 years prior to the damaging interview, when the Gallo assignment was executed. In the unlikely event that the daughters had already at that stage even been born, they would at best have been very small children. What would they have known about their father's administrative and financial affairs? When their father died in 1962 the only asset in his Estate was a bank account standing at R147. He thus clearly operated a bank account at the relevant time. How would he have opened a bank account and operated it, i.e., made deposits and withdrawals from it, if he was not able to sign his own signature? It is not a difficult or insurmountable problem to learn how to sign your own name even if you can't read and write. It makes you think, doesn't it?

The crucial question is: was Solomon Linda's signature on the 1952 assignment genuine? The daughters were shown the document and the actual signature on it purporting to be Solomon Linda's was magnified. Viewing this material is what caused the daughters to claim that it was not genuine. No doubt they had seen this document before, because they had instructed Hanro Friederich to argue the whole question of the validity of the assignment with the lawyers who had previously represented them. An interesting point arises at this juncture.

Solomon Linda in fact executed three assignment documents in favour of Gallo. All were on the face of it perfectly effective instruments achieving the desired objective, namely transferring the ownership of the copyright in *Mbube* to Gallo. They were executed on respectively 14 January, 26 February and 9 April 1952 (see paragraphs 9.1 – 9.3 of the Particulars of Claim – Annexure III on page A3). It is not apparent why the same transaction was done three times. The difference between the second and third assignments, on the one hand, and first one on the other hand, is that they related to two songs, namely *Mbube* and *Ngi Hambiki,* whereas the first one dealt only with *Mbube.* There was, however, another important distinction between them.

Unlike the first one, the other two were executed before a Notary Public who certified 'Signed in my presence by SOLOMON LINDA' (see Annexure I on page A1). It is not apparent which version of the assignment was shown to the daughters when the relevant scene in the documentary was filmed, but my guess it that it was the first one because it would have been difficult for the daughters to have made their startling claim if they had been shown a document which carried the abovementioned attestation.

Cullman and his researcher were given access to the pleadings in the court case. He must have been aware of the existence of the three assignments, copies of all of which were annexed to the pleadings. He obviously made a copy of at least one of them. If I am correct in my supposition, why did he choose to show the daughters the unattested one? It would certainly have suited his purpose to show them the one that was not notarised. If he had shown them a notarised one surely, he should have asked them to comment on the Notary's attestation in the light of their assertion. This is most perplexing!

I say that it is improbable that the daughters' evidence is true. However, be it as it may, the incontrovertible fact is that the damning statement publicly made by intimate relatives, is on record, and is there for the world at large to behold. Unless it is publicly retracted and satisfactorily explained (why, and what prompted, the making of the untrue statement) it will be accepted as plausible evidence of the fraudulent nature and invalidity of the 1952 assignment. This could sound the death knell of the family's claim to copyright in *Mbube* and any entitlement to derive any revenue whatsoever from the exploitation of *The Lion Sleeps Tonight*. This would be tragic, but really the daughters' fate in this regard lies entirely in their own hands. Perhaps they should consult their lawyers in this regard.

I can only theorise about these matters. I don't know the answers to these questions. That is the preserve of the daughters and Cullman. I am merely posing them because they highlight dramatic issues which are cardinal to *The Lion Sleeps Tonight* case and its outcome and implications.

In conclusion on this issue, on his version of the 'truth', Cullman's film has arguably brought about the downfall of the whole case. It has shown that the daughters should have received no money at all let alone that they have been deprived of *the lion's share*. His quest and obsession to find a controversial issue that could be sensationalised might prove to have been dramatically successful to an extent way beyond his contemplation. At all events, if he had the daughter's interests at heart, it was most injudicious, to say the least, for him to have presented this material in his film. It was a horrendous gaffe on his part.

In the dying embers of the film Rian Malan woefully says that he believes that he failed the daughters: 'I let them down, ja, I did'. He feels he should have gotten a better outcome for them, but the prevalence of White guilt got the better of him. Prior to my viewing the film, I did not share that view at all and said as much on camera. On the contrary, I believed that his intervention on their behalf was marvellously successful and that the daughters ought to be eternally grateful to him. However, on the strength of the shot-in-the-foot interview in which he collaborated I am inclined to think it may turn out that he was actually correct. He may well have failed them completely in the final analysis by assisting in comprehensively destroying their claim.

What the choreography and inclusion of this shot-in-the-foot scene in the film makes abundantly clear is that Cullman never actually understood the case that he was pontificating about. If I may say so, it is not prudent to cause the making of extravagant far-reaching allegations while standing on shaky unfamiliar ground. One would have expected better from a seasoned and celebrated documentary film maker.

SUMMING UP

Sam Cullman came to South Africa with the predetermined objective of making a controversial film about *The Lion Sleeps Tonight* case in pursuance of his mandate from Netflix to relate a story about the case that 'told the facts you don't know'. He fixed on the money that was generated by the case, and what became of it, as the optimum focus and subject matter of the film. He capitalised on the daughters' deluded fixation that they were entitled to all their father's money from the exploitation of the song, being all the proceeds of all versions or derivations of *Mbube* from 1952, which would amount to millions upon millions of dollars, and that this would be brought to fruition by our court case.

Knowing full well that this belief was totally unfounded (the true position was painstakingly explained to him in detail by me), Cullman chose not to disabuse the daughters of it but instead capitalised on it in order to achieve his objective. He used Rian Malan and his views on White guilt to further his cause. He built up a narrative that money that ought to have gone to the daughters had been filched by White South Africans carrying out their longstanding supremist practices and attitudes towards Black South Africans. The lawyers acting in the case had, according to him, been active participants in this misdeed and so, probably, had the trustees of the Trust. This had resulted in the lion's share of the proceeds of the case being diverted from the daughters, so the story went.

In carrying out his mission he made selective use of the facts, ignoring those which did not support his narrative, and with poetic licence wove them into a scenario which would achieve his objective. This resulted in a skewed and distorted picture of the case and its outcome, with strong political overtones (whereas, in fact, there had been none at the time of the case) being created.

The film is sadly lacking in integrity. It does an injustice and a disservice to all those individuals who, with selfless motives, worked hard and gave of their best to serve the welfare of the family. It also has fanned the flames of the daughters' discontent by promoting and enhancing their illusions, whereas it could have brought them down to earth and made them face realities. In the long run this might have made them happier. After all, becoming multi-millionaires is really not a bad outcome if they come to think about it.

The irony is that along the way before his denouement in his grand finale Cullman actually did give a reasonable resumé of the circumstances and the conducting of the actual court case (save for his omission of the information of the launching of the trial action without funding). If he had left it at that he would, in my view, have produced a good and interesting film which had integrity. When I think of the worth of his end product, the well-known phrase (attributed to Mark Twain), 'never let the truth get in the way of a good story', immediately springs to mind.

The Lion's Share won the 2020 Emmy award for Outstanding Arts and Culture Documentary. Taken at face value, this was probably a fitting accolade, since the court case and its outcome indeed made 'a good story', but the fact that the real truth has been obscured detracts from the merit of the award. This recognition granted to the film exacerbates the depth of the wound that it has caused.

XVIII

Postmortem

EFFECT OF THE SETTLEMENT

When in 2006 the settlement of the court case was announced at the press conference that we held, it met with public acclaim both in South Africa and internationally. The general view was that we had achieved a remarkable success. We, the lawyers who had handled the case, were feted as heroes. Against considerable odds and risks to ourselves we had scored a outstanding victory for the indigent family of Solomon Linda and had placed them in a position to obtain a considerable amount of money. Although political considerations were irrelevant at the time, it turned out that we were an all-White legal team working without any immediate expectation of financial reward for the benefit and to improve the well-being of an indigent Black family. Contrary to Rian Malan's view of things, we were moved by a desire to obtain social justice for a previously disadvantaged family.

We had obtained judicial recognition and approval of an obscure but important point of law and had used it to triumph over the mighty Walt Disney. Moreover, we had established the South African origin of *The Lion Sleeps Tonight* and had overnight converted the hitherto largely unknown Solomon Linda into a national cultural hero and an internationally celebrated composer. *Mbube* came to be regarded as a treasured piece of South African indigenous culture. South African parenthood of *The Lion Sleeps Tonight* was recognised.

We had also spectacularly broken new ground in South African law and court procedure by attaching, as a form of property, some of the most world famous trade marks registered in South Africa in order to found the jurisdiction of the South African court over one of the world's most prominent and powerful foreign based companies.

I gave talks on the case at numerous public meetings and seminars and was interviewed by the press and on television and radio both in South Africa and internationally on services such as the BBC. The case was mentioned in dispatches in the South African parliament. It featured as a significant milestone and achievement in my career.

I published an article entitled 'Stalking the Sleeping Lion' in the legal journal, *De Rebus*, which won the journal's award for the best article of the year. I also published similar articles in a variety of South African and international journals. These articles and the news of the case spawned communications with legal scholars and practitioners from all over the world. Several articles written by other authors appeared in journals published in a variety of countries. The case enjoyed considerable fame and good repute.

PRICKING THE BUBBLE

This success bubble was burst some thirteen years later, in 2019, by Sam Cullman's Netflix documentary, *The Lion's Share*. With its diversionary politicised approach and its emphasis on the role of White guilt it altered the thrust of the story significantly. It skewed the narrative of the case and presented a distorted picture of its outcome. Instead of being the heroes of the story, the lawyers who took up the cudgels on behalf of the family were cast in the role of the villains of the piece, avaricious gold diggers who diverted *the lion's share* of the spoils of the litigation to themselves.

Sam Cullman, despite having been fully apprised of the folly of their beliefs and how the monies were in fact distributed, pandered to the delusional mythology of the daughters regarding the vast fortunes that they ought to be receiving. There was not one shred of evidence to substantiate his assertions of dishonourable conduct on the part of the lawyers. On the contrary, the investigation conducted by Rian Malan failed to disclose any evidence of malfeasance on their part, nor indeed by anyone else. His entire message was one of convenience to support the pre-conceived story that he wished to sensationalise. His true colours were revealed by his dismissal out of hand of my suggestion that he might appoint forensic auditors to make a thorough investigation and assessment of how the monies were dealt with and report on the propriety of the whole process.

The upshot of the film was that it cast aspersions on Spoor & Fisher, Hanro Friederich, me, the advocates, the trustees of the Trust and the Executor of the Estate and suggested that we had acted dishonourably to say the least, in our handling of the case and the distribution of the monies. The uninformed viewer of the film could not fail to gain the impression that our conduct was lacking in integrity and that we indeed had taken unconscionable advantage of the daughters. In this vein Rian Malan said on screen, *'Is Owen going to say I put my own selfish interests paramount? No, I don't think that he is going to say that. Which lawyer does?'*

I submit that the personal risks I took and the prejudice I suffered in handling the case, and my willingness to commence the South African court proceedings on a self-funding basis without any assurance of financial support from a third party, belies the veracity of this statement.

Rian Malan further sounded off on this theme by saying, *'Let's just say every lawyer involved in this made a sh*t load of money!'*

Is that really so? Let's take my own case as an example. I billed the Department of Arts and Culture for my services in this matter. In doing so I charged them in the standard manner of billing them on the basis of the time I spent on the case. I had plenty of other opportunities of alternate work, and had I not been working on this case I would in all probability have billed for the same number of hours, or more, to other clients for the cases that I would have been handling on their behalves. The income I would have generated in this manner would have been at least the same as I generated in the Disney case. I would have sold the same number of hours of my time to other parties at the same rate. I was thus no better off billing the Department than I would have been if I had not been handling the Disney case.

The amount I earned in handling the Disney case was thus by no means exceptional and I gained no particular financial advantage from handling the case. I sold hours of my time that I would otherwise have sold to other clients at the same rate. I was thus in a financially neutral position.

Indeed, in actual fact I earned less in the Disney case than I would have earned had I been handling other cases. This was because I only billed Arts and Culture for the services I performed after we had entered into the funding arrangement. All the work I did after Gallo bailed out of the case and before Arts and Culture entered the picture went unbilled. This means that I acted *pro bono* for a period of around six months while doing the following: replacing the Executor of Solomon Linda's Estate; searching for and obtaining copies of Disney's two hundred and fifty registered trade marks from the Register of Trade Marks; drafting the court application to attach Disney's trade marks; drafting the Particulars of Claim for the trial action; bringing the court application for attachment of the trade marks; consulting with and briefing counsel to act in the matter; serving the court papers on Disney in the United States (which involved paying the fees of the American attorneys who carried out the actual service of the documents); and effecting the actual physical attachment of the trade marks. In normal circumstances these services would have generated a substantial debit, but this was willingly forgone.

Contrary to Malan's assertions, from an earnings point of view, the Disney case was at best done by me in the ordinary course of conducing my normal practice. Nothing more. Once again, his assertion was unfounded and made in the cause of furthering Cullman's mission.

To add further insult to injury there was the intimation in the film to the effect that what else could one expect from White South Africans! Given the true position and what we had gone through and achieved, these were extremely unkind and unwarranted suggestions. I was left with a very bad taste in my mouth after viewing the film.

Surprisingly, once he had viewed the film, even Rian Malan expressed unhappiness to me about the thrust of it. He was critical of the unfavourable light in which the protagonists of the case had been portrayed. Since Cullman told his dark story mainly through Rian's mouth and in his words this was incongruous. It caused me to wonder how Rian came up with some of his unfavourable comments featured in the film. Why had he now made this disclaimer? Do some of his statements made on screen perhaps not reflect the views that he expressed? Alternatively, it is a possibility that he had been seized with a guilty conscience at having turned on people with whom he had originally identified and collaborated. Only he can tell.

THE BULL AND ITS HORNS

As time went by, the more I thought about the film the more aggrieved I became. My feelings were fortified by the comments I received from friends and colleagues who knew what had been involved in handling the case. The commonly held view was that the film did not reflect the true story of the case and did a disservice to the protagonists of it and was reprehensible on that account.

I decided to take the bull by the horns, and I entered into a dialogue with Sam Cullman. I advised him of my disenchantment with his end product and in particular the conclusion he had reached that the lawyers had succumbed to greed and had usurped the lion's share of the spoils of the case. I also criticised his politicisation of the story and the manner in which he had distorted the tale of the case. He had presented a skewed picture of it. I considered that his message of White guilt was at odds with what most responsible South Africans were seeking to achieve, namely a balanced society untrammelled by racial prejudices.

He staunchly defended his version of the story and said that he had told both sides' view of it. I challenged him on this and said that he had by no means been objective and had clearly favoured the daughters' hard luck story. The debate became somewhat acrimonious.

PAYING THE PIPER

In the end it got down to his saying outright that he believed that the lawyers ought to have acted entirely *pro bono* and were wrong to have taken any remuneration whatsoever out of the case. I considered this to be an astonishing proposition. We had made the daughters into multi-millionaires but yet were not entitled to earn our own bread and butter!

The hundreds of hours that we had collectively spent on the case, which was time that we could have sold to others in going about the ordinary course of our professional activities, would simply have to be donated to the daughters so as not to spoil their party spending the millions of Rands which we had earned for them. If they had simply gained a paltry sum of money, it might have been different, but we had made them rich, and they could easily afford to effectively pay reasonable compensation to us.

It should be borne in mind that as far as the lawyers were concerned only counsels' fees were paid out of the proceeds of the case – Spoor & Fisher fees had been paid by the Department of Arts and Culture. Obviously, the Department considered that we were entitled to be paid for the services that we had rendered. Was he saying that the Department was wrong in this respect? Moreover, counsels' fees had been paid strictly in accordance with the mandatory rules laid down by the Bar Council for acting on a contingency basis. Is the policy and governance of the Bar Council in his view at odds with what is fair and just in the circumstances? By what higher order were we being judged?

It is rather incongruous for an American to look askance at lawyers acting on a contingency basis as this is a practice that is widely adopted and accepted in the United States. As practised in that country, lawyers undertake litigation on behalf of a client (generally someone who is indigent) free of charge subject to their right to obtain payment when there is a successful outcome resulting in a monetary award to the client. The payment takes the form of a percentage of the proceeds. This percentage commonly varies from thirty-five percent to fifty percent of the monetary award obtained. In these circumstances there is no opprobrium attached to lawyer obtaining payment by this means. Why should contingency remuneration be viewed differently when it takes place in South Africa? It is approved by the professional authorities in South Africa, and it takes a much milder form. It is, however, seldom employed in South Africa as proving damages is very difficult under our law and procedure. In terms of the Bar Council rules the contingency payment is not determined by a percentage of the payment obtained, but rather it takes the form of payment of double the counsel's normal fees.

In the present instance, counsels' fees (the only legal charges deducted from the payment received) probably amounted to less than ten percent of the total. Hardly the lion's share!

I asked Cullman why he expected the lawyers alone to bear the entire financial burden of the litigation? What about other possible philanthropists, if philanthropy was considered necessary? If he felt that strongly that the daughters ought to have gotten off the litigation scot-free, despite their bounteous rewards, perhaps he personally, or Netflix, must compensate them for the 'losses' that they had incurred through having to pay some legal fees. After all, he and Netflix would no doubt be handsomely rewarded by the film that they had made on the strength of the case, and the cost to them for compensating the legal fees would be the proverbial drop in the ocean. The case and the daughters' plight had enabled them to undertake a successful project, and they had thus gained from it financially and in other ways. They were winners on the strength of it and this would be an opportunity for them, themselves, to practice the selfless altruism that they preached. This suggestion had no attraction for him.

Had he considered suggesting to the fiscus that they should in the circumstances of the matter waive the estate duty (35% of the receipts) that had been deducted from the proceeds of the litigation? No, as far as he was concerned it behoved the lawyers, and them alone, to make the required sacrifice. Perhaps he had bad experiences with lawyers in the past (contingency fees?) and had a jaundiced view of the breed!

I asked him whether he had considered interviewing Abilene, or investigating their fulfilment of their obligations to pay royalties out of the settlement? Perhaps if they had not done so fully, this may provide a solution to some of the 'missing millions' of which the daughters had allegedly been deprived. He had nothing to say on this question. Perhaps they were not considered to be a part of White guilt.

The upshot of it all was that he was happy with his version of the financial situation and was not interested in exploring any other possibilities. He obviously had no intention of disturbing the punch line of his film of which he was no doubt proud.

CARRYING ON THE CRUSADE

Cullman also suggested that I had left the daughters in the lurch once the case had been concluded, and that I ought to have continued my crusade on their behalf indefinitely, presumably at no cost to them. I advised him that, having spent six years on the case, I had other commitments (with the Soccer World Cup looming) on hand. I successfully completed my role in the matter, had put the platform in place for the matter to be taken further and I had to move on. Moreover, I was disenchanted by the ungrateful attitude of the daughters, who had not even thought fit to thank me for my efforts which were the result of years of stress and work, but instead had stabbed me in the back and insulted me. I owed them nothing.

Nonetheless, in correspondence with Folkways, I had prepared the ground for a claim to be made against them in respect of *Wimoweh* and I had passed this opportunity on to the trustees of the Trust holding the funds and administering the copyright. There were still another six years to go before the copyright in expired in South Africa and most other countries, and another 31 years in the United Kingdom, and Canada etc. There was the possibility of more money to be made (assuming that some way could be found to get around the daughters' public claims on film that the original assignment was invalid). Here was a further opportunity for Netflix and him to serve the interests of the daughters, about whose welfare they were supposedly greatly concerned. They could become knights in shining armour. They could sponsor another round of litigation and create a further filming opportunity for themselves. This did not fall on fertile ground. His caring for the lot of the daughters had definite bounds and required financial sacrifices to be made only by lawyers, and definitely not by film makers.

At his behest I agreed that even at this late 2019 stage (I had already long since relocated to the Western Cape and retired from active practice but remained a consultant to Spoor & Fisher – albeit it not in the role of a litigator), and in spite of everything, I would be prepared to manage or oversee pursuing further claims on the daughters' behalf, subject to two conditions. First, they must retract all spurious claims made by them against Spoor & Fisher and the other lawyers and, second, that any such future claims would be conducted on a formal contingency fee basis. The latter was a concession to them because I had never before acted on that basis, and my standard approach (and that of most lawyers in South Africa and elsewhere) was to bill for the time I spent irrespective of the outcome of a matter. He said that he would convey this offer to the daughters.

I subsequently heard that he had made disparaging remarks about me, and, finally realising that he was not the kind of person that I cared to be associated with, I then severed all communications with him. I never heard again from him nor from the daughters. Apparently, they had no wish to invoke my assistance if it was not forthcoming at no charge!

TRUTH WILL OUT

These exchanges that I had with Cullman fuelled my feelings of aggrievement about the film and I resolved that something should be done to set the public record straight. It was necessary to address the inaccuracies and the misinformation contained in the film. I accordingly wrote an article entitled 'Awakening the Lion in the Jungle' in 2019. In this article I adopted the approach of not pointedly addressing and criticising the fallacies and inaccuracies in the film, but rather of unambiguously stating the correct facts wherever appropriate in the course of the narrative. This article was published on the Stellenbosch University IPSTELL website, Spoor & Fisher's website and in the legal journal, *Without Prejudice*.

It was subsequently suggested to me by a legal colleague, who had viewed the film and read my article, that my corrective writing, which was well warranted, should be made available to a wider audience. This comment spurred me on to write this book. Another factor that prompted my decision was the fact that the film won an Emmy award in 2022 for Outstanding Arts and Culture Documentary. This led to the film being billed on the Netflix platform as being 'Award Winning'. Apart from the dubious nature of this accolade given the film's lack of integrity, from my perspective this probably enhances the perceived credibility of the film and heaps coals on the fire. I now want to take steps, as slight as they might be, to counter the misinformation contained in the film.

To the uninformed, *The Lion's Share* may be an interesting and entertaining film, and the award may appear to be well deserved when it is taken at face value. The rub is that it unfortunately gives what I say is a distorted and ultimately inaccurate portrayal of what really happened in the Disney case and in the return of *Mbube/Wimoweh/The Lion Sleep Tonight* to its home in South Africa. This contaminates its worth and value. This is a pity. It could easily have been otherwise.

I invite you, the reader, now that you have heard my story, to view the film and to form your own judgment on what is the real truth of the story of the case and the worth of the film. To quote William Cowper, 'The truth lies somewhere, if we knew but where.' In this day and age of pervasive fake news in the media, the world out there is entitled to be enlightened.

Amen!

SOLOMON LINDA

for value received, do hereby cede, transfer
and make over to, and in favour of

GALLO (AFRICA) LIMITED

all my right, title and interest in and to the
copyright (including all mechanical rights and
performing rights) of my arrangement of the following
traditional tunes :

"MBUBE"
and
"NGI HAMBIKI"

Solomon Linda

AS WITNESSES :

1.

2.

ACCEPTED by me, ALEXANDER DELMONT, for and on
behalf of GALLO (AFRICA) LIMITED

_____
DIRECTOR

AS WITNESSES :

1.

2.

SIGNED in my presence by SOLOMON LINDA and
ALEXANDER DELMONT at JOHANNESBURG on the 26ᵗʰ day
of February 1952.

_____
NOTARY PUBLIC.

230

5. Ownership of copyright etc

(1) Subject to the provisions of this Act, the author of a work shall be the first owner of the copyright therein:

Provided that—

(a) where, in the case of an engraving, photograph, or portrait, the plate or other original was ordered by some other person and was made for valuable consideration in pursuance of that order, then, in the absence of any agreement to the contrary, the person by whom such plate or other original was ordered shall be the first owner of the copyright; and

(b) where the author was in the employment of some other person under a contract of service or apprenticeship and the work was made in the course of his employment by that person the person by whom the author was employed shall, in the absence of any agreement to the contrary, be the first owner of the copyright, but where the work is an article or other contribution to a newspaper, magazine, or similar periodical, there shall, in the absence of any agreement to the contrary, be deemed to be reserved to the author a right to restrain the publication of the work, otherwise than as part of a newspaper, magazine, or similar periodical.

(2) The owner of the copyright in any work may assign the right either wholly or partially, and either generally or subject to limitations to the United Kingdom or any self-governing dominion or other part of His Majesty's dominions to which this Act extends, and either for the whole term of the copyright or for any part thereof, and may grant any interest in the right by licence, but no such assignment or grant shall be valid unless it is in writing signed by the owner of the right in respect of which the assignment or grant is made, or by his duly authorized agent:

Provided that, where the author of the work is the first owner of the copyright therein, no assignment of the copyright, and no grant of any interest therein, made by him (otherwise than by will) after the passing of this Act, shall be operative to vest in the assignee or grantee any rights with respect to the copyright in the work beyond the expiration of twenty-five years from the death of the author, and the reversionary interest in the copyright expectant on the termination of that period shall, on the death of the author, notwithstanding any agreement to the contrary, devolve on his legal personal representative as part of his estate, and any agreement entered into by him as to the disposition of such reversionary interest shall be null and void, but nothing in this proviso shall be construed as applying to the assignment of the copyright in a collective work or a licence to publish a work or part of a work as part of a collective work.

(3) Where, under any partial assignment of copyright, the assignee becomes entitled to any right comprised in copyright, the assignee as respects the right so assigned, and the assignor as respects the rights not assigned, shall be treated for the purposes of this Act as the owner of the copyright, and the provisions of this Act shall have effect accordingly.

IN THE HIGH COURT OF SOUTH AFRICA

TRANSVAAL PROVINCIAL DIVISION

Case no:

In the matter between

STEPHANUS GERHARDUS GRIESEL   Plaintiff

and

DISNEY ENTERPRISES INC   First Defendant

NU METRO HOME ENTERTAINMENT (PTY) LIMITED   Second Defendant

DAVID GRESHAM ENTERTAINMENT GROUP (PTY) LIMITED   Third Defendant

DAVID GRESHAM RECORDS (PTY) LIMITED   Fourth Defendant

PARTICULARS OF CLAIM

1.

1.1.   The Plaintiff is Stephanus Gerhardus Griesel, a male adult acting in a representative capacity as the duly appointed Executor of the Estate of the late Solomon Masazeni Ntsele, also known as Linda (hereinafter referred to as "Linda").

1.2.   The Plaintiff conducts business in partnership as a chartered accountant under the style Griesel Nel and has his principal place of business at 7 Centuria Park, von Willich Avenue, Centurion, Gauteng.

2.

2.1.   The First Defendant is Disney Enterprises Inc, a company organised and existing under the laws of the State of Delaware, United States of America, having its principal place of business at 500 SO Buena Vista Street, Burbank, United States of America. The First Defendant was previously named The Walt Disney Company Inc.

2.2.   The First Defendant conducts business as a producer and distributor of cinematograph films and is the owner of various intellectual properties which it licences to others for use by such other parties.

2.3.   The First Defendant has no place of business in South Africa, or within the jurisdiction of the Honourable Court. The Plaintiff has founded jurisdiction against the First Defendant by attaching property belonging to the First Defendant located within the jurisdiction of the Honourable Court, more particularly by attaching the trade marks registered under the Trade Marks Act, 1993 in the name of the First Defendant and the copyright in the cinematograph film entitled THE LION KING, which copyright is registered in South Africa under the Registration of Cinematograph Films Act, 1967, under no 94/0106. The Honourable Court thus has jurisdiction over the First Defendant. A copy of the Court Order issued in case no. 16361/2004 is annexed and marked "A".

3.

3.1.   The Second Defendant is Nu Metro Home Entertainment (Pty) Limited, a
        company organised and existing under the laws of South Africa, having its
        principal place of business at Gallo House, 6 Hood Avenue, Johannesburg
        Gauteng. The Second Defendant carries on business as the manufacturer and
        distributor of copies of cinematograph films in South Africa.

3.2.   The Second Defendant is the South African licensee of the First Defendant in
        respect of various intellectual properties owned by the First Defendant, and
        more particularly in respect of the cinematograph film entitled THE LION KING.

                                          4.

4.1.   The Third Defendant is David Gresham Entertainment Group (Pty) Limited, a
        company organised and existing under the laws of South Africa, having its
        principal place of business at 59 Bowling Avenue, Kramerville, Sandton.

4.2.   The Fourth Defendant is David Gresham Record Company (Pty) Limited, a
        company organised and existing under the laws of South Africa, having its
        principal place of business at 59 Bowling Avenue, Kramerville, Sandton.

4.3.   The Third and Fourth Defendants carry on business in conjunction with each
        other *inter alia* as licensors under the copyright in various musical works and as
        manufacturers and/or distributors of sound recordings of musical works.

5.

5.1.   Linda was at all material times domiciled in South Africa and was a South African citizen and permanent resident of South Africa.

5.2.   Linda died on 8 November 1962. Upon his death his Estate was administered and wound up by the Office of the Bantu Affairs Commissioner, Johannesburg. The sole known assets in his Estate were the proceeds of a savings account at the Allied Building Society, Johannesburg in the amount of R148.00. These assets were distributed to his heirs and his Estate was closed. The Estate was administered under reference 1192/62.

5.3.   In 2004 the existence of a hitherto unknown asset of the Estate of the late Linda became known to his surviving heirs. In order to deal with this asset the Estate of the late Linda was re-opened and one Hugh Melamdowitz ("Melamdowitz") was appointed by the Additional Magistrate, Johannesburg as the Executor of the re-opened Estate in March 2004. Annexed and marked "B" is a copy of his Certificate of Appointment.

5.4.   On or about 22 June 2004, the Plaintiff was substituted for Melamdowitz as the Executor. Attached and marked "C" is a copy of his Certificate of Appointment.

6.

6.1.   During or about 1938/39 Linda composed an original musical work, being the melody of a song entitled MBUBE. The musical work was recorded and copies of the sound recording of the work were issued to the public in South Africa during or about 1938/39. A copy of such sound recording may be inspected and played at the offices of the Plaintiff's attorneys of record during normal business hours.

6.2.   The issuing of such sound recordings to the public in South Africa constituted the first occasion anywhere in the world when copies of the musical work MBUBE were issued to the public.

6.3.   In the premises, Linda was the author of the musical work MBUBE and copyright subsisted in it by virtue of the provisions of Section 1 of the Third Schedule to the Patents, Designs, Trade Marks, and Copyright Act, 1916 (hereinafter referred to as the "1916 Act") read together with Section 143 of the 1916 Act.

6.4.   In terms of Section 5(1) of the said Third Schedule, Linda was the initial owner of the copyright in the musical work MBUBE.

6.5.   In terms of Section 3 of the said Third Schedule the term of the copyright in the musical work MBUBE would have endured for a period of 50 years after the death of Linda, (i.e. until 8 November 2012).

7.

In the premises, and by virtue of the provisions of Section 41(1), read together with Sections 1, 2, and 3 of the Sixth Schedule to the Copyright Act 1965 (hereinafter referred to as the "1965 Act"), read together with Sections 3, 5, and 48(1) of the 1965 Act, copyright subsisted in the musical work MBUBE under the 1965 Act for a period terminating 50 years after the death of Linda, (i.e. until 8 November 2012), and the initial ownership of such copyright vested in Linda.

8.

In the premises, and by virtue of the provisions of Section 43 of the Copyright Act, 1978 (the "1978 Act"), copyright subsists under the 1978 Act in the musical work MBUBE for a period terminating 50 years after the death of Linda (i.e. until 8 November 2012), and the initial ownership of such copyright vested in Linda.

9.

9.1.   On 14 January 1952 Linda executed a written Assignment of the copyright in the musical work MBUBE to Gallo (Africa) Limited. A copy of such Deed of Assignment is annexed and marked "D".

9.2.   On 26 February 1952 Linda executed a further written assignment of the copyright in the musical work MBUBE to Gallo (Africa) Limited. A copy of such Deed of Assignment is annexed hereto and marked "E".

9.3.   On 9 April 1952 Linda executed a further written assignment of the copyright in the musical work MBUBE to Gallo (Africa) Limited. A copy of such Deed of Assignment is annexed hereto and marked "F".

9.4.   The said assignments of copyright were subject to the provisions of the proviso to Section 5(2) of the Third Schedule to the 1916 Act. Accordingly, notwithstanding their terms, the said Assignments vested in the Assignee, or any successor in title to the Assignee, ownership of the copyright in the musical work MBUBE only for a period comprising the lifetime of Linda and 25 years after his death, (i.e. until 8 November 1987).

9.5.   Furthermore, in terms of Section 5(2) of the Third Schedule to the 1916 Act, as read with Section 144 of the 1916 Act, a reversionary interest in favour of the Executor of the Estate of Linda was created, which reversionary interest would take effect on 8 November 1987. On 8 November 1987 the Executor of the Estate of Linda would acquire full and complete ownership of the copyright in South Africa in the musical work MBUBE free of all licences or other encumbrances which might previously have existed.

9.6.   In the premises, and by virtue of the provisions of Section 27(1) of the Sixth Schedule to the 1965 Act, the aforesaid limitation of the effect of the assignment of copyright was operative under the 1965 Act and the reversionary interest in the said copyright would have devolved on the Executor of the Estate of Linda, (i.e. on 8 November 1987).

9.7.   Accordingly, the right of the Executor of the Estate of Linda to receive the ownership of the copyright on 8 November 1987 existed under the 1965 Act.

9.8.   In the premises, and by virtue of the provisions of Section 43(a)(1) of the 1978 Act, the right of the Executor of the Estate of Linda to receive ownership of the copyright in the musical work MBUBE on 8 November 1987 continued to exist and on that date the Executor of the Estate of the late Linda became the owner of the copyright in the musical work MBUBE free of any licences or other encumbrances which might have existed prior to that date, and with the duty to administer that copyright as part of the Estate.

10.

By virtue of the aforegoing, the Plaintiff is the owner of the copyright subsisting in the musical work MBUBE.

11.

11.1.   In or about July 1950 one Pete Seeger, a resident of the United States of America, wrote a musical work called WIMOWEH. This work was a reproduction, alternatively an adaptation, of the musical work MBUBE or a substantial part thereof.

11.2.   In or about 1961 George Weiss, Hugo Peretti and Luigi Creatre, residents of the United States of America, wrote a musical work entitled THE LION SLEEPS

TONIGHT. This work was a reproduction, alternatively adaptation, of the musical work MBUBE or a substantial part thereof and/or the musical work WIMOWEH.

11.3.   In the premises the musical work THE LION SLEEPS TONIGHT embodies a reproduction, alternatively an adaptation, of the musical work MBUBE or a substantial part thereof and was copied directly or indirectly from that work.

12.

12.1.   In or about 1992 to 1994 the First Defendant caused a cinematograph film entitled THE LION KING to be made in the United States of America. The First Defendant became the owner of the copyright in the cinematograph film THE LION KING and is currently the owner of such copyright.

12.2.   In or about 2003 the First Defendant caused a cinematograph film entitled THE LION KING 3 – HAKUNA MATATA to be made in the United States of America. The First Defendant became the owner of the copyright in the cinematograph film THE LION KIND 3 – HAKUNA MATATA and is currently the owner of such copyright.

12.3.   The cinematograph film THE LION KING 3 – HAKUNA MATATA is for the present purposes an adaptation of the cinematograph film THE LION KING and both such cinematograph films are hereinafter referred to collectively as THE LION KING.

12.4.   The First Defendant is a licensor of rights under the copyright in the cinematograph film THE LION KING.

12.5.   The First Defendant has made or caused to be made multiple copies of the cinematograph film THE LION KING, *inter alia*, in South Africa. It has also distributed or caused to be distributed in South Africa copies of the cinematograph film THE LION KING on 35mm prints, videotapes and/or DVD discs.

13.

13.1.   The musical work THE LION SLEEPS TONIGHT has been embodied in the cinematograph film THE LION KING and the said cinematograph film therefore contains a reproduction and/or an adaptation of the musical work MBUBE and/or a substantial part thereof.

13.2.   Performing any act in relation to a copy of the cinematograph film THE LION KING entails performing that action in relation to a reproduction or adaptation of the musical work MBUBE and/or a substantial part thereof

14.

The Plaintiff has not authorised:

14.1.   The making of a reproduction or an adaptation of the musical work MBUBE
           and/or a substantial part thereof in the cinematograph film THE LION KING by
           anyone.

14.2.   The publishing, performing in public, broadcasting, causing to be transmitted in
           a diffusion service of the cinematograph film THE LION KING containing a
           reproduction or an adaptation of the musical work MBUBE and/or a substantial
           part thereof by anyone

14.3.   In general the performing of any acts in relation to the cinematograph film THE
           LION KING containing a reproduction or an adaptation of the musical work
           MBUBE and/or a substantial part thereof by anyone.

15.

15.1.   From a date unknown to the Plaintiff, the Second Defendant has without the
           licence of the Plaintiff reproduced in any manner or form, made adaptations of,
           performed in public, and/or caused to be transmitted in a diffusion service, the
           cinematograph film THE LION KING. In so doing it has acted in such manner in
           relation to the musical work MBUBE and/or a substantial part thereof.

15.2.   In the premises, the aforesaid conduct of the Second Defendant has infringed,
           and is infringing the Plaintiff's copyright in the musical work MBUBE in terms of
           Section 23(1), read together with Section 6 of the Copyright Act, 1978.

15.3.   The First Defendant has caused, authorised, instigated, and/or aided and abetted the aforesaid conduct of the Second Defendant and it has in so doing, infringed, and is infringing, the Plaintiff's copyright in the musical work MBUBE.

16.

16.1.   From a date unknown to the Plaintiff, the Second Defendant has without the licence of the Plaintiff:

16.1.1.   imported into South Africa for a purpose other than for its private and domestic use;

16.1.2.   sold, let, or by way of trade offered or exposed for sale or hire in South Africa;

16.1.3.   distributed in South Africa for the purposes of trade, or for any other purpose to such an extent that the Plaintiff is prejudicially affected;

copies of the cinematograph film THE LION KING, being infringing copies of the musical work MBUBE, with the knowledge that the making of such copies constituted infringement of the Plaintiff's copyright in the musical work MBUBE or would have constituted such infringement if the copies in question had been made in South Africa.

16.2.   By virtue of the aforegoing, the Second Defendant has infringed, and is infringing, the Plaintiff's copyright in the musical work MBUBE in terms of Section 23(2) of the Copyright Act, 1978.

16.3.   The First Defendant has caused, authorised, instigated, and/or aided and abetted the aforesaid conduct of the Second Defendant and it has in so doing infringed, and is infringing, the Plaintiff's copyright in the musical work MBUBE.

17.

17.1.   From a date unknown to the Plaintiff, the Third and Fourth Defendants have, without the licence of the Plaintiff, reproduced in any manner or form, made an adaptation of, published, performed in public, broadcast and/or caused to be transmitted in a diffusion service the musical work THE LION SLEEPS TONIGHT, and/or caused, authorised, instigated and/or aided and abetted another to do so. In doing so it has acted in such manner in relation to the musical work MBUBE and/or a substantial part thereof.

17.2.   In the premises, the Third and Fourth Defendants have infringed, and are infringing, the Plaintiff's copyright in the musical work MBUBE in terms of Section 23(1), read together with Section 6, of the Copyright Act, 1978.

18.

18.1. From a date unknown to the Plaintiff, the Third and Fourth Defendants have without the licence of the Plaintiff:

18.1.1. imported into South Africa for a purpose other than its private and domestic use;

18.1.2. sold, let, or by way of trade offered or exposed for sale or hire in South Africa;

18.1.3. distributed in South Africa for the purposes of trade or for any other purpose to such an extent that the Plaintiff is prejudicially affected;

copies, in the form of records, tapes, compact discs and the like, of the musical work THE LION SLEEPS TONIGHT, being reproductions or adaptations of the musical work MBUBE and/or a substantial part thereof, with the knowledge that the making of such copies constituted infringement of the Plaintiff's copyright in the musical work MBUBE or would have constituted such infringement if the copies in question had been made in South Africa.

18.2. By virtue of the aforegoing, the Third and Fourth Defendants have infringed, and are infringing, the Plaintiff's copyright in the musical work MBUBE.

19.

The Plaintiff's attorneys addressed letters of demand to the First, Second, Third, and Fourth Defendants drawing such Defendants attention to the unlawfulness of their conduct as aforesaid and calling upon them to desist from such unlawful conduct. Despite these demands, the Defendants have declined to furnish the Plaintiff with appropriate undertakings that they will refrain from acting unlawfully as aforesaid in the future. The Plaintiff apprehends upon reasonable grounds that the Defendants will not desist therefrom unless restrained by Orders of the above Honourable Court.

20.

The Defendants have at all times relevant hereto been aware of, or have had reasonable grounds to suspect, that copyright subsists in the musical work MBUBE.

21.

The Plaintiff apprehends upon reasonable grounds that the Defendants have in their possession copies of the musical work THE LION SLEEPS TONIGHT, being infringing copies of the musical work MBUBE.

22.

22.1.   In the premises, the Plaintiff is entitled, in terms of the provisions of Section 24 of the 1978 Act, to payment of an amount calculated on the basis of a reasonable royalty which would have been payable under the circumstances by a licensee in respect of the work or the type of work concerned, namely a musical work.

22.2.   The said reasonable royalty would be calculated as follows:

22.2.1   In respect of records, tapes, compact discs and the like: 6,76% of the Published Price to Dealer (being the wholesale price of records, tapes, compacts discs and the like sold to retailers for distribution to the public);

22.2.2   Reproductions of the cinematograph film: 6,08% of the Published Price to Dealer (being the wholesale price of records, tapes, compacts discs and the like sold to retailers for distribution to the public);

22.2.3   Mechanical reproduction and synchronisation in the cinematograph films: all net sums received from the exploitation in the Republic of South Africa of the mechanical rights, reproduction rights and television synchronisation rights and all other rights in the musical work THE LION SLEEPS TONIGHT collected by or, alternatively, which ought to have been collected by, collecting agencies such as, but not limited to, SAMRO and NORM.

23.

The Plaintiff is currently unaware of the Defendants' extent of use of the musical work THE LION SLEEPS TONIGHT. Once the Defendants have made full discovery, the Plaintiff will apply to amend these particulars of claim.

24.

The Plaintiff estimates that a reasonable royalty pertaining to paragraph 22.2.1 will amount to R5 million.

25.

The Plaintiff estimates that a reasonable royalty pertaining to paragraphs 22.2 and 22.3 will amount of R10 million.

WHEREFORE the Plaintiff claims:

1.   An Order interdicting the First Defendant from infringing the copyright in the musical work MBUBE by performing the acts set out in paragraphs 15.1 and 16.1 above.

2.   An Order interdicting the Second Defendant from infringing the copyright in the musical work MBUBE by performing the acts set out in paragraphs 15.3 and 16.3 above.

3.   An Order interdicting the Third and Fourth Defendants from infringing the copyright in the musical work MBUBE by performing the acts set out in paragraphs 17.1 and 18.2 above.

4.   An Order directing the First, Second, Third, and Fourth Defendants to deliver up to the Plaintiff for destruction all copies of the musical work THE LION SLEEPS TONIGHT and all plates used or intended to be used for making the aforegoing in their possession or under their control.

5.   An Order that, for purposes of determining the amount of a reasonable royalty to be paid to the Plaintiff by the Defendants, an enquiry should be held and that, if the parties cannot agree upon the procedure to be adopted, the Court should prescribe such procedures for conducting for such an enquiry as it considers necessary.

6.   Costs of suit, including the costs of two Counsel.

7.   Further and/or alternative relief.

DATED AT PRETORIA on this 2nd day of July 2004.

pp C E PUCKRIN SC

    R MICHAU

    _____

COUNSEL FOR THE PLAINTIFF

SPOOR AND FISHER
Attorneys for the Plaintiffs
c/o Van Zyl Le Roux Hurter
13th Floor SAAU Building
cnr Andries & Schoeman Streets
PRETORIA
LC3004421-23/OHD

2006 BIP 299

DISNEY ENTERPRISES INC v GRIESEL NO

A

IN THE HIGH COURT OF SOUTH AFRICA
(TRANSVAAL PROVINCIAL DIVISION)

2004 SEPTEMBER 7 DANIELS J

_____

B

An application to set aside an order attaching certain assets belonging to the applicant ad fundandam jurisdictionem—*Executor of the respondent found* prima facie *to be representative of the estate—Respondent having established a* prima facie *case of contributory infringement of copyright* C *'though open to some doubt'—Court exercising its discretion in favour of the respondent—Application dismissed.*
Copyright Act 98 of 1978, s 23

In an application to recall and set aside an order made earlier by the Court attaching certain D
assets belonging to the applicant *ad fundandam jurisdictionem* in an action to restrain
the alleged infringement of copyright brought by the executor of the late copyright
proprietor, it was contended by the applicant that the first respondent had failed to
make out a *prima facie* case for the relief sought for the reasons that (1) the first
respondent had not been appointed as executor by the Master of the High Court and E
accordingly did not have authority to represent or act on behalf of the deceased estate;
and (2) the applicant did not infringe nor did it cause the infringement of the copyright
allegedly vesting in the first respondent, and the Court
Held, insofar as the argument relating to the respondent's appointment was concerned, that
the document relied upon by the respondent had been attached to the founding F
affidavit and nothing more was required of the respondent at the relevant stage of
the proceedings.
Held, further, that the respondent had made out a case that the applicant had 'caused,
authorised, aided or abetted the second defendant to make reproductions of the film'
and, once that was understood, the applicant's complaint fell away.
Held, further, that the Court in any event had an overriding discretion to grant or deny relief to G
a litigant who might be guilty of a failure to disclose material or relevant facts and that,
having regard to the facts at the Court's disposal, the Court would in any event have
exercised its discretion in favour of the respondent.
The application was, accordingly, dismissed.

H

Daniels J: The applicant seeks an order recalling and setting aside an order sought *ex parte* and granted by Swart J on 29 July 2004 attaching certain assets belonging to the applicant *ad fundandam jurisdictionem.* No reasons were furnished by Swart J and none were called for. At this stage the *onus* is upon the first respondent to show upon the affidavits filed in I the *ex parte* application and in the present application that it was and still is entitled to the relief sought.

It was said in *Simon NO v Air Operations of Europe AB and Others* 1999 (1) SA 217 (SCA) at 228 that,

A

'the remedy of attachment *ad fundandam jurisdictionem* was an exceptional remedy, and one that should be applied with care and caution. Once all the requirements for attachment had been satisfied, however, a court had no discretion to refuse an attachment.'

B

At the same time it was explained that an applicant had obviously to establish that he or she had a *prima facie* cause of action, although open to doubt, and this requirement was satisfied if an applicant showed that there was evidence which, if accepted, would establish a cause of action.

C The mere fact that such evidence was contradicted would not disentitle an applicant to the relief sought, not even if the probabilities were against him. It was only where it was quite clear that the applicant had no cause of action, or could not succeed, that an attachment had to be refused. (228B–D.)

D The accepted test for a *prima facie* right in the context of an interim interdict was to take the facts averred by the applicant, together with such facts set out by the respondent that were not or could not be disputed, and to consider whether, having regard to the inherent probabilities, the applicant should on those facts obtain final relief at the trial. The facts set

E up in contradiction by the respondent should then be considered and, if serious doubt was thrown upon the case of the applicant, he or she could not succeed. (228F–I.)

It was contended on behalf of the applicant that the first respondent failed to make out a *prima facie* case for the relief sought by reason of the

F following:

(1) The first respondent was not appointed as executor by the Master of the High Court. Accordingly he did not have, and does not have, authority to represent or act on behalf of the estate of the late Mr

G Solomon Ntsele (also known as Linda);

(2) the applicant did not infringe nor did it cause the infringement of the copyright allegedly vesting in the first respondent.

H ## The first respondent's appointment as executor

I do not intend dealing in any detail with the arguments presented by counsel. Suffice it to say that, however one views the matter, the fact remains that Griesel purports to act on behalf of the estate. It is the estate 'represented by ...' whomever, that will be cited as the plaintiff in the

I matter. The Master and/or the magistrate regard Griesel as the duly appointed representative of the estate and they will individually or collectively look to him for reporting on the estate, and to account for the assets recovered. The first respondent was appointed, in terms of reg 4(i) of the regulations published under GN R200 of 6 February 1987, to represent the estate. It is true that he is not named 'executor' of the estate, but this does not detract from the fact that he was appointed '... to represent the ... estate, to assume responsibility for the collection of the assets, to pay all claims to the value of the assets in the estate ... and to award the balance of the estate, including the immovable property if any, to the rightful heir(s)', which is exactly what an executor does. Whether Griesel is called an agent or executor cannot impact upon his entitlement to institute the action. If the applicant has a problem with the appointment such as it is, but which is *prima facie* proper and regular on the face of it, it can bring a substantive application to have it set aside. The Master will obviously be joined as a respondent and he or she will be able to explain the manner in which the Act is applied and the measures taken to implement the *Moseneke* judgment in a practical and sensible manner.

At this stage of the proceedings and having regard to the test to be applied, the Court is to be satisfied that Griesel has shown, no more than *prima facie*, that he as the representative of the estate is entitled to recover whatever is allegedly due. That much he succeeded in doing.

The applicant's alleged infringement

The first respondent's case appears from para 12 of his proposed particulars of claim. The essence of his case is that the applicant caused certain cinematograph films to be made in the United States of America, that it made or caused to be made multiple copies of that film and distributed or caused to be distributed in South Africa copies, videotapes and DVD discs thereof. The first respondent will have to prove these allegations at the trial. At this stage he need only show a *prima facie* case 'although open to doubt'. With this end in view he need go no further than to show that there is evidence, which if accepted, would establish a cause of action.

The applicant's case is that no such a case was made out, and that no such a case is made out in the matter now before me. The Copyright Act, 1978, s 23 thereof, provides as follows —

'23. Infringement.

(1) Copyright shall be infringed by any person, not being the owner of the copyright, who, without the licence of such owner, does or causes any other person to do, in the Republic, any act which the owner has the exclusive right to do or to authorise.'

It is the applicant's case that it was at all relevant times the owner and licensor of the copyright in the relevant cinematograph film and that it was never a producer or distributor of the film, neither in South Africa nor elsewhere. The production and manufacture, copying and distribution were undertaken by the various licensees, all of whom incidentally

A are its subsidiaries. It is alleged that the first respondent through his attorney should have been aware of that fact. I do not believe that the testimony of the applicant is seriously disputed by the respondent. This, however, is not the end of the matter.

The first respondent's case is not of the limited extent it may appear to be.

B It was common cause between the parties that copyright can be infringed by a person who causes another to do 'a restricted act without the authority of the copyright owner'. Accordingly copyright can be infringed by both the actual perpetrator and the person who instigates or instructs the doing of that act. Upon the authority of *Bosal Afrika (Pty) Ltd*

C *v Grapnel (Pty) Ltd and Another* 1985 (4) SA 882 (C); and *Esquire Electronics Ltd v Executive Video* 1986 (2) SA 576 (A) the applicant submitted that some subjective knowledge of the unlawful act was required in order to hold the instigator liable. There was, however, no evidence that the ap-

D plicant did so knowingly at any stage or that it was knowingly personally involved in any copying.

The respondent confirmed and repeated in his answering affidavit that it was not his case that the applicant was itself actively involved in the alleged infringement, but that it is involved to the extent that, by granting

E a copyright licence to the second defendant in the infringement action, it 'caused, authorised, aided or abetted the second defendant to make reproductions': the respondent obviously does not have evidence, at this stage at least, directly linking the applicant to the alleged infringement of the copyright by its subsidiary in South Africa. These are early days. At this

F stage the applicant appears to rely upon the existence of the various licensing agreements and the obligations imposed by the applicant licensee upon its subsidiary licensor to exploit and promote the licence to its full extent, the argument also being that this had to be so since the applicant was sharing, on the probabilities at least, in the income gene-

G rated by way of royalties. This approach and argument is certainly not without merit. He need do no more than establish a *prima facie* case. I am satisfied upon the argument presented that such a case had been made out. I prefer to believe that Swart J was similarly not unimpressed and that

H this led him to grant the interim relief. It follows that the application must fail on the second ground also.

The applicant finally criticised the granting of the order on the ground that the respondent failed to disclose material facts which might have influenced the Court in arriving at the decision arrived at. It was sug-

I gested that the respondent should have disclosed:

- the initial debate surrounding the question of the respondent's appointment as executor in the deceased estate of the late Mr Ntsele (Linda);
- the 1983 assignment of copyright by the late Regina Ntsele and her receipt of substantial royalties;
- the 1992 assignment of the copyright by the late Solomon Ntsele's daughters;
- the 1994 documentation relating to the registration of the applicant's copyright, including the statement of case prepared by the first respondent's attorneys, which demonstrated that the applicant was neither a producer nor a distributor of cinematograph films and never made or reproduced the film here involved.

1. The respondent's appointment.

I have dealt with the debate surrounding the respondent's appointment. There was no reason to embark upon an extravagant explanation to warrant the allegation that he was the duly appointed executor in the estate. The document he relied upon was attached to the founding affidavit. Nothing more was required at that stage.

2. The 1983 and the 1992 assignment of the copyright.

Awareness on the part of the then presiding Judge of these alleged or purported assignments would have had little effect upon his decision. In this regard I refer to the first respondent's answering affidavit at 394 and further, read with that of attorney Dean at 504–509. At best there might have been a suggestion, extremely remote I suggest, that a court might have adopted the attitude that there might have been uncertainty, but, having regard to the test to be applied, it would nevertheless have granted the order sought.

3. The non-disclosure of the 1994 documentation.

I need go no further than to say that the applicant might have had a case if it was the respondent's case that the applicant as the principal party infringed the copyright by itself producing, manufacturing, copying and distributing the film here involved. We know that the respondent alleges that the applicant 'caused, authorised, aided or abetted the second defendant to make reproductions' of the film. Once this is understood the complaint must fall away.

The court in any event has an overriding discretion to grant or deny relief to a litigant who might be guilty of a failure to disclose material or relevant facts. The principle is well established that it is the duty of a litigant who approaches the court *ex parte*, to disclose to the court every circumstance which might influence the court in deciding to grant or to withhold relief. Among the factors which the court will take into account in the exercise of its discretion to grant or deny relief to a litigant who has breached the *uberrima fides* rule are the extent to which the rule has been breached; the reasons for the non-disclosure; the extent to which the court might have been influenced by the proper disclosure in the *ex parte* application; the consequences, from the point of view of doing justice between the parties, of denying relief to the applicant on the *ex parte* order; and the interests of innocent third parties, such as minor children, for whom protection was sought in the *ex parte* application. (*Cometal-Mometal S A R L v Corlana Enterprises (Pty) Ltd* 1981 (2) SA 412 (W) at 414G – H.) Having regard to the facts at my disposal and then in particular the comprehensive explanation offered by attorney Dean and the first respondent, I would in any event exercise my discretion in favour of the respondent.

It follows that the application cannot succeed. Although it can be argued that the applicant was ill-advised in launching this application and that costs should follow the result, the fact remains that the applicant may be successful in the main action on the very grounds here debated. I would prefer to order the costs of this application to be in the cause. This does not involve attorneys Spoor & Fisher, against whom no order of costs is made.

The following order is made:

1. The application is dismissed.
2. Costs are to be costs in the cause.

www.ingramcontent.com/pod-product-compliance
Lightning Source LLC
Chambersburg PA
CBHW040145200326
41519CB00035B/7601